S0-CCA-148

The Peopling of Silicon Valley,

1940 to the Present Day:

An Oral History

By

Tim Stanley

2 Timothy Publishing
Irvine, CA

The Peopling of Silicon Valley, 1940 to the Present Day:
An Oral History

© 2017 Joseph Timothy Stanley

Cover Photos: Tim Stanley

All rights reserved. No part of this book may be reproduced in any manner or stored in a retrieval system of any kind without prior written permission from the publisher.

ISBN 978-0-9842391-5-3
Library of Congress # 2017908915
First Printing, September 2017

2 Timothy Publishing
P.O. Box 53783
Irvine, CA 92619-3783
USA
www.2timothypublishing.com

Printed in USA

For a copy of this book by mail, order online or send a check or money order to the P.O. Box above. Shipping and handling are included in the amounts stated. Total cost: $24.00 (CA mailing addresses, add $1.60 sales tax); Canada: $40.00 total.

See website for discounts on bulk purchases.

Dedication

In memory of my father and mother, Joe and Helen Stanley.

Contents

The Peopling of Silicon Valley, 1940 to the Present Day: An Oral History

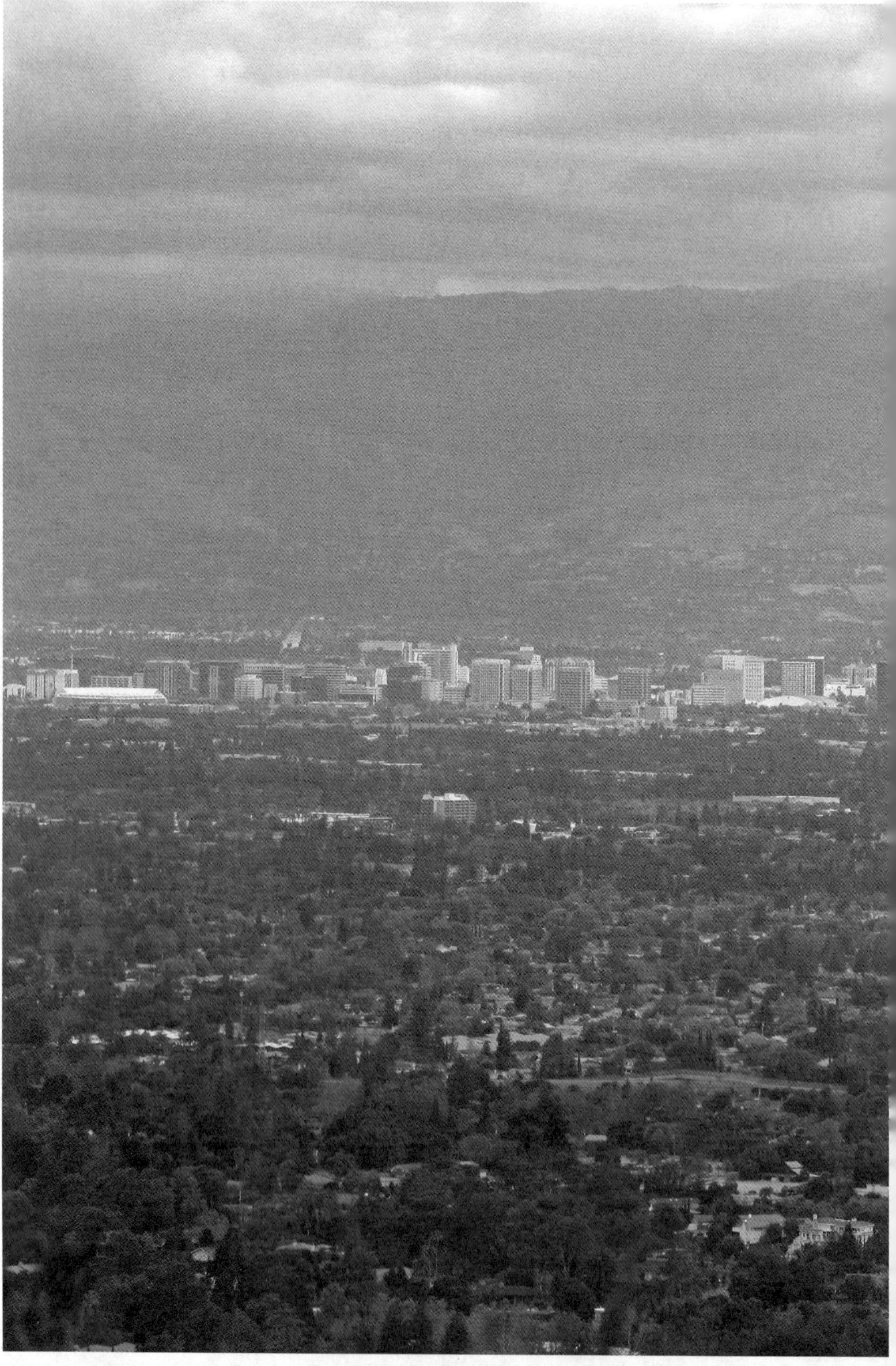

Preface

The Peopling of Silicon Valley, 1940 to the Present Day: An Oral History puts a human face on the Valley. It does not pretend to be a history of the entire Valley during this period or of the technology industries for which the place is now famous. This is a personal history of a cross section of the people who have settled here and of the place they call home with just enough of the technology story to make it interesting.

The book is a compilation of more than 180 stories, or personal accounts, of people who live here, have lived here, or are otherwise connected to the Valley. Some stories are only a few lines; others require a few pages. Many of these stories are as interesting as any I have ever read, and they open up the history of the Valley in a way it cannot be known otherwise.

If you ask five people where Silicon Valley is, you may get five different answers. Old-timers will tell you the Santa Clara Valley became Silicon Valley. Older technical people may tell you it's San Jose and the southern San Francisco peninsula. Younger techies, who live in Fremont, San Mateo, or other places around the San Francisco Bay, and like to say they are from Silicon Valley, often assert that it encompasses the entire Bay Area. For brevity, some just say, "San Jose." Others get philosophical about it and say something like, "It's where the technology is happening." Since I was here long before the term was used, I will stick with the first definition—Santa Clara Valley. But in fact the term "Silicon Valley" has been a misnomer for decades because the silicon fabrication plants, though once numerous, are now about as rare around here as prune orchards are. Both are from bygone eras.

Most of the history of the Valley is not spectacular; it is of ordinary people doing ordinary things in the midst of what became an extraordinary place. The stories in this book, by being candidly told, give voice to the human experience in the midst of what has often been an out-of-control environment.

The book encompasses the five major migrations to the Valley since World War II: the GIs, Lockheed, the chip makers, the minicomputer folks, and the software and web developers. Each is, if not the dominant group, at least a group representative of a particular period that lasted fifteen years or more. Each wave of people brought with it both increased economic prosperity and social change. This is their story, told as much as possible in their own words. I have used narrative sparingly to provide adequate historical context.

If you are frustrated by books that repeat well-known information without telling you what is crucial—that is, the why and how of events—you will enjoy this one. For example: A dozen books may tell you that the blimps stationed at Moffett Field Naval Air Station used helium for lift without telling you the fascinating story of that helium. Likewise, an equal number of books tell of the rapid development of the Santa Clara Valley after World War II but fail to say why that development did not begin in earnest until 1950. And so it is, too, with many matters fundamental to the discussion of semiconductors, integrated circuits, programming languages, and search engines. As with *The Last of the Prune Pickers: A Pre-Silicon Valley Story* and all my books, this book is meant to educate, not merely to entertain.

Throughout the book I have respected the saying, "You do not really understand something unless you can explain it to your grandmother." This saying has been attributed to Albert Einstein. Whether he said it or not, I don't know; but I do agree with the statement, and for that reason I present technical matters in a way that is easy to understand.

In a history book, if the author leaves out everything that might be regarded as sensitive, you end up with what I call a mayonnaise sandwich. It has little or no value, is so sanitized that it has no substance, and the facts of history have been withheld or, worse yet, distorted. For this reason, I have included many stories from people who prefer to remain anonymous. For the most part, these occur in the later chapters and are from individuals who were very candid in private conversation but did not want their identity disclosed. In a few cases, I have changed some insignificant details of someone's story to further protect their anonymity.

Some of the stories were told to me by people I did not know, or I have forgotten who they were. These are credited as "Unknown."

I have also included some of my own stories where I thought they would be helpful in rounding out a chapter. These begin with my initials, *T.S.*

Additionally, to fill what I perceived to be gaps in the book, I included about a dozen stories from people who have not lived in the Valley but in other parts of the San Francisco Bay Area, elsewhere in California, or in other technology centers.

Last, we all see things from different perspectives, our own perspective can change over time, and memories are not always accurate. For this reason I researched many of the claims found in the oral histories and have done my best to see to it that historical facts are presented as fairly and accurately as possible.

So come along with me and take a look at the human side of the Valley, past and present.

Photo on next page: Valley view, about 1940   >>>
Courtesy of San Jose Public Library, California Room

Chapter 1

The Valley of Heart's Delight and Stanford's Woes

The Lord God took the man and put him in the garden of Eden to cultivate and keep it.
                                        —Genesis 2:15

If you looked out onto the Santa Clara Valley of California from the surrounding hills in the spring of 1940, what you would see below you was a glorious display of the cooperation between God and humanity. Millions of fruit trees bursting with white and pink blossoms covered the Valley, and the scent of the air was heavenly.

The Valley was blessed with some of the most fertile soil in the world, abundant underground water, and a mild climate. But that was not all. A lot of people had done a lot of hard work to transform the Valley into that scene.

I will tell you a little about who these people were, where they came from, and why they came. Better yet, I will let them tell you. As you will see, despite the beauty of the area and its great fertility, it was not Eden. Although the place had become known as the Valley of Heart's Delight, there are always at least two sides to any story.

I will begin with a story from a father and daughter who were third- and fourth-generation Santa Clara Valley fruit growers.

Linda Lester
As a young man in his early twenties, my great-grandfather, Nathan Lester, heard that there was a lot of fertile soil out here in the Santa Clara Valley. The soil in Connecticut, where he was from, was rocky and not much good for farming, so he came to California in 1861 thinking this would be a better place to start. There were no roads back then, and the maps were not very good, so he ended up in the Napa Valley. At the time, both the Napa Valley and the Santa Clara Valley were mostly in wheat production. He worked at the Bale Grist Mill, which was a very early mill and is now a state park.

Nathan stayed in the area for several years and while there corresponded with his brother Amos. He told him there was indeed plenty of good, fertile land here and encouraged him to come out, saying, "This is the best place to live." His brother wrote back, telling him, "Yes, but you need to come back here—the women are here."

So Nathan went back to Ledyard, Connecticut, and found a bride. As it was, three Lester brothers married three Spicer sisters.

Then in 1883, Nathan and his wife, Sarah, came to the Santa Clara Valley to pursue a life of farming and fruit production. They bought thirty-one acres on the northeast corner of Lincoln Avenue and Curtner in what was then called the Willows, now Willow Glen. They planted a prune orchard and that became the home ranch. Later they added other ranches.

Nathan and Sarah had five children and did very well on their fruit ranch. Amos and his wife also came out a little later and farmed.

The Lester ranch out on Almaden Road, near Koch Lane, was purchased during the Depression. That is where my father grew up, and where I grew up. My dad said, "The land was not used that much then—the price of prunes was way down, maybe one-half cent per pound, dried. That was giving it away."

When in his nineties, Linda's father still had not forgotten the Depression. He added this.

Lee Lester

After grammar school at the Willow Glen School, for high school we boarded the Peerless Stages bus, which dropped us off at Los Gatos High School. We had the most fun on that bus. The bus driver, a fellow named Henry, was real nice. One day I left my lunch pail on the bus and he drove all the way out to the ranch with it so I'd have it the next day.

One of the highlights was a class that I joined, the Future Farmers of America. I had more fun building equipment, hog pens, things like that. It was really an education. I was pretty handy at welding and I fabricated a lot of equipment.

I would sit there and eat my lunch and George Yamamoto, a Japanese boy, would sit next to me, and he'd say, "Hey Lester, is there any chance we can trade sandwiches? I'll give you my sandwich for yours." Well, my mother was very frugal. She made sandwiches out of anything she had on hand. Maybe it would be a fried egg or it could be anything else.

Sometimes the kids made fun of me because of the sandwich I had. One day I had a lima bean sandwich. I was ashamed of my lima bean sandwich, but George wanted it.

We had Italians working for us in those days. One thing that fascinated me was the food they ate. They had salami, sausage—things they made.

I was working for my dad, and early in the morning he would send me down to the Farm Labor Office. I'd stand outside the door and hijack those workers.

People worked hard in those days. [1]

Henry Petrino

Of my four grandparents, one, my paternal grandmother, was born in San Jose in 1898. The other three emigrated to the U.S. from Italy between 1907 and 1913. I once said to my dad's father: "What a great adventure coming here must have been for you! A new country, new people, everything fresh!" He looked at me like I had two heads and said, "Adventure? In Italy we had meat in the soup on Sunday if it was a good week. We lived in what was essentially a feudal system. We had no hope of improving our lives there. At least here we had a chance!"

My maternal grandfather worked in the Illinois coal mines. He told my grandmother they needed to get out of the mines if they expected him to live past age forty. He told her of young men he had met in boot camp who were from California. They told him there were orchards and field crops to dream of in California and how beautiful it is. She said to him, "What about my parents and my eight brothers and sisters? I can't leave them and go all the way to California!" He told her, "Don't worry about that. They'll all follow us." That's exactly how it turned out. They all ended up in the Santa Clara Valley except my great-grandfather. He was killed in a hunting accident sometime around 1923.

My uncle was born in the San Jose Hospital on Santa Clara Street in 1927. When it was time to check my grandmother and the new baby out, my grandfather didn't have the money he needed to settle the bill. It was late summer so he did have his freshly dried prune crop. He offered the hospital the equivalent value in prunes to settle the bill. They accepted his offer. Then, the real kicker to this story—they called him the following year wanting to purchase his prunes.

They worked twenty acres of vineyard and prunes in Evergreen from 1923 until 1946. During that entire twenty-three years they cooked and heated bathwater on a wood stove, used kerosene lanterns because they did not have electricity, pumped water by hand, used an outhouse because there was no plumbing, and had no telephone. My grandfather worked the land all those years with a team of mules because he didn't have a tractor. Then, in 1946, they sold the place in Evergreen and purchased a place near El Camino Real and Lawrence Station Road that had apricots, prunes, and walnuts. Suddenly it was the early twentieth century. There were electric lights, a telephone, a real bathtub, and a toilet. A windmill pumped water from the well into the tank house. There was a 1918 Ford Model T one-ton truck and a 1919 Holt orchard tractor. No more mules! [2]

***

In 1940, relatively few Valley residents were descendants of the Californios from the Spanish and Mexican eras. Many more were descendants of people who came from the Midwest and East during the middle or late 1800s. For twenty-five years, beginning with the gold rush, most of the people who came worked the wheat fields that covered the Valley. After the advent of canning, most people who moved to the Valley did so to grow fruit. Perhaps as large as any group were those who were economic or political refugees of the early twentieth century. Most of these came from southern and eastern Europe, Japan, and, during the 1930s, from the Dustbowl states. The Valley of 1940 was a diverse mix of Italians, Slavs, Portuguese, Japanese, Dustbowl refugees, and those who had arrived earlier.

Along with the others, a large number of San Franciscans came to the Valley, especially after the 1906 earthquake. Many left the city entirely, others had summer homes here, and not a few commuted to "The City" by train.

Wherever they came from, they worked hard, raised their families here, and sent deep roots into the Valley.

With the exception of the colleges and universities—Stanford, San Jose State, and Santa Clara University—virtually all industry in the Valley revolved around agriculture. Banks, stores, and other businesses served the farmers and canneries.

More than ten million fruit trees graced the Valley in 1940—about sixty for every man, woman, and child living here. At the time, the

Santa Clara Valley was the largest fruit-canning and dried fruit-packing center in the world. The dried, canned, and fresh produce shipped out of the Valley annually exceeded 300,000 tons. [3]

More than ten thousand farms grew that produce. The great majority were family operations of between ten and one hundred acres.

In the 1940s the Valley had between fifteen and twenty canneries. There had been many more, but modernization and the Depression had caused several to close. Del Monte Corporation was one of the largest employers in the Valley.

Most of the canneries were unionized under the American Federation of Labor, and, beginning in the early 1930s, cannery workers received unemployment compensation during the off-season.[4] This was a kind of forced savings plan. To my knowledge the farmworkers had no such system.

Both Continental Can Company and American Can Company had large operations on Taylor Street next to the railroad tracks. [5]

Fruit and vegetable packinghouses were everywhere. The largest were owned by Sunsweet.

Sunsweet

Sunsweet Growers Association was by far the largest processor and distributor of dried fruits, not only in the Valley but probably in the world in 1940. It was a cooperative, formed in 1917 as the California Prune and Apricot Growers, Inc.

The association had a rough start, partly because the members were accustomed to selling their crops to independent buyers or marketing them themselves. They were not accustomed to abiding by the rules of an association. So, if a member grower could get more money for his crop, or part of his crop, by selling independently, he typically did. This was especially true if a grower had done well before joining the association or had premium fruit. The practice undercut the association, but by 1940 most of the kinks had been ironed out and the association was a powerhouse in the Valley with more than half the Valley prune and apricot growers happy to be members and abiding by its rules.

Population and Enrollment Statistics, 1940

Santa Clara County: 174,949
San Jose: 68,457
Palo Alto: 16,774
Santa Clara: 6,650
Sunnyvale: 4,373
Mountain View: 3,946
Gilroy: 3,615
Los Gatos: 3,597
Alviso: unknown, probably fewer than 1,000

San Jose State College: 3,950
Stanford University: 5,242
Santa Clara University: probably fewer than 2,000

Sources: US Census, *The Spartan Daily,* and Facts.Stanford.edu.

Lois McPherson

It delights me to write this story about the great time I had with my grandmother, Lena Brodies, on her ten-acre ranch of prunes and apricots at the corner of Senter Road and Coyote in San Jose. I was born in San Francisco, but my mother died when I was one and a half years old, so my dad took me to live with Grandma. She was a great lady, originally from Germany, and was the biggest influence in my life.

We had, growing, all kinds of fruit, vegetables—and a grape arbor, chickens, a cat, and a German shepherd. Every year, her grandchildren would come to help with the fruit harvest. I was the youngest, and I can remember they were all so excited because the "Okie" family Grandma hired every year was coming and the lady was expecting a baby. I was only a young girl at the time and knew nothing about where babies came from. Why all the excitement? Then someone said they heard some screaming, and—lo and behold—the baby was born perfectly well and normal in a tent under a prune tree. Everyone was so happy.

Grandma didn't even have a bathroom for the workers to use—just an outhouse with a Sears and Roebuck catalog for toilet paper. [6]

John Giacomazzi

My mother and father both had Swiss immigrant parents who were in agriculture. My mother was raised on a dairy and grain ranch in San

Luis Obispo, my father, on a ranch in Nipomo, near Santa Maria, California. When my parents married, they bought their first ranch in Almaden with relatives. Later, they sold that ranch and bought their own ranch on Ross Road. The ranch did not have available water, which had to be purchased. When I was ten years old, our family moved to a forty-acre prune ranch on Almaden Road.

Besides doing chores for the family, my first job, at age twelve, was to work on the dipper crew for John Withers, who owned a forty-acre ranch across the street. I loaded empty trays onto a conveyor, John Withers did the dipping—the prunes were dipped in hot lye water— and his wife spread the prunes out on trays. [i] Art Blake, who owned a twenty-acre ranch north of our property, stacked the trays on a miniature railcar that would be rolled into a dehydrator. [ii]

We [did not have a dehydrator, so we] put our prunes out in the sun to dry, using three-by-eight wood field trays. The trays were placed on the ground in the sun, and the prunes would dry after a few days. The prunes needed to be rolled over with a tool so they would dry on both sides. When dry, the prunes would be taken to the barn and dumped in a pile to further cure. [iii] Eventually, the dried prunes would be shoveled into sacks so they could be delivered to the buyer. One of the buyers was Valley View Packing Company located on Almaden Road at Hillsdale Avenue.

We had major changes, which had to be addressed when my father died in 1946 when I was sixteen years old. We needed to hire people to do things that my father normally did, such as irrigating, pruning, and cultivating. Since all these things added cost to our farm, we had to look for better options.

We realized we needed to change many things. We joined Sunsweet Growers so that [we could take our prunes to their dehydrator and so that] the marketing and sale of our prunes would be simplified. This eliminated the problem of determining what your prunes were worth, since independent fruit buyers changed the price often, and every grower did his own negotiations independently. We also addressed the major cost of irrigating the orchard by putting in a pipeline from our

---

[i] The lye perforated the skin of the prunes which kept them from fermenting.

[ii] A dehydrator is a metal shed with large fans that blow hot air across the prunes to dry them.

[iii] For storage, prunes are dried to an 18 percent moisture content. Before packaging they are re-hydrated to 25 percent or a little more.

water source. Formerly, we directed the water into a ditch, and it flowed by gravity nearly a quarter-mile to some parts of the orchard.

The underground pipeline also made it possible to rent out about four acres of land (that had been our drying area) to a Japanese farmer who planted strawberries.

We did one other thing at that time. There was a continued need to buy hardware and things such as fertilizer and spray materials for the orchard. A group of farmers formed a cooperative organization that eventually became Orchard Supply Hardware. . . . We purchased one share of stock for $36, which entitled us to receive a small discount on everything we bought at the store. The original store was located on San Carlos Street in San Jose.

There were some problems we faced that could not be easily fixed. Most of the farming areas in San Jose were hay [or grain] fields before they were planted to fruit trees. And most of these fields had occasional oak trees. When prune orchards were planted, and the trees grew to their normal size, their roots would come into contact with the old oak roots and get a disease called oak root fungus. Eventually, the tree would die. Unfortunately, this disease would be transferred to adjacent trees, which would also die. There was fumigation available to try to stop this, but it also involved the healthy trees and it was very expensive. As a result, in certain areas of the ranch we had to let the trees die.

Farming requires not only a lot of hard work but also working odd hours—either early morning or at night—under a variety of weather conditions. Once you are exposed to these experiences, anything else you do in your life seems really easy. [7]

Joan Huff Marschall

My family moved to San Jose when I was seven because of a job transfer with the telephone company—a new experience, especially for my mother, who grew up in England. My parents built their home in a new part of town near the San Jose Municipal Rose Garden, which was right at the western edge of town. A pear orchard was at one end of the street and the Rose Garden was at the other end. The only downside was in the coldest part of the winter when smudge pots were burned in the orchard and everything got black! [i]

---

[i] Smudge pots, or orchard heaters, were used to protect fruit from frost. They were basically just a steel can filled with fuel oil and fitted with a valve and a chimney. The soot-producing devices were later replaced by orchard fans.

In the late forties I cut 'cots and picked prunes for the Pitmans in Saratoga, along with my friend Marilyn Whaley, who later married Mr. Pitman's son, Bob. Working there was a great experience, and one I learned a lot from. Mr. Pitman hired several of us from his church to come out to the farm. We had great fun, but we also knew we had to get the fruit cut before the day was over. Some memories I have include knowing that the 'cots must be laid flat or they wouldn't dry evenly, wrinkling our noses when the fruit came out of the sulphur house, and learning that "slabs" were the sweetest 'cots. ⁱ It seems as if the packinghouses didn't figure out the value of slabs for a long time, since I used to buy them from Sunsweet for my family at a cut-rate price!

I also learned that, no matter how smooth the ground looked when it was rolled, it wasn't when you got down on your knees to pick prunes! A friend and I devised some sort of spongy kneepads in order to survive. We managed to find time to flirt with the boys who took away the full trays of apricots and who shook the prunes down for us to pick. Wages were 35 cents per tray of 'cots and 25 cents per box of prunes. In those days the prunes were sun dried, and the whole Valley smelled sweet when they were all laid out.

Older high school and college students worked in the canneries in the summer. These were coveted jobs. A friend and I walked a couple of miles every morning to the Richmond Chase cannery on Stockton Street to see if they were hiring. The number of hires depended on how many trucks full of fruit came in that day. The day we finally got hired was exciting for us but a real life lesson for me. As the forelady chose us to go to work, a woman who was also waiting in line burst into tears. For the first time in my sheltered life, I realized that some people needed those jobs in order to live. Fortunately, the forelady took pity on her and took her as well. My first purchase with my earnings was a beige cashmere sweater from Roos Bros. downtown that I had coveted. My family could never have afforded that.

Canning freestone peaches meant wearing long sleeves and gloves. Any peach fuzz that got on your skin or under your gloves meant you would be itching for the rest of the day. It was hard work, and the canneries treated the students the same way as the permanent workers. Canning apricots meant seeing the ladybugs go into the vats with the ripest ones to make nectar. It took me years to come to terms with drinking it. Just a little protein with your juice!

ⁱ "Slabs" were the overripe apricots that were mushy and didn't keep their shape when cut in half.

At the end of the season one summer we worked at another cannery that would be OSHA's worst nightmare.[i] They were canning tomatoes, and although we stood on pallets, we were swimming in tomato juice on the floor. The debris around there was unbelievable. We were glad when school started. [8]

Prune pickers
Courtesy of San Jose State University

Rose Lesslie

When school was out for summer, we immediately looked for work, and all of my family, all the kids in the area, worked the fruit. So there were apricots and peaches and pears and prunes. A lot of them picked prunes. And the [straw]berries and the nuts. We were all working, so that was good. Then one year I graduated to Libby's Cannery [in Sunnyvale]. . . . I must have been about fifteen then.

[It was] predominantly young women. They would send out county workers during the day to catch the kids that were under age, so they caught my sister who was older than me because she was working days. They never caught me because I was working nights, and the city workers didn't come out at night to see who was working there that shouldn't have been.

---

[i] OSHA was not formed until 1971.

I would work ten, twelve hours a lot of nights right through. Forty-three and a half cents an hour is what I made on the night shift, and that was acceptable good pay at that time. I hated it. It was cold, it was miserable, it was wet, and the cans never stopped coming down that belt. They're just as fast at the end, the last hour, as they are the first hour. [9]

Workers at canning tables
Courtesy of San Jose State University

Bob Norona

San Jose was a small city in 1940. On the east, King Road was the edge of town; at the north, Hedding Street; to the south was Alma; and to the west was Bascom. The Rose Garden was at the west edge of town. At the east edge was the dump. There was an incinerator 135 feet tall at the end of Empire Street, where Empire Gardens Elementary School is now.

There were two slaughterhouses in town. The San Jose Meat Company slaughtered horses and the Garden City Meat Company butchered cattle. The cattle came in by rail and were put in holding pens near the rail yard. The canneries worked 24/7 in the summer. Kids could always get a job picking crops or working in the canneries. [10]

Next pages: Santa Clara (below) and San Jose, 1940   >>>
Courtesy of Santa Clara University Library Archives

Stanford

It was a different world at Stanford, in the upper left-hand corner of the Valley. The following story is a little window into what was going on there.

Edward Ginzton

I did my undergraduate work, as well as the first year of graduate work, at Berkeley. I started in January of 1933 as a student and graduated in three and a half years. I tried to get a job—any job—and found it next to impossible, so I went to graduate school simply because there wasn't anything else to do. . . . That gave me an opportunity to do some research along certain lines called negative feedback, that became important later on. [i] *I did my thesis under a professor of electrical engineering, Abe Thulis. He didn't know much about electronics but there wasn't anyone else to supervise me. . . .*

I once again looked for a job after my first year of graduate work and came across some kind of announcement that at Stanford there was a fellowship available in electronics under Professor Carrol, who was head of the High Voltage Laboratory at Stanford. I went to see him, and described who I was, and what my ambitions were. He said, "Well, you don't belong with me, but there's a young professor here at Stanford by the name of Frederick Terman, who is trying to build up a department; why don't you go see him?" So I did, and he became interested in the research work on negative feedback which I had done on my own without supervision. He was interested that I could do as much as I did without help or advice. So he invited me to become a research assistant in his new department and to continue with graduate studies towards the PhD.

At that time, as I recall, the [Electrical Engineering] department had sixteen graduate students altogether, very small, and Terman was very busy teaching courses, being head of the department, trying to develop the department. . . . He provided guidance, supervision, and advice to all his students. He came into the laboratory, usually at late afternoon, and he would talk to the students until a very late hour, until around dinnertime. He was very much the moving spirit in the laboratory.

Terman's book [Radio Engineering], was the most important document. [It] first came out in 1932 and then was revised later.

---

[i] Negative feedback stabilizes amplified radio signals. This was, and is, crucial for ship-to-ship and ship-to-shore communications. To send a radio signal over long distances, it must be amplified. The problem was distortion. (See chapter 5.)

My knowledge of Terman's activities between late 1939 and 1942 is meager because one branch of the activity at Stanford was focused on the klystron[i] per se, and many of us, including a fair number of EE students, were pursuing the invention, its implications and ramifications. . . . Something else was going on in radio engineering under Terman. The first branch, the klystron group, almost entirely went over to Sperry in Garden City, New York, to work.

When we went to work in Sperry Laboratories [in late 1940], the war was obviously imminent. Any thinking person would recognize that the war was coming. With the wartime activities and its implications, one didn't know what to expect from the future. . . . I hoped to be able to come back to the university when it became possible. [11]

***

Even before the threat of war loomed large, Professor Terman was losing nearly all his graduates to the East Coast, where the jobs were. He tried to talk them into doing something locally, but that fell largely on deaf ears. A couple of young men, Bill and Dave, liked his idea of starting a company and were inspired when he took them on a tour of some local laboratories, but they had no idea what they wanted to build—and what could they do, anyway?

---

[i] The Klystron, invented in 1937 by Russell and Sigurd Varian, is a specialized vacuum tube used to amplify radio signals. It was crucial in the development of radar. (See Chapter 5.)

Chapter 2

Wartime

The attack on Pearl Harbor on December 7, 1941 caught the United States completely off guard. Three days later, when Germany and Italy declared war on the United States, we were immersed in a global war, and, at least on the West Coast, we could hardly have been less prepared for it. I will have Earl Warren, attorney general of California at the time of the attack, begin the chapter.

Earl Warren

[Shortly after Pearl Harbor, I had] a phone call from Abe Brazil down in San Luis Obispo. He was the district attorney there, and he told me that that morning there was an explosion off the coast there that awakened the whole town, and that [the town's residents] got up and they went down to the shore—the seashore—and they learned when they got down there that a submarine had sunk a tanker of ours. . . .

[Brazil said to me], "Gee, I don't know who to call, but we immediately phoned the Air Force"—they had an air base just three miles from town—"and [we waited] for hours. They never showed up!" So, he called me. He said, "I don't know who to call, so I just called you."

I said, "Of course, I don't have anything to do with it, but I'll go over and see Admiral [John] Greenslade." (He was the commandant of the Twelfth Naval District.) I told him the story, and he said, "I'm sorry to say that's true, but there's just nothing we can do about it." He said, "I only have two submarines between San Luis Obispo and Vancouver, British Columbia." He said, "All the rest of ours have gone out into the Pacific Fleet." [1]

***

The tanker SS Montebello was sunk in the early morning of December 23, 1941. Fearing a mass panic because the Japanese had gotten so close to shore, the government confiscated newspaper reports about the sinking and did not release them for many years afterwards. In seven days, from December 18 to 24, nine Japanese submarines, sent to strategic points along the West Coast following the attack on Pearl Harbor, attacked eight U.S. merchant ships off the coast. Two were sunk and two others were damaged. Thankfully, the Japanese were not accurate with most of their torpedoes, and the submarines had no way of being resupplied. [2]

William Kays, Stanford University, class of 1942

It wasn't any question I was going to go into ROTC when I got [to Stanford]. My father insisted on it. But the only ROTC was artillery. Horse artillery. So I went into the horse artillery, and we had horses here, and that's how we did it. . . . As a matter of fact, my sophomore year all we did in ROTC was ride horses, and the horses,—you didn't ride them, you were pulling things,—caissons and guns and things. [3]

***

Although we were ill-prepared for the war, there was a silver lining. Unlike our other wars, nearly everyone recognized the threat, and there was a sense of unity in the country. Everyone had gone through the Depression together, and everyone was involved in the war effort in one way or another. These factors brought about a unity of heart and purpose that the country had probably never known before and has certainly not known since.

The next story is from a young Stanford history professor.

Rixford K. Snyder

Pearl Harbor occurred in 1941 and immediately thereafter we had the drawing for the draft. . . . I didn't want to go in as an enlisted man, and I thought somewhere and somehow I could get a commission. . . . I taught through to 1942, and then I was due to be called up in the early part of 1943. In November, Dr. Wilbur called me into his office and said that a naval lieutenant commander had come from San Francisco and had asked him "to recommend young instructors who had had experience teaching groups of men—approximately thirty to thirty-five men." Wilbur had come up with a number of names and wanted to know would I want to be included? I said yes. I was then interviewed by Lieutenant Commander Pierce. He'd come down from San Francisco from his recruiting office, and he explained to me what was then known as the V-5 program, which was the academic program for the young men who were to become Navy pilots. He explained to me what was required and he said, "Do you think you could do that?" I said, "I think I can." He said, "Your country needs you, my boy." . . .

We had been told by Pierce, and in our indoctrination program at Chapel Hill [North Carolina], that we would be teaching Navy history so we would inspire these cadets to go out and do deeds comparable to John Paul Jones, and Perry, and Dewey and others. When we arrived. . . we reported to the captain, and he said, "What are you here for?" "We're going to teach history of the United States Navy to your cadets, sir." "We're not going to win this war on history. What we need to teach these cadets about is aerology so they can fly through this weather." One of us spoke up and said, "But sir, we don't know anything about aerology." "But you can teach, can't you?" "Yes, we can teach." "Go into the classes tomorrow morning and start teaching aerology." Which is what we did. . . I taught aerology, which is meteorology [but] the Navy called it aerology. [4]

Student soldiers at Santa Clara University
Courtesy of Santa Clara University Library

Dave Cochran
Having grown up in Palo Alto from the second grade, I didn't pay much attention to goings-on. World War II started and I made a blackout curtain for our bathroom. There was a bucket of sand near the front door with an air-raid warden's helmet hanging on the hook. My dad was in the army during World War II; my mom was the air raid warden for our block. The sand was to put out fires. [5]

Joan Huff Marschall

The beginning of the war saw a number of changes in the Valley of Heart's Delight. Very soon tents appeared on the grounds of Hoover Junior High, with young soldiers occupying them. Blimps were housed in the Moffett Field hangar and often flew over our houses. Lighter-than-air training involved free-flying balloons, which frequently ran out of fuel when they got as far as San Jose. Then, everyone with a bike raced to the site where they put down, usually at a ranch, and watched handsome young soldiers talking on walkie-talkies while they waited for a truck to pick them up. Sixth-graders each built a model airplane, and we learned to recognize the different military planes that flew over. My father had young signal corpsmen riding in his telephone company truck, learning the ropes of communication. As a junior high girl, I was in awe of them. [6]

George I. Rodriguez

I was raised on Morris Avenue in Sunnyvale. Later my dad sold the place and bought a farm on Wolfe Road. In the 1930s and '40s the streets were gravel. There was a horse-drawn wagon that watered the streets down. There were oak trees all over the place in the lowlands.

Before the war, I went to work at IBM at 15 Battery Street in San Francisco. My work was with the wiring boards that the IBM equipment used for punch card accounting. I also worked at Hendy Iron Works and at the shipyard in Emeryville on their IBM equipment. The equipment was out, and people were using it, but only the big operations had it. Libby's had it and so did the canneries in San Jose.

The war changed everything. After a while I enlisted. That was better than waiting to be drafted. If you enlisted, you could choose which branch and type of service. So I enlisted in the paratroopers.

I was sent off to basic training, but when the train got to L.A., I was pulled off the train by a fellow who had been given orders to pick me up. I had no idea what the situation was, and he wouldn't tell me anything. I thought I was being arrested or something. We got back to San Francisco and he took me to the California Hall building at Polk and Turk streets. We went into the basement and there was all this clanking away of IBM equipment. I said, "Oh, s___!" The major who had been put in charge of me said, "What did you say?" I said, "Oh, crap! That's an IBM installation, isn't it?" I told him I signed up for the paratroopers, not to be stuck in some building with all this. He said I could put in for a transfer and I did. I was eventually assigned to General MacArthur's headquarters and sent to the South Pacific—Sydney, Brisbane, New Guinea, Mindanao, Luzon, Leyte—all over the place. There were IBM installations in all those places. That is how they kept track of the men and everything else. Everything was on cards. If a general needed, say, twenty riflemen, we could find them readily in the Fifth Replacement Depot. [7]

***

 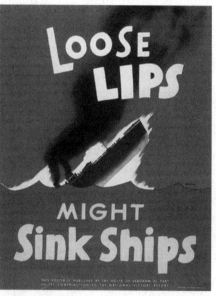

Posters like these were ever-present reminders that we were at war.

Joshua Hendy Iron Works had been a large equipment manufacturer since the gold rush days. Among many other pieces of heavy machinery, Hendy manufactured the large water cannons and pumps that were used for hydraulic mining in the Sierras. After being shaken out of San Francisco by the 1906 earthquake, the company settled in Sunnyvale. By the middle of the Great Depression, the once thriving company with more than a thousand employees was barely afloat, and employed about sixty people. That all changed dramatically with the coming of the war. By the time the war was over, there were more than eleven thousand people working at Hendy. Here is a story from one of Hendy's early wartime employees.

Lola Vaughn

I thought, "I've got to do something for the war effort," so I decided, "well, it's either going into the service or coming down here [to Sunnyvale] and get a job in the war plant." . . .

There were five of us, at the very beginning, but then they employed many more girls. My sister came too, as a factory worker. And we were given uniforms, coveralls, and hats, and hard toed shoes. Then I was instructed how to use the pentagraph machine, and what we did on the pentagraph machine was engrave the sight that went on the torpedo mount. . . . It had this sight that was mounted on the top to find a range and fire a torpedo. All the engraving of the numbers and degrees was done on the pentagraph. I worked as an engraving machine operator until 1944. At that time I went into the hospital; I had a thyroidectomy.

When I came back, I was rehired not as an engraver but as an inspector. . . . They had the five-inch guns that were already assembled brought into the plant [that] had to be wired. They had special teams of people that did the wiring, which included women. . . . They also had 40-millimeter guns that were brought in that were to be repaired that had been used and they were inoperative. . . .

Now, everyone in our plant, Plant 2, we were isolated from the rest of the plant; in fact, we never got over to see what was going on in the other buildings because there was tight security in our plant. The other plants were located on the other side, but they couldn't come to us and we couldn't go over there. Only for the rallies. We were allowed to go to the rallies. It was not until after VE [Victory in Europe] Day that they opened the plant up and you could go about and see what was going on. . . .

[The women] came from all walks of life. Most of the ones I can recall were housewives. I mean, they needed the manpower. . . . [The women] worked in the storerooms—they were particularly good in the storerooms. . . . Then there were a lot of middle press operators, also broaching machines. . . . Some of them had training beforehand, like the women on the lathes. Myself, I had no training; I was trained on the job. . . .

You knew America was in the war. Men were over there fighting and here you were trying to. . . supply them with what they needed. We were ready to sacrifice to do it. [8]

***

Top: inside Hendy Iron Works, Sunnyvale   Credit: Hendy Iron Works
Bottom: 500th Liberty Ship engine produced by Hendy.
Courtesy of Sunnyvale Historical Society

Aside from Hendy Iron Works, the canneries, the packinghouses, and the colleges, Food Machinery Corporation (later FMC) was the only other large employer in the Valley when the war broke out. Like Hendy, and to a lesser degree some of the canneries, Food Machinery was also enlisted for war materiel work.

The company was the result of the 1928 merger of the John Bean Manufacturing Company and the Anderson-Barngrover Company, both of which had their beginnings in the Valley. According to the company's 1935 annual report, "The company [was] the world's largest manufacturer of machinery and equipment for the handling of fruits, vegetables, milk, fish and meat products from the time the commodity comes from the orchard, field, farm, or sea until it is packed or canned and ready for the consumer."

Food Machinery had also bought up a wide array of companies and was involved in many pursuits. One in particular caught the attention of the War Productions Board. At a facility in Florida, where FMC had a plant that made citrus packing machinery, one of the engineers had developed a tracked amphibious vehicle for rescuing people trapped in the Everglades. The Marines and the Navy had shown interest in the vehicle's development before the war, but as the war neared they got serious and ordered two hundred Alligators, as the vehicles were called at the time.

The Navy's specifications for the vehicles were considerably different from what the company had produced, but Food Machinery's chief engineer, Jim Hait, saw it as "really a water propulsion problem" and somewhat boldly told them, "Yes, I think we can do it."

And do it they did. Although, according Hait, "costs at that early stage were totally unknown to us," they had to put a price tag on the vehicles and did. The next thing Hait knew, Food Machinery had an order for one thousand LVTs, or Landing Vehicles Tracked, as they were now called. The $60 million order was seven times the company's total sales volume for the previous year, 1940.

Food Machinery built the vehicles in three locations: Dunedin, Florida, and Riverside and San Jose, California. The company made hundreds of modifications to the vehicles during the war to match the perceived conditions at the various beaches where they were to land.

Although the engineering challenges were significant, perhaps the most difficult matters were keeping trained workers and procuring parts. The company would hire and train workers only to lose them to the draft. As for parts, one manager complained, "Everything you needed was grabbed by other manufacturers." Usually, the company could prove its project had priority. If that was the case, company representatives would find out where the parts were and the Navy would authorize them to literally go and get them. Such were the times.

There were also many technical problems. My own father, who was trained in the craft while in the Army, told me that one of the vehicles flipped over in the surf during a training exercise and all the men aboard were killed. But the company learned as they went along and kept refining the vehicles. In the end, LVTs proved to be one of the most effective weapons of the war.

By the time the war ended, Food Machinery had produced more than eleven thousand LVTs, many of which were built in San Jose. [9]

Food Machinery Corporation Landing Vehicle Tracked
US Navy

Rose Lesslie

I was good with my hands, and back then, when things were still kind of rough for us, my mother would say, "If you want clothes, learn to make them." Well, that was a challenge that left me wide open. I did learn to make them. And I would make a lot of clothes that I wore, which led me into what was to happen later.

I found out that, if you could take a piece of material and lay it out properly and cut the pieces out to make full use of the material that you have, and put it all together one piece at a time, following the pattern that comes with the dresses, it would sure help with putting together aircraft parts later in life. . . . You learn quickly. And just the same way you can lay out a pattern, you could follow a blueprint. . . .

After the war started . . . my sister applied for work at Moffett Field. For some reason, the man that was going to be her boss came to the house. She was going to be working in a ship's service store, which is a place where the military go for coffee and soft drinks and sandwiches and ice cream. . . . So this man came to the house to talk to my sister, and he saw me walking around and he says, "Well, how about you?" I said, "I can't go out there." He says, "Why not?" I said, "I'm too young." You had to be eighteen, I guess, to go out there, and I was sixteen at the time. He says, "No, you're not!" He says, "I'll take both of you." He says, "You're eighteen, she's nineteen, you're on." So we went to work at Moffett. . . .

The year after I worked in [the] ship's service store, I went out to Moffett . . . looking for work, and at that time they said, "Well, we don't have much going on around here, but we have a class starting. We're going to train women to work on blimps." I said, "Would we learn to be mechanics?". . . I never had a tool in my hand before, but I said, "I can do that." So I did start. We went to school in Palo Alto.

They set up a school in a hurry, and I didn't even know how to drive. I didn't know how I was going to get there. I thought, "If push comes to shove, I'll get a bike and I'll ride seven miles," because I was young and strong. . . . But I got in with a woman right next to me. She had a car, and she picked me up because we were all in carpools at that time. So I went with her and we went to school for three months. We got eighty-three cents an hour. We started out with about two hours of book work in the morning, then we went down in the shop and had hands-on with tools. So we took little pieces of metal and we drilled holes in them, and we cleaned them all up, and we put rivets in. We riveted them by hand, and then with different kinds of machinery and tools and stuff. I was quickly using everything, all kinds of hand tools and all kinds of power tools, anything that they had. And it was no problem, I liked it. It was easy.

We started out in the fin room. . . we were making new fins and rudders for blimps. And believe it or not, that room was full of women only. We had a male lead, and we didn't really need him. This particular case— [She shows a photo] *here's one of the jigs that was there. It's a very large jig, this one. In nothing flat I was running this jig by myself.*

You have to get extrusions, materials that are much like this [gestures], *put in here; and we'd get it all together. If you're working on the top, that's easy; but on the bottom, we'd get on scooters and we'd be lying right on our back, just barely off the ground scooting, around on wheels. And we'd be riveting and drilling. . . up above our head. . . .*

We would work. . . twelve days, and [then] two days off; so we'd work right through the weekend. We would work two shifts, and we were busy. Some [of the women] were married and some of them weren't. [She shows another photo] *They were a good bunch. . . .*

Blimps were important because they were our shore patrol. They were out there looking for submarines. They carried depth charges, and they carried a machine gun. There were two other blimp places on the West Coast. There was one in Tillamook, Oregon, and one down in Santa Ana [California] that had blimp stations where the blimps came in. They would go out and do their patrolling, and then they came back in again. At the time, Moffett Field was the only place that was outfitted for overhaul and repair. So we got blimps from the other two stations. [10]

***

Helium provided buoyancy for the blimps. It is a nonflammable component of petroleum, but most of the world's petroleum does not contain it in quantities that make isolation and extraction worthwhile. However, north Texas crude does contain a significant amount, and a helium extraction plant was built in Amarillo.

Buoyed by helium, the U.S. blimp fleet had a tremendous reconnaissance advantage during the war. No other nation had access to helium in useable quantities. Hydrogen, the other means of lift for lighter-than-air craft, is explosive, and after several disasters the other nations abandoned their lighter-than-air programs. The value of the blimps—those "eyes in the sky" during World War II—was similar to the value of superior reconnaissance satellites today.

Blimps at Moffett Field
Made of rubber, the bottom one is being deflated

US Navy

Gene Arnold

I grew up in Palo Alto. During the war there was very little meat for too many people. Lucky's Market opened in town, though, and I got a job there. I became friends with the butcher so I always knew when meat was going to be delivered. There was only one delivery of meat a week. Some of the meat was horse meat. It was a little tough, but it was good to have it. So we didn't suffer too bad.

Rationing was serious. All the gas coupons were for four gallons of gas. I also worked at the Chevron then. Gasoline was controlled very tightly. You took the pump readings at night and again early in the morning. And the readings had better match up with the number of gas coupons you had taken in. We had it OK though because the PG&E, telephone, and city trucks would come in and they'd just say "Fill it up." Well, it's never going to be an even multiple of four, and they didn't care. So almost every day there were a few extra gallons that could be sold without a coupon. So I'd call my mother up and tell her to come down and get it.

When I was old enough, I got a job at the shipyard at Hunter's Point. There were people standing around everywhere doing nothing. I suppose we won the war because there were a lot of people who worked fifteen minutes a day. The cleaning women just stood around for nine-tenths of the day.

I started out as a welder's helper and the welder didn't need me, so he just sent me to scamper off. Then I went to welding school and became a welder. We were always short welding leads. They would be very long, extending from the dock down into the ship. So you had to keep watch or someone else would take off with your lead. You'd go down into the hold to start welding, but the machine would not be set right, so you had to go all the way back up to the dock to adjust it. Up and down, up and down, until you got it adjusted right. I suppose I got an hour or an hour and a half of productive work done out of a ten-hour day.

I took the train that ran from San Jose up the peninsula. By the time it got to Palo Alto, it was full. But more of us got on. People just packed in. And then there were stops at Menlo Park, Redwood City, San Carlos, all the way up the peninsula where more people got on. The next train would be just as full. There was no way the conductor could collect the tickets. People passed them forward, but. . . . There were people hanging out of the cars. Hanging off the vestibule, hanging out of the train and holding on to the handrails. [11]

***

As war materiel plants neared peak production, the shortage of agricultural workers in the Valley and in other agricultural regions became problematic. A friend of ours came with his family from southern Oregon to pick prunes in Los Gatos for two seasons. Others came from greater distances. Something had to be done about the labor shortage and eventually was when Mexico declared war on the Axis powers in May of 1942. That declaration gave Congress the way to institute the Bracero Program, which it did that August.[i] The program allowed Mexican nationals into the country to work in agriculture and made them an official part of the war effort. [12]

In recent times much has been said about the poor treatment of these men by American agriculturalists, so I do not think it is necessary to repeat any of that here. However, the story has another side that is often not told. I will let two of these men tell that side of the story. The first is from an interview conducted in San Jose in 2006.

Interviewer: Like almost all the men I have met, (F.V.) is grateful for the life here that was made possible because of the Bracero Program, and he would rather not recount his negative experiences. In his words, "I don't eat from a plate and then talk about the plate I'm eating from." Instead, he talks about another part of the story.

F.V.
I was poor in Mexico. I lived in poverty. I couldn't even manage to pay for a cup of coffee. The poverty was so bad that I lost three children in one year. They died because I had no money for medical care to save them. If you've got money, then you eat, get medical care, everything. But if you don't, then you are in the hole; you die.

I will never forget it. One son and two daughters—they all died on me. One was already talking. He said, "Papa." He said, "Papa," and then he died. The last was a little girl named Carmelita. She died talking too because I did not have the money to save her. Because of this I cursed the government of Mexico.

Interviewer: And he warns about some of the corrupt profiteers who were attracted by the guest worker program.

F.V.
What I am telling you is true. The Bracero Program was a business. For each work permit, the Mexican lawyers, middlemen, and government

---

[i] Bracero: Roughly translated "arm," a manual laborer.

would charge three to four hundred pesos. They were robbing us. You had to pay or they would not give you a contract. They got rich on us. There were a lot of people making money. [13]

***

The second bracero story comes from an attendee at the 2010 "Braceros in California" program at the Mexican Heritage Plaza in San Jose. The program was part of a traveling Smithsonian exhibit, and there were several speakers, mostly educators, who told something of the local story. After they finished, the moderator opened the meeting for questions and comments. During that time, a man in the audience stood up and related the following story.

Unknown

My father was a bracero during the war. He was living in Mexico City and wanted to come up here to earn some money so he could go back and marry my mom. They had this recruiting center, and he waited there for several days. If you had money, you could buy food from the women there who were selling tacos right along the railroad tracks. If you didn't have money, you were out of luck.

So he went through processing and they sprayed him with all that stuff.[i]

To give you a perspective of how poor the people were who joined the Bracero Program (at least in the case of my father), when he got to [the U.S.] he was working for the Southern Pacific near Fresno. . . . Once he got there, he went up to the kitchen and they asked him, "How many eggs do you want?" No one had ever asked him that question. So he said, "How many can I have?" And they said, "As many as you want." He thought about it for a minute (he was a little embarrassed), and he said, "How about eight?" So she cooked up eight eggs and he ate that. As he was telling us the story, [he said] he thought three might be typical, maybe four—but eight!

All the talk about the exploitation of the braceros is true, and he related that also, but he had never eaten so well in his life, and he was twenty-three years old.

***

---

[i] He was referring primarily to de-lousing powder and DDT. American soldiers in the South Pacific were also fumigated. I don't know which chemicals were used on them.

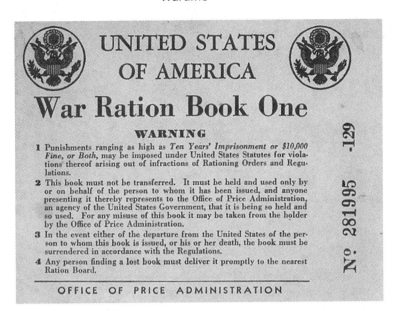

WWII ration book

Clarence Robert Tower

When World War II broke out, my intermediate school initiated numerous drives and programs connected to the war effort. Sometime in 1942, the school conducted a large paper and materials drive, and offered prizes for the students who could amass the most points based on a system devised especially for the drive.

Although I'm not certain why there was a demand for large quantities of paper, everyone knew that aluminum was one of the critical materials needed in large quantities by the aircraft industry and by manufacturers of other necessary wartime equipment, such as lightweight canteens and mess kits. Wartime workers in our neighborhood constructed a wooden enclosure at the front corner of the big open field opposite Washington School where people could deposit anything made of aluminum.

People tossed buckets, pots, pans, vacuum cleaner pieces, coffee pots, and all sorts of aluminum goods in the enclosure for the war effort.... Housewives saved large cans of cooking grease that were collected and processed to make materials for explosives. Smokers saved the tin foil from cigarette packages, rolled them into balls, and donated them to special material drives. [14]   ***

Unlike wars we have known since, World War II was a total effort. One part of that effort was Victory Gardens. Americans were encouraged to plant gardens and grow as much of their own food as possible to save the food supply for the troops.

Lee Lester's victory garden certificate
Courtesy of Linda Lester

Richard Mesa

Our mother was one of a few teenage girls who would go to catch a bus to work at a convent in Mountain View. The family lived across from Washington Park on Pastoria Avenue at the time. New recruits were getting preliminary training at the park.[i] The drill sergeant would bark, "Eyes right! This is what you're fighting for!" and order a whistle. My mother, her sister, and one other girl would scurry off, giggling and blushing and embarrassed all at the same time. [15]

T.S.

My dad was twenty years old when he went off to war, and like so many other GIs he left his sweetheart, my mom, back home in Pennsylvania. After basic training and radio school in Kentucky, his unit waited at Camp Stoneman, near Pittsburg, California, for transport to the war in the Pacific. Although Dad never talked about it, we know from the photos he took that getting a good look at California was a priority for him while he was on leave before going overseas. He spent Christmas

---

[i] The soldiers were with the 607th Antitank Battalion and were a common sight along Murphy Avenue during the war. The battalion was sent to Europe for the invasion of Normandy in 1944. (Jeanine Stanek, Sunnyvale Historical Museum, e-mail to author.)

1943 with an Army buddy and his family in Richmond, and New Year's Day 1944, with Ed and Mildred Parker in San Jose.

Dad met Mr. Parker at the USO (United Service Organization) in downtown San Jose.[i] Mr. Parker was at the USO installing a lockset on a door, and when he heard Dad ask where he could get a good, hot meal, he turned around and told him, "Right at my house." He took him home and Mrs. Parker cooked a nice dinner for him. That night Dad came down with a bad case of the flu, and Mrs. Parker nursed him for a few days. Mr. Parker, who was a Coast Guard reservist, even called Dad's commanding officer to tell him where Dad was. Thus began a wonderful relationship between the two families.

The Parkers had a son stationed overseas, and they took Dad in as their own.

My father, Joe Stanley, with Ed Parker, January 1, 1944

Henry Petrino
My dad graduated from San Jose High in 1937. Immediately following graduation, he went to work in his dad's bakery, Louis Bakery, which was at 180 West St. James Street. The building was brick and had a storefront in front, a residence in the middle, and the bakery to the rear.

---

[i] The USO house in San Jose was built before the war with locally donated labor and materials. (*Reflections of the Past.*)

Out back was a long building that housed three or four Model T delivery trucks, a gas pump, and an apartment for an employee. As with many boys his age, he joined the U.S. Navy shortly after the attack on Pearl Harbor, in the spring of 1942. He was gone for a little over four years, with a few visits home in between.

Meanwhile, my grandfather continued to operate his bakery, working double hard because my dad was gone. One of the stores he sold bread to was the Lucky Market on East Santa Clara Street (at around Fifth Street). During his daily bread delivery visits he met a "beautiful redhead," who at that time was about nineteen or twenty years old. She managed the produce department, setting up great displays of whatever fresh produce was in season. He liked her and told her, "I have a son for you. He's away in the war, but he'll be back and he's perfect for you!"

My dad was discharged in early 1946. He married the beautiful redhead on January 5, 1947. I was born in December 1947.

My grandfather always liked redheads. [16]   ***

This photo was taken on Castro Street in Sunnyvale during the war.
The people in it are unidentified.
Courtesy of Sunnyvale Historical Society

As for Bill and Dave, Professor Terman's students, they did start a little company. Their first financially successful product was an instrument called a precision audio oscillator, which they developed in a lab at Stanford. The device was used to test sound equipment and was based upon Bill Hewlett's master's thesis. It had a simple but effective design; its output signal was constant, with low distortion; and it was received by a waiting market, most notably by the Walt Disney Company, which, in the late 1930s, bought eight of them for $71.50 each. The HP200A (so named to make it appear that Bill and Dave had an established company) put Hewlett Packard in position to win several small, but significant, wartime contracts. [17]

After Pearl Harbor, Bill went off to war and Dave kept the shop going.

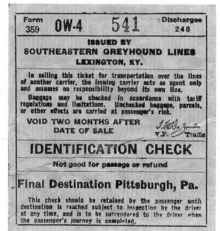

This blimp came out to meet my father's troop ship as it neared the Golden Gate in January 1946. The men on that ship, like millions of others, had waited for months after the war ended for a transport ship to bring them home. I found my father's bus ticket for the ride home among his few keepsakes after he passed away.

Chapter 3

The First Wave: The GIs

As stated in the preface, the Valley has seen five major waves of migration since 1940. The first was the World War II GIs.[i] Once again, I'll let Earl Warren, by then the governor of California, set the scene for the chapter.

Earl Warren

These were not normal times when I became governor. We were in the middle of a war. The war started in 1941, and I was elected in '42, November '42. Now there were a lot of [infrastructure improvements] that were entitled to high priority, but you just couldn't possibly get them done at that time, because it would involve manpower and materials, and the war restrictions on those were such that you couldn't get any materials, and you couldn't get any manpower for them. So there was no use wasting time on those right at the moment. The only thing to do was to start [the projects] you could get done, and then save the money for when you could get those other things done. So I selected things where we could get something done at the moment, and then, because of our inflated revenues, which we had at the time, to lock up every dollar that [we] didn't need for governmental purposes in a building fund, to take care of it when the restrictions were off of labor and materials.

And then, so we'd be ready at that time, I had the [Division] of Architecture go into all these various departments, [and] see what they needed. And we had plans and specifications on the drawing board, or on the shelves, at the time the [U.S.] government was ready to release materials and manpower [after the war ended]. Because we were one of the few states to make those preparations beforehand, it was wide open to us from the beginning [of the postwar era]. We got in and built like crazy. . . . The [U.S.] government was glad to see it done, and we needed to do it, too, because with the war over, we had eight hundred thousand boys of our own who came back from the war in a very short time. [They] came back with no jobs or anything, don't you see? We had to have a lot of things going for ourselves or we'd have been in bad shape.

Also, all those youngsters who trained here—so many of them wanted to come back. And by the time I left [office in 1953], there were a million

---

[i] The term *GI* comes from "government issue."

out-of-state veterans who came here—a very large percentage of them with wives and babies, and they had to be taken care of too. So we had to look forward to the future, and some of our priorities were determined by that situation.

The problem was to keep this money—to keep the big taxpayers from reducing taxes and getting rid of those surplus funds, on the one hand, and [keep] the legislature [from] spending it for something other than capital investment. I argued to keep our funds intact, don't you see, for building purposes; and we were able to do it. [1]

Anonymous
My dad was stationed at Moffett Field during the latter part of the war. Coming from northern Minnesota, he thought he had died and gone to heaven. There was not snow on the ground for half the year. As a matter of fact, there was no snow, period. The sky was blue. He got used to that real quick. The work he was doing was important to the Navy, and at the end of the war they still needed him, so he re-enlisted. [2] ***

One of the immediate challenges Valley residents faced after the war was where to house the large number of incoming veterans who either never returned home after the war or moved here shortly thereafter. One emergency solution, funded by a $300,000 state grant, was Airport Village. More than three hundred temporary war surplus housing units were brought in on trailers and set on piers on an unused plot of ground by the airport, just outside of San Jose. But this effort hardly made a dent in the housing shortage.

Airport Village, San Jose, 1946   Courtesy of History San Jose

People were accustomed to the government taking action on their behalf on many, if not most, fronts. After all, they had lived through the Works Progress Administration and Civilian Conservation Corps days as well as the war years. But now, everything seemed to be on hold. What was going to happen? Would there be another depression? Money was tight. The banks were not in a mood to lend money. And millions of returning GIs were asking themselves, "Where do I go to live?"

A well-disciplined workforce was ready to go to work, but in the aftermath of the war the largest employers in the area, Hendy and Food Machinery, were not hiring—they were laying off workers.

The returning GIs had known hard times. They grew up during the Great Depression and had survived the war. Now, at least, times were hopeful, and many of the GIs were determined to stay in the area at any cost. In fact, many had no good alternative.

There had been almost no private construction during the war years because all building materials were needed for the war effort. Furthermore, people from out of the area had moved in to do the war materiel work, and when the GIs came home, someone else was in their room—often literally. The problem was considerably worse in some cities, but it was significant in the Valley.

In late 1945, a small group of veterans got together to discuss their housing situation. Or, rather, their lack of housing situation. Most were married; some had children or had children on the way. Some were living with relatives, others were in doubled up living quarters, some lived in barns or sheds. After talking the thing into the ground, and realizing they would have to help themselves, they formed a cooperative to benefit veterans and incorporated as a nonprofit called Valley Homes, Inc.

The members found a thirty-acre prune and apricot ranch on the outskirts of Campbell that the owner would give them an option on, and, after much frustration, and being tossed out of every bank they entered, they found a local resident who was willing to take a chance on them. He put up the money to purchase the land and offered them a $32,000 mortgage for one year at 5 percent. They subdivided the land into eighty-two building sites—eighty home sites for veterans and two for a neighborhood store. They also set aside two and a half acres for a park that would encircle the community.

The veterans built their houses over a few years with varying degrees of professional help, and, at least initially, a lot of helping each other. Much of the construction was done on evenings and on weekends. City water was available, but sewer lines were not, so each lot had a septic tank. There was no natural gas in the area yet, so the houses relied on electricity for heating and cooking.

The labor unions, which since gold rush times had been stronger in San Francisco than anywhere else in the West, had made their way down the peninsula years earlier. The unions did not have a problem with the veterans' housing development as long as each owner worked on his own house. But as soon as they swapped labor, the unions ordered all union workers off the job. Despite this and other problems, the association was able to refinance the loan before the year was up and also obtain an additional $5,400 to help with general development costs. By the time a few houses were completed, they even had gravel on some of the streets. The tract was eventually named Aquino Park. [3]

Valley Homes, about 1947
Courtesy of Sourisseau Academy for State and Local History, San Jose State University

Valley Homes, house under construction, about 1947
Courtesy of Sourisseau Academy for State and Local History, San Jose State University

Robin Chapman

My father was from Homewood, Alabama, where his father worked in the advertising business and hardly ever removed his tie. My mother was from Spokane, Washington, where her father was a sheriff's deputy. They met when Captain William Ashley Chapman, serving along with millions of other men in World War II, was stationed at Geiger Field, near my mother's hometown.

They knew each other for just six weeks before they married. They were together for six more weeks before my father headed overseas for the last and greatest battle of the war in the Pacific—the Battle of Okinawa.

Reunited, they came to the Santa Clara Valley in 1947 when my father, an engineer, took a job at Ames Aeronautical Research Laboratory at Moffett Field. Ames was a branch of the National Advisory Committee for Aeronautics, a federal agency that later morphed into NASA. It was one of the first places in the Santa Clara County to explore the new technologies that would one day transform the area into Silicon Valley.

Ames was built on the site of what once had been orchards and bean fields.

At first, my parents lived in Palo Alto, the nearest city of any size to Moffett Field that had housing for them—and there wasn't much housing available even there. Next to nothing had been built for civilians during World War II, so all the returning veterans found housing a challenge.

My parents took what they could find—a rented room in a little house on Palo Alto's Emerson Street that my mother dubbed "Denman's Dump." If that seemed cramped, things got even tighter when my sister arrived that autumn. My mother hoped they could one day buy a house in Palo Alto. My father, it turned out, had other ideas.

All during the last year of the war, in the midst of nightly air raids, kamikaze attacks, and anti-aircraft guns booming around him on the little island of Ie Shima, he spent his free time building a house on paper. He sketched in his pyramidal tent as he worked twelve-hour shifts as commander of C Company, 1902 Engineer Aviation Battalion, United States Army Corps of Engineers. As the war wound down he wrote my mother [the following]:

> "You speak of buying a house. I wouldn't buy someone else's house or one that someone else had built unless it was pretty cheaply priced. I don't believe we'd ever be satisfied unless we planned exactly what we wanted."

When he got home, he began to plan what he and his family would need. My mother, never much of a risk-taker, wasn't so sure. She may not have liked "Denman's Dump," but she liked Palo Alto. Home to Stanford University, its lovely old homes were large and its neighborhoods neat, with sidewalks and mature shade trees. Unfortunately, these same features meant fewer houses to choose from and higher prices.

The prices may have made the difference. In the winter of 1947, my mother gave in, and the Chapmans bought a set of house plans and a lot in an apricot orchard in Los Altos.

Los Altos was then an unincorporated town on the peninsula that stretches along the western edge of San Francisco Bay. It was just a few miles south of Palo Alto and 4.9 miles west of Moffett Field. In the late 1940s, it was transforming itself from a rural village into a pretty town.

Almost all of the lots in Los Altos were being subdivided from land that had been in orchard production for at least half a century.

The construction project took two years of weekend work. I heard this story all my life. What a sacrifice my father made for his family, I always thought to myself. It just goes to show you how little I knew him.

When he died in 2010 at the age of ninety—just three months after the death of my mother—I found an old memorandum book in the top drawer of his dresser. It had rested there for many years with other things he had saved: some old coins that had belonged to his father; notes to himself about how to be a good husband; homemade cards from my sister and me; a Valentine's Day poem from my mother. Among them was this little green notebook.

I opened it and saw a chronological notation of all the hours he had spent building the house, what he had done on each day he worked, and who had helped him. . . . I realized then, after he was gone, how much it meant to him, building that house for his family. He had made a safe return from the war—"home alive in '45!" as the soldiers repeated to one another during that last terrible year in the Pacific. He was young and strong. He was in love. He had a family. Now he was giving his family a home and making it with his own hands. Life was very good. [4]

***

In the Santa Clara Valley, in the years following the war, comparatively few houses were built by cooperatives or by the homeowners themselves. The overwhelming majority were built on large tracts that had been subdivided for fifty to two hundred houses or more. I discuss how this mass-produced housing came into being in chapter 7, but for now will continue with some additional GI stories.

T.S.

I think Dad knew where he wanted to live after the war, and his immediate prospects upon returning home reinforced that. There was no work in Washington, Pennsylvania, where he and Mom grew up, so he moved to Detroit, where his uncle Frank lived. Dad's experience with radios in the Army probably helped him get hired at International Detrola, a company that made car radios. After a short time Mom packed a bag, went to Detroit to meet him, and they married.

But Detroit was not safe, and Dad had seen the beauty of California and knew that opportunity awaited there. However, they were not in a financial position to buy a car. Cars had not been produced during the war years, and supply and demand kept prices high for a few years. But Dad was so desperate to get out of Detroit and go west that he and Mom even discussed traveling cross-country by bicycle. They had good reason to be serious about it.

Detroit was a violent city at the time, largely because of the racial tension that lingered after the Detroit race riot of June 1943. Before the war, and especially between 1910 and 1930, millions of people had moved from the rural areas of the southern states to the industrial cities of the North and West seeking factory work. Most were African Americans, but many were not. After the Great Depression, and with war on the horizon, this migration began again in earnest as even more workers were needed for the production of war materiel. These two migrations together became known as the Great Migration, and no city was affected more than Detroit, where enormous factories ran day and night during the war. The population of the city increased by 350,000 between early 1941 and mid-1943. Obviously, the need for additional housing was very great. The U.S. government stepped in to build two huge housing projects, one for white workers and one for black workers. For some reason, the Roosevelt administration, apparently against the recommendation of the Detroit Housing Commission, decided to build the project for the black workers in a predominantly white neighborhood. Tensions rose over several months and eventually boiled over on June 20-22, and the National Guard was called in to restore order. By the time some semblance of order was restored, thirty-four people were dead, hundreds more had been wounded, and millions of dollars' worth of property had been destroyed. The feeling of ill will continued after the Guard left, and Detroit was the scene of violence for years, especially after nightfall. [i] 5

So, when Mom went into labor with my older brother in the middle of the night, and they had no telephone, she refused to let Dad go out to get the doctor. She told him, "No! It's not safe!" Although as a child of nine, she had helped her father clean up a large amount of blood after her mother suffered a miscarriage, she felt it was safer for Dad to stay and deliver the child than it was for him to go out into the night. After all, her mother had given birth to eleven children at home, and for the most part all turned out well.

---

[i] Add in the flight to the suburbs by those (almost all white) who could afford to move out of the city, and this is a summary of how U.S. inner cities became predominantly African American. There were many lasting effects of WWII. This was one of them.

In the summer of 1947, after my brother was born, International Detrola shut down for the season, so Dad was out of a job. He immediately came out to San Jose by himself to look for work. Mom went back home to Pennsylvania with their four-month-old baby until Dad could get work and send for her. [6]

After Dad got work, Mom and my brother flew out to join Dad. Mom wrote in her journal: "California—three of us now. Arrived in San Francisco in August. Thought I'd freeze to death. I love Pennsylvania summer walks in the evenings. It's cold in California in the evenings and the hills are brown."

The first work that Dad was able to get was making deliveries for a restaurant supply house. That was not at all what he or Mom had hoped for, and they were more than a little concerned about it. But they needed to be together, and after a short time Dad was hired on at Pacific Bell and had a good stable job. Things could have turned out very differently.

Dad and Mom were part of another great migration—that of the GIs and GI families to the West Coast after the war. It seems that in all our generations large numbers of Americans have been pioneers, leaving where they had grown up. A high percentage moved by necessity.

When the family was reunited, they lived in a house on Ruge Lane, near Capitol Avenue and Penitentia Creek Road. The house, which was surrounded by orchards, they shared with a Mrs. Long and her son. Dad worked downtown, but they lived out in the country, so he hitchhiked to work because he still didn't have a car. Early on a man named George picked Dad up, and thereafter Dad had a regular ride with him.

About a year later, they moved to 140 East Santa Clara Street in downtown San Jose, where they rented an apartment on the third story of a building. Phil and Mary Drew, another young couple of about the same age, and who were also beginning a family, lived on the second floor below them, and there was a meat market at street level.

A building boom began in the Santa Clara Valley about 1950, as the need for housing had increased greatly, and both the Drews and the Stanleys went out to look at new homes. Both couples looked at some of the same tracts and were impressed that the El Quito Park homes, at the northeastern edge of the Saratoga district, had an extra half-bath.

At that time most houses had only one bathroom. But the houses were way out in the country, and neither Mary nor Mom liked the concrete slab floors.

One day Mary called Mom and told her, "You are now talking to the homeowner Drews." "Mary! You didn't buy one of those houses with cement floors, did you?" Well, yes, as a matter of fact they had, and the Stanleys followed suit shortly afterward and bought a house on the next block. [i]

The terms for GIs were pretty good: $25 down for the cost of the blueprints, a twenty-five year mortgage, and payments of $57.55 a month. My folks had considered a house in Willow Glen, but they could not qualify for the loan. So the Stanleys—now a family of four, moved out to a street called Paseo Flores on July 7, 1950. My brother was three years old, my sister was four months old, Mom was twenty-five, and Dad was all of twenty-six.

***

The massive flow of World War II veterans to the Valley, however, did not begin in earnest until early 1950, mostly because the infrastructure, that Earl Warren talked about at the beginning of this chapter, was not yet in place. I will tell you the story behind that infrastructure in chapter 7, but since those GIs who came at that later time make up the largest part of this first wave of migration to the Valley, I will have a few of them tell you their stories here.

Geoff Goble
My dad was from near Syracuse, New York, and joined the Army Air Corps near the end of World War II. He was trained to fly, but the war ended before he shipped out. After he finished his time in service, he and my mother moved to Albany, New York.

My mother had a bad case of asthma, and her doctor told her there were only two places she could live that would be beneficial to her. One

---

[i] Concrete slab floors were a new cost-cutting measure, and not everyone liked them. The original sales brochure for our tract stated: "The homes of El Quito Park are constructed on a thoroughly proven foundation principle which is as practical as it is modern. The concrete slab and attached footings are steel reinforced and poured on a built-up waterproof membrane which will stop all moisture from the soil below." Although many people disliked the slab floors, the majority ended up buying houses built on a slab. In those days of leather-soled shoes, my mother wrote: "My legs were wrecked in three months."

was in Greece, because of its Mediterranean climate; the other was Saratoga, California.

So my folks came out to California in late 1949 or early 1950 when I was just a year old. They bought a small trailer, loaded up everything they had, and set out. There were no freeways then, and it was not so easy driving across the country.

The trailer was attached with a bumper hitch that kept coming loose, so they had to stop frequently to tighten it. You couldn't tighten it too much or it wouldn't work at all. They also had flat tires along the way. Going across the desert, the radiator needed water too. All this with a one-year-old!

Along the way, they stopped to see my uncle in Texas and then drove up through Southern California to see my mother's parents in Paso Robles. They had recently located there after giving up on the farm in Kansas where my mother grew up.

When my parents arrived in San Jose, they lived on the east side, on Cragmont Avenue off of Alum Rock.   Eventually, they bought a new home in the Cambrian area (for $9,700), which is where I grew up. [7]

Goodwin Steinberg

Like so many other post-war GIs, I was drawn to the memory of the San Francisco Bay Area I had visited while in the service as I pondered where to establish my career. Drawn by the beauty of the bay itself, by majestic spans that bridged land to land, by the solid mooring of the already bustling city of San Francisco, many veterans who had passed through on tours of duty were determined to return after the war.

To me, the San Francisco Bay Area presented an irresistible opportunity to build an architectural practice. More importantly, it seemed to me to be a perfect place to raise a family.

Then there was the San Francisco Peninsula, abundant in flat, open space, with good north-south traffic flow. It was home to an intellectual center that proved ripe for an ambitious architect seeking to invest himself in building a career. The temperate microclimate, generally ranging from 50 degrees in the winter to 90 degrees in the summer, was mild enough for outdoor sports, dining and entertaining while still variable enough to display seasonal changes: hillsides turning spring green to summer gold, autumn leaves, and sometimes even frost.

Locked in by the bay on the one side and the Santa Cruz Mountains on the other, the Valley was largely protected from the high winds that sometimes plagued San Francisco.

Abundant and inexpensive land offered newcomers to the Santa Clara Valley an opportunity that they could seize. Post-war GIs, Stanford graduates, and others attracted to the area could realize their dreams largely because they could afford to buy land—for their businesses, homes, and, often in the early years, both.

Stanford University, already well established at sixty years old, was the biggest enticement of all. . . . Speakers came from all over the world to discuss their artistic pursuits at the design conferences. To me, the artistry was paramount, and a big draw. . . . The serenity of the Stanford campus was also rejuvenating: picnicking in natural oak groves, enjoying pastoral landscapes, and slowing the everyday workaday pace recharged a driven man's batteries. In combination with the discussions of functionality that students from the School of Engineering brought to the conference, attendees came away with a new appreciation for the balance between utility and aesthetics.

If we stayed in Chicago, both my father and my father-in-law would be looking over my shoulder, second-guessing every move. But the idea of leaving the security of family and financial stability did not come easily to my wife, and even I had my doubts from time to time as we mulled over the decision to move to California with two small children and no job. It was as much effort to convince myself as it was an attempt to persuade my wife when I assured her, "I know that we will make a living. Trust me."

Eight years and two children later, we finally made our way back to the Bay Area, to make the South Peninsula town of Los Altos our home. By then I had received my architectural degree from the University of Illinois. [8]

Bill O'Dell

I was in the Army, stationed at a little artillery post on the Pacific side of the Panama Canal, when the war broke out. If the canal had ever been attacked there is no way we could have defended it. The artillery pieces we had were old, undersized, and had short range. We got supplies by taking packhorses down to a village that was hours away. Later, I was called Stateside and became a drill instructor.

What about all the yelling that I had to do? You knew the lives of many of those boys depended on how well you did your job. If you didn't train them right, they would be less likely to survive in a combat situation.

When the war was over, there was little opportunity for work in the little hamlet on the Ohio River where I was from. My sister moved out to Sunnyvale first. After she got the franchise for the Foster's Freeze on Sunnyvale-Saratoga Road, I moved out and went to work for her as a fry cook. Later I took a job at the miniature golf course on El Camino, which I enjoyed. I played golf whenever I could. [9]

Al Thompson

I was born and raised in Chicago. In 1944, toward the end of the war, I enlisted in the Naval Air Corps V-5A program (similar to V-12) to become a Navy pilot. They sent us to naval school—in North Dakota, of all places.

The Navy had enough pilots, so we were sent to naval engineering college. My class went to Dickinson, North Dakota, to a state teachers college that was converted to Navy standards. The curriculum included general courses with emphasis on engineering. It was a concentrated schedule, and after one year it was equivalent to one and a half years of college credits.

Those of us who scored high on flight aptitude were accepted for preflight training. I was assigned to St. Mary's College in Moraga, California. Our intense training consisted of four hours of naval flight subjects and four hours of athletics every day. Upon completion I was assigned to Glenview Naval Air Station, Illinois, where we learned to fly in Stearman biplanes, which are still used today for crop dusting.

In 1946 the war was over, so the Navy offered us the opportunity to stay in the service for five more years as naval flyers or be discharged. I chose the latter in order to get my college degree at UCLA under the GI Bill.

After graduation, I had several jobs but longed to get into the aviation industry. So I was hired by Lockheed Aircraft Company in 1952 at Burbank, California, in labor relations. After a few years I transferred to the new missile division in Van Nuys. That division grew rapidly, which led to a move to the Bay Area.

Lockheed had purchased 160 acres in Sunnyvale, California, and I moved north in the first wave of transfers. We started in an insurance building off the Alameda in San Jose. Then, in September of 1956, when building 201 was completed, we moved to Palo Alto. Across from us was the headquarters for Hewlett Packard.

We had no air conditioning in those days. One of my administrative jobs was to issue fans to deserving scientists. They had to justify their need for one as we had only a limited number of them.

Our location was ideal. We ate our bag lunches on the patio looking at the western hills where Japanese gardeners planted flower gardens in the hills beyond—a very peaceful setting. It was beautiful! [10]

Grady Hall

I grew up in rural Louisiana, a poor kid who picked cotton. (Although, admittedly at the time we didn't know we were poor.) When the war came, it was my way out. At seventeen I joined the Navy. But the Navy was not much better than Louisiana because I spent my days in the engine room as a grease monkey down in the lower deck of a ship.

After the war, with the GI Bill available, I applied to the University of Southern California. California was about as far away from Louisiana as you could get and still be in the United States. I had heard nothing but good things about California, so I applied at USC. The fellow in the admissions office took one look at my high school transcript, shook his head, and with a half-smile said, "You better go back to Louisiana and make up some classwork. You're not close to being qualified to come here." The whole appointment lasted about one minute. So I went back, enrolled in a junior college where I made up what I didn't do in high school, and then, when I had gone as far as I could there, went on to Louisiana Tech in Rustin, where I got my degree in mechanical engineering.

I had always admired the guys who flew the crop dusters. I thought they were really something. After all, they were up there flying those planes; I was down on the ground picking cotton. As soon as I graduated, my wife and I put everything we had in our 1949 Ford and headed out to Southern California. I hoped to get into the aircraft industry but couldn't right away and had to take a very poor job for a while. After almost a year, I got on at Lockheed in Burbank, and after the Missiles and Space Division relocated to Sunnyvale, we moved north. We lived in an apartment on Hamilton Avenue for several months while our house was being built in Saratoga.

The best job I ever had in Louisiana was wheeling sawdust from the lumber mill into the surrounding woods with a wheelbarrow. That was when I was in college. Without the GI Bill, I don't want to think about how things would have turned out. [11]

T.S.

Many GIs in the early wave of postwar migration were entrepreneurs, although the term was not used at the time. Until the late 1950s, when Lockheed came, very few were involved in what today we would call technology. Our neighborhood was typical of many, if not most, of the new neighborhoods that sprouted up all over the Valley in the early to mid-1950s. Below is a snapshot of our neighborhood.

Mr. Van Riper, across the street, operated a hamburger stand he built on Saratoga Avenue. Mr. Scott had a trenching machine that he operated and parked out in front of his house. Mr. Green was a masonry contractor. Mr. Tiffany owned and operated a print shop in San Jose. Mr. Mullis drove a milk truck for Foremost Dairy. Mr. Comeford was a newly minted attorney. The Cains, Whiteners, and Mr. and Mrs. Juice were all retired. Mr. Kutslip was a maintenance foreman at Varian. Mrs. Cronk, Mrs. Hopkins, Mrs. Fowler, and Mr. Van Dyke were teachers. Mr. Walsh and Mr. Beechie were carpenters. Mr. Kelly owned the local liquor store. Mr. Drew was a chemist for one of the food companies. Dad and Mr. Miller worked for the phone company. Most of the women were stay-at-home moms.

The new housing tracts were filled with young married couples and almost all had children—probably an average of three per household. The lack of experience of these young couples, combined with their being away from home, took its toll and many divorced. Thankfully, there were some older couples, like Mr. and Mrs. Whitener and the Van Rippers in our neighborhood, who added much-needed stability and wise counsel when asked for.

That is pretty much what the new neighborhoods on the west side of the Valley looked like before the late 1950s when Lockheed moved in. Almost all the residents were Caucasian, and that remained the same until the middle to late 1960s.

A number of Japanese families owned and worked small strawberry patches or nurseries nearby. The Yamashita children and some other Japanese American kids attended our elementary school. A few families of Hispanic descent also lived nearby—some in our housing tract, some in the company housing located in the cherry orchard at the back of the Campbell Cage Company. Other than that, I remember one Filipino family and an Asian family named Sue. The rest were of European descent.

Many World War II veterans who eventually came to the Valley stuck it out in the eastern cities for many years before making the move to California. My uncle Chet was among them. He finally gave up on Detroit in 1960. Lockheed recruited heavily in Michigan, and he had a job waiting for him here when they moved out. I still remember him driving up to our house with my aunt Alice and their four girls in their new, green 1960 Ford station wagon. It had been a long trip, but they were all excited to see us and to start their new lives in California. As with many of the GI families that came later, they required a significant amount of coaxing (from my dad in this case) before they were ready to pull up stakes and head west. Had they taken a trip out to visit, a lot of postage stamps could have been saved.

***

As for the people who had lived in the Valley of Heart's Delight before the war—they had no idea what was coming upon them. I once asked Dave Pitman, whose father was an old farmer for whom I worked in the 1960s, "What did you think about so many people moving here after the end of the war?" Surprised by my question, he paused, shook his head, and replied, "We thought there was plenty of land."

Snapshots of what newly arriving GIs came to after the war:

Above: the corner of Stevens Creek and Saratoga-Sunnyvale roads, 1939.
Cupertino consisted of the train station, a general store, a few shops, and
maybe a couple dozen houses.

Photo courtesy of California History Center, De Anza College

Next pages: New Owens-Corning fiberglass plant in Santa Clara, 1948 >>>>

Courtesy of Santa Clara City Library

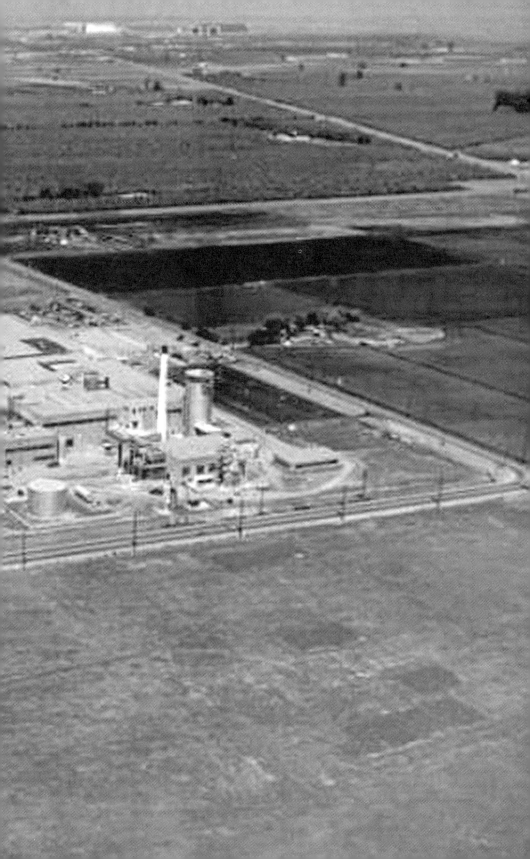

Chapter 4

The Changing Countryside, 1940s to Mid-1950s

The stories in this chapter are typical of the times and portray the gradual, disarming, and even confusing nature of the transformation that took place as the Valley began to shed its agricultural roots after the war.

Henry Petrino

I was born in San Jose in 1947 (a third-generation native), and started working on my grandfather's ranch of apricots, prunes, and walnuts at the age of eight. Like the other younger children, I started out picking up "ground fruit" from under the trees. I remember vividly how pleased with myself I was after the first tree and my sense of achievement as I approached the end of the first row. Then reality sank in—the next row. That was certainly a lesson that would serve me well for the next sixty years or so.

In the middle 1950s we learned that there was to be a new component added to our valley. Something called Valley Fair was to be built way out on Stevens Creek Road. It would be a shopping center, whatever that might be. I very clearly remember the adults, and in particular those adults of my grandparents' age, griping to each other about it. "Who the heck is going to go all the way out there to shop? Are they crazy? That's what downtown is for." When construction started, I can remember riding my bicycle through the construction site. When it opened (in 1956 or 1957, I think) the world of shopping changed forever.

Around that same time, maybe a little later, my aunt, uncle, and two cousins, who lived on Coleman Avenue near the airport, were advised by the state that their home would be required for construction of the new Highway 17 freeway. They relocated to the east side, up near the San Jose Country Club, so things turned out well for them. Of course, that didn't dampen the griping. "What do we need a freeway there for? It's a total waste of money. No wonder our taxes are so high!" Their house sat on the south side of Coleman just about where northbound 17 goes under it today. [1]

Gene Arnold

In the 1950s, while I was at Hewlett Packard, a friend of mine from Varian and I contracted with the Libby's Cannery to deliver fifteen tons of fresh apricots and twenty tons of dried during the season. We picked and cut the 'cots in the evenings and on the weekends in our spare time. That was our vacation money.

In those days, the housing developers were selling houses with quarter-acre lots, and they'd leave a lot of the fruit trees on the property. So all these people had apricots, and we'd go by and ask them if they wanted their apricots. If they didn't, and a lot of people didn't, we'd pick them. That is, as long as the fruit was big. We avoided asking at the houses where the fruit was small. We didn't have any trouble finding 'cots to pick. It worked out good for everybody.

I lived in Cupertino in one of those new tract houses, and we cut and smoked the 'cots there. There was just a little road coming out to the highway (now DeAnza Boulevard) from the tract through the orchards. The highway was two lanes.

I built a sulphur shed in back of my house out of lath and tarpaper, and we even had a little railroad track and pushcart to roll the trays of 'cots into and out of the sulphur shed. The house had a flat roof, so that was perfect. We'd put the trays of 'cots up there to dry. Libby's supplied the boxes and we had trays from somewhere. We'd make about $500 for the season. That was a good bit of extra money in those days. [2]

Rhonda Bump
My folks moved several times and in 1951 ended up building a home in Campbell, where they lived until my father passed away in 2000. My brother was born in 1949, and I was born in 1953. The land our folks purchased was part of an eighty-acre farm. They bought the one-acre plot that had the well on it, then later subdivided it and sold one third of it to pay off the mortgage. My father built our house around an existing shack using scavenged materials. He began working the soil, and with water available for irrigation, he had a huge garden and maintained the existing orchard of apricot and prune trees. Every year he grew massive quantities of tomatoes, corn, green beans (always Blue Lakes), yellow squash, crookneck and zucchini, rhubarb, and various herbs. We pretty much grew everything we ate except meat, although I did have a 4-H lamb. In later years, my father relied on a friend, Angelo Troquato, who was known as "the sharecropper." Angelo mostly grew basil that he sold to local restaurants and grocery stores. After my father's death, the home was sold, bulldozed, and replaced with three McMansions. The well was capped, as required upon transfer of property, and there is no evidence of the once-lush land that was there. [3]   ***

Tully Rd. at Hwy 101, 1953, looking east.
Eastridge Mall is now on golf course land.
Courtesy of History San Jose

N.M.

I moved with my family in 1943 to what was then Cupertino. My parents had purchased a summer and weekend home on Titus Avenue, which runs between Prospect and Cox. When Saratoga incorporated, everything up to Prospect was included in Saratoga. Our summer home became our residence, and my dad commuted by train to San Francisco. After the war, Dad retired, and in 1951 he completed building a house across the street. In 1956 my husband and I purchased the home, and my parents moved to Santa Cruz, selling the rest of the property.

While ranching was still going on, we encountered many of the situations you wrote about in your [Prune Pickers] book, such as farm equipment and getting workers. Those old farm trucks always knew when the season was over and just died on the spot. [4]

Eugene D. Sharp

Our family moved to Mountain View in the spring of 1943 because my father was in charge of installing the electrical equipment at the forty-by-eighty wind tunnel and two other wind tunnels at Moffett Field for Westinghouse.

We lived on two acres, between Church and Center streets, south of Calderon and cattycorner to the baseball field of the Highway School. The back acre contained about a hundred apricot trees, and the fruit became ripe in late June and early July. In 1947, we had a bumper crop of juicy apricots. I picked most of the sixty thousand pounds of apricots from a three-legged ladder. The result was ten thousand pounds of dried apricots, which we sold to Marianni Fruit Packing in Cupertino.

The summer of 1944, when I turned twelve, I became a Tenderfoot Scout in Troop 42, led by Skipper Montgomery, and took my first Boy Scout hike to Stevens Creek Reservoir. . . . We put on our packs somewhere in Mountain View and hiked along Grant Road with the Permanente Cement trucks roaring past us in both directions and raising dust all around. After a few hours, we got to the corner of the road leading to the Permanente Limestone Quarry, which was to the right, and stopped at the Rodeo Inn for some refreshments. After being refreshed, we hiked toward Stevens Creek Dam.

When we got a little past the dam, we went up to two miners' cabins across the road from the reservoir. We were to stay in one or both of them. Along the way, the older scouts talked about hunting snipe. At night, one would take a bag and a flashlight out into the woods. The snipe would see the light and jump into the bag. This sounded really weird to me, but I listened carefully. We cooked our supper and put our sleeping bags in one of the miners' cabins. Some of the other guys went out to look around. Suddenly, they came running back and said that they had seen a dead miner in the other cabin. We all huddled together in our sleeping bags waiting for the scoutmaster to arrive.

The snipe hunt never happened, Skipper Montgomery did not show up, no dead miner was found, and we had a nice hike home. [5]

Evelyn Stevens-White

My husband, Dave, and I moved to Sunnyvale on Valentine's Day 1954. Our new housing tract of about a hundred homes was called Sunnyvale Acres. It encompassed Georgia, Carolina, Glendale, Ferndale, and Morse avenues. The homes were about a thousand square feet. We came from San Francisco and couldn't find affordable housing until [we came to] Sunnyvale.

It seemed like we were coming to the country. . . . Shortly after we moved in, the pear orchard on Morse was removed and Morse Elementary and Madrone Junior High were built. We were naive gardeners at that time. As the pear trees were being uprooted, we took one to our house and planted it. Soon we found that it wouldn't bear any more fruit.

Beyond our tract, at what is now Fairoaks Avenue near the 101 freeway, were another pear orchard and a few cattle. Early Saturday mornings in the spring a crop-dusting plane came over our house very low. Since both of us were commuting to San Francisco during the week (by train) and wanted to sleep in, we were not thrilled.

When my mother would come to visit, we would drive on Evelyn toward Mountain View in the spring to see the trees in bloom. What a beautiful sight it was! Mary Avenue was a small country road with many flower growers with their greenhouses. Westinghouse, on Hendy, was a busy place still, even after the war. The canneries—Libby-McNeil and Schuckyl—were full of workers during the harvest season. Murphy Avenue was the main downtown street with city hall, Kirkish Department Store, the Bank of Italy, and other businesses. [6]   ***

Next pages: portion of Sunnyvale, 1955, Fremont High School at upper left
Courtesy of Sunnyvale Historical Society

T.S.
According to people in San Jose, we lived "way out in Saratoga." Of course, today you cannot tell where one city stops and another starts, but it was not so then.

My mother later wrote in her journal about her move to Saratoga in 1950: "Downtown San Jose was good. Moving to Saratoga, we were eight miles out of town. Having no means of transportation, I was stuck." [i]

Separated from the rest of the world by orchards, life was a little different then. People in the outlying housing tracts like ours burned their rubbish in their backyards—a standard Saturday morning chore for kids my age. Even in San Jose, in the fall, people raked their leaves out onto the street to burn. (The streets were paved with concrete.) We would drive down some of the streets on Sunday morning on the way to church, and there would be all these fires—some tended to, some left smoldering.

Another thing: People knew each other. We knew a lot of the people in our area. Although we lived out in Saratoga, we had many friends in San Jose, and it was amazing how many people we ran into in various places who knew our family or at least had heard about us. That happened frequently, and other people have told me that was a common experience for their families too.

People we knew from the Evergreen Dairy delivered milk to the door in glass bottles. We knew the butcher and the baker, although I have forgotten their names. Our mailman, Art, lived around the corner. He knew all our goings on from handling our mail and would ask how I was coming along on one project or another. Kid stuff, but he took interest in it. He did not have children of his own, so, looking back on it, I suppose he kind of adopted a lot of the kids on his mail route.

Joan Fox
We came out from Ann Arbor, Michigan, in 1958. I remember driving up into the hills and looking down on the Valley. It was so exciting. All the trees were in bloom. It was all pink and white. [The development] was just starting. There were groups of houses, and then there was flat land. Valley Fair had just opened up—it was just two stores then—but it was

---

[i] There was bus service, provided by the Peerless Stage bus company, but it was minimal.

in the middle of nowhere. You had to drive on these little two-lane roads to get there. It was all farmland between downtown Sunnyvale (which was one or two streets at the time) and Valley Fair. When you got to Valley Fair—all of a sudden there was this store sitting there. We did not have the freeways we have now, so getting around was different. [7]

Dave Pitman

We had two electric fences at the farm. One was around the back to keep the sheep out of the orchards. The other was around the garden to keep the cow out. The one in the back was set a few feet inside the perimeter fence. At ten thousand volts but very low amps, the jolt from it was not enough to hurt you, but it sure would get your attention. Cows are curious. After we put it up, our cow saw the wire, was curious, and touched it with her wet nose. She didn't do that again. A rooster hit it with his comb. That wasn't pretty.

As the land was developed around us and houses were built, sometimes one of the dogs from those houses would get inside the perimeter fence. One day someone's dog was out there yelping up a storm. He'd obviously touched the electric fence and was not happy about it. Another time, one of the neighbor kids decided he wanted to do some exploring, I guess. He got over the perimeter fence and got shocked. His mother got up in arms, and she complained to PG&E.

So a PG&E person came out and advised Dad that he had an illegal fence. (It wasn't illegal, they were just trying to—you know.) Dad had some PG&E stock, so he called up PG&E corporate headquarters and told them, "I want to speak at the next shareholders' meeting." "What do you want to talk about?" "My electric fence." Well, they didn't want that, so the San Francisco office sent someone out to take care of this man, and make this go away. The instructions were, "Make it safe but keep the sheep in."

I guess they did something; I don't know. [8]

***

A few years ago, I was at the Santa Clara Art and Wine Festival to sell my book *The Last of the Prune Pickers: A Pre-Silicon Valley Story*. About five or six people came up to my table and told me this next story with minor variations.

Unknown

*We used to sneak into the orchard across the street from our apartment
to play. We'd climb in the trees, have walnut fights, play hide-and-seek,
and otherwise have a good time. The farmer wasn't too keen on all that,
and would come out with his shotgun, which he loaded with salt. I never
got shot at, but I guess some kids did. Once my mother decided to go
and collect some walnuts in the orchard. She had her apron full of them
and when she turned around the farmer was standing there with his
shotgun cradled in his arm. She said, "I guess I better leave these here."
He replied, "I think that would be a good idea."* [9]

***

Meanwhile, at Stanford, the realities of population growth and
increased financial need led to the decision to build the Stanford
Shopping Center. Stanford's endowment stated that the university
could not sell any land; but it did not say anything about leasing it. So
in 1954, Stanford broke ground for the shopping center on land that
had been vineyards, and the first shops opened the next year. The
project was well planned, set the standard for new shopping center
development, and provided the money that helped catapult Stanford
into a top research university.

As Henry Petrino pointed out earlier in this chapter, the shopping
center was a new concept. And, like its counterparts all over the
country, the new Stanford Shopping Center struck a heavy blow to
local merchants. Many were forced out of business, but the growing
population eventually healed the wounds of those who survived.

The cows that had grazed on the hills above the campus were kicked
out too. Although almost everyone was sad to see them go, renting
pastureland to Piers Dairy barely covered the taxes on that land and
soon would not.[10] So plans were drawn up for an industrial park, the
likes of which had not been seen before but that would set a
precedent for major universities in the future.

Cuttin' Cots and Pickin' Prunes

(A Minor)   Daddy, born on the frozen prairie,
Landed northwest down by the sea.
Wanderlust just captured his soul;
Life of adventure became his goal.

Arizona called his name
And things were never the same.
A Kingman girl, oh so fine,
A hidden gem down at the mine.

Just seventeen, he captured her heart,
Swept her away, a brand new start.
California, paved with gold;
Packin' their bags, they were sold.

(A Maj)   To the Valley of Heart's Delight,
Their new home, oh so right.
Life was simple then, all things right;
Oh, so right, Heart's Delight.

> *Chorus:*
> Growin' up in a carefree world,
> A fifties child in a family,
> Workin' hard, summer afternoons
> Cuttin' 'cots and pickin' prunes,
> Cuttin' 'cots and pickin' prunes.

Before they knew it, children three,
Brother, sisters, family;
Growing, scouting, twirling, whee,
Kids on bikes, we were so free.

Cuttin' 'cots, a quarter a tray,
Back then, it went a long way.
Bubble in time, perfect day,
But that was then, not today.

> *Chorus*

(A Minor)   Seasons passed, the children grew,
Subdivisions made the orchards few;
Shopping malls, not county fairs,
The simple life, no longer theirs,
Cuttin' 'cots and pickin' prunes,
Cuttin' 'cots and pickin' prunes.

Rhonda Bump[11]

Chapter 5

Early Electronics: IBM, Varian, HP, and Others

Due to a strong maritime trade and the presence of several local naval bases, the San Francisco Bay Area became one of the leading centers for the development of radio and radar.

Bell Labs was back east, in New York and New Jersey, but around San Francisco Bay was perhaps the highest concentration of amateur, or "ham," radio operators anywhere in the world.[i] These amateur enthusiasts were constantly figuring out better ways to send or receive a radio signal.

By 1920 many local, mostly young, men had caught the radio bug. Among them were a few notable teenagers: Bill Eitel, Jack McCullough, Charles Litton, and Frederick Terman.

Eitel picked up his mechanical skills in shop classes at Los Gatos High School and at his father's granite quarry. McCullough gained his at the California School of Mechanical Arts (later, Lick-Wilmerding High School) in San Francisco. Litton was a child prodigy, who at age eleven in 1915 operated an amateur radio station from his parents' Redwood City home. Later, he, too, attended the mechanical arts school. Terman, the son of a Stanford professor, began operating his own amateur radio station in Palo Alto in 1917. He was seventeen. [1]

These young men and many others were fascinated with radio and competed intensely to come up with new ways to solve practical problems. In the joy of solving a problem, they shared their knowledge with other hams at radio clubs throughout the area. This friendly competition and sharing of information led to many innovations among them and eventually to the founding of Litton Engineering (in 1932 in Redwood City) and Eitel-McCullough (in 1934, in San Bruno). Eitel-McCullough designed and manufactured high-powered vacuum tubes; Litton built equipment for making vacuum tubes. [2]

Both businesses were at the cutting edge of tube development and were propelled by the amateur radio market, which was constantly

---

[i] Originally a derogatory term, akin to a "ham" actor or an inept telegraph operator, the term eventually became a badge of honor in amateur radio circles.

clamoring for more powerful tubes that could transmit and receive radio signals at greater and greater distances. In the late 1930s, when Radio Detection and Ranging, or radar, was proved to be practical, these companies were in prime position to win large government contracts. And the local electronics industry began to blossom.

Vacuum tubes: These vacuum-sealed glass jars with electrodes in them were the main components of radio sets, as they were called. By running an electrical current through them, depending upon the design, they were used to generate, detect, or amplify radio signals. [3]

Courtesy of IBM Archives

Suddenly math became very important. It wasn't always that way, as a former Stanford mathematics professor tells us.

Harold Bacon
When I got my bachelor's degree and then my master's degree [in mathematics], what could I do? Well, I could teach mathematics in a high school. Or maybe I could try to be an actuary for an insurance company. That's what I thought I was gonna do, partly because I was an office boy in the actuary's department during the interval between my graduation from Los Angeles High School in 1923 till I came [to Stanford] as a freshman in 1924. And I thought, "This is great stuff." So I went back to L.A. and worked a year. . . before I came here on a PhD program. That was an outlet for people who were mathematicians, and

of course, if they went on and did graduate work to a fair extent, or even on to a PhD. . . then there was the university opportunity for teaching too. But there wasn't much. But my goodness, the technological revolution, to say nothing of the computer revolution and everything else. . . . The importance of mathematics in all fields has increased so much that, if you get a degree in mathematics, you may become a doctor of medicine. . . . It's a much wider market (that's a nasty word), for people who have degrees in mathematics now. . . . This is a matter of the whole society changing. [4]

***

With the government getting involved, Bay Area tube development got a huge push forward. At the request of Professor Terman, Charles Litton set up a tube research laboratory at Stanford that proved to be highly beneficial to the university, to Litton Engineering, and to the advancement of electronics in general. [5]

Into that lab at Stanford came Russell Varian, a genius with learning disabilities who needed six years to complete his bachelor's degree. In the Stanford laboratory, he and his brother, Sigurd, a college dropout, would invent by far the most powerful vacuum tube. It was called the klystron, and it changed everything in the fields of radar, microwaves, and telecommunications.

After the invention of the klystron, Stanford and the Varian brothers became formal partners in its further development. The brothers and others in their group would have access to the physics lab and to William Hansen, one of the top mathematicians on campus. The university and the group would split the profits from the group's innovations fifty-fifty.[6] This agreement continued until the threat of war became great, at which time the entire Stanford klystron team went east to Sperry Gyroscope to advance its development. The military urgently needed the klystron in order to perfect radar into the defensive weapon it could be but was not yet.

After World War II the Varians and almost all of the Stanford team returned to California and to Stanford University. In 1948 the brothers, along with William Hansen and Edward Ginzton, a physics professor at the university, formed Varian Associates. From the beginning, their directors included Frederick Terman and Leonard Schiff, the head of the physics department at Stanford. By then these men had worked together for several years, and many people who had been associated with them followed them into the company.

Varian, Eitel-McCullough, and Litton Engineering were not typical companies and they set a pattern for later Bay Area electronics businesses on many fronts.

From the gold rush years, San Francisco had taken the lead in the labor union movement in the United States, and by the late 1930s and early 1940s the region's unions were probably stronger than those anywhere else in the western states. Consequently, once Eitel-McCullough began landing government contracts, the unions wanted (as is commonly said) a piece of the pie, and began a union-organizing drive. But the unions were not dealing with dockworkers, merchant marines, or carpenters. They were dealing largely with engineers and highly skilled machinists.

Eitel-McCullough was unwilling to lose control of production to shop stewards so it established a profit-sharing program and a generous pension plan, made provisions for job security, and established a medical clinic for employees and their families. The company even opened a cafeteria and subsidized the meals. Litton took similar steps, and union organizers moved on to easier targets. [7]

The Varian brothers took the employer-employee relationship further. They had been born and raised in Halcyon, California, a utopian society on the central coast, and idealism was in their blood. Their company would be employee owned—a cooperative and "an association of equals." [8]

Likewise, in the 1940s, Sigurd Varian became an early member of the Ladera community in the Portola Hills above Stanford. Ladera was a cooperative, incorporated as the nonprofit Peninsula Housing Association. It was a nice idea but soon failed, as it needed money to build and maintain the community, and its directors refused to adopt restrictive covenants in the title deeds.

The idealism at Varian Associates was also sorely tried. The Cold War, and especially the Korean War, greatly increased the klystron market and to compete, the company had to accept help from Wall Street. Varian was playing with the big boys now, and the rules were different.

The relationship with Stanford, however, remained strong, and Varian Associates and the university would grow together. In an era when academic and industry relations were frowned upon or even forbidden, Stanford and industry thrived.

Edward Ginzton

Varian, like Hewlett Packard, began to develop very rapidly after the war, and it became obvious that very soon we would outgrow the tiny facility at San Carlos where the company was formed, [and] that we ought to identify some piece of land where we could build our own laboratory. One of the cornerstone ideas of the Varian Associates' enterprise was that we wanted to be close to the research being done at American universities, but Stanford University in particular. It was obvious to this group, both at the board level and to consultants, that we would push our ideas even further with access to Stanford faculty, Stanford students, and some of the Stanford facilities.

I believe it was my idea to try to convince the university to lease us some land, and this was debated at Varian, because even though it might have been a good idea, people said that Stanford land was more expensive, and might have other limitations. But we decided to try it and made the proposal for leasing a piece of land to the business office of Stanford. Terman was asked for his advice and obviously supported the idea. For one thing, he was on Varian's board of directors, and for another he saw the beginning of further development of industry in the proximity of Stanford.

We started with six acres and increased holdings to seventy-five acres over time. Hewlett Packard made a decision to follow our example, and Terman helped provide Hewlett Packard a site of leased land. After that, Terman's ideas began to generalize. You could see this growing into a very large enterprise, and he became the spokesman at Stanford [for] developing the idea that this could grow into something that might be called a park. [9]

***

And a park it was, and by 1960 Stanford Industrial Park had added many tenants. The early ones, besides Varian and Hewlett Packard, included GE, Lockheed, Eastman Kodak, and Zenith.

Hewlett Packard also had a profit-sharing plan and a stock option plan for employees. Originally, the company sold stock to employees at a small discount, but was disappointed when some employees who bought discounted stock turned around and sold it right away. Out of necessity the company added a vesting period. [10]

Before I go on to more stories about early Hewlett Packard, I need to say something about "the HP Way." Perhaps it was best expressed in an article in *Stanford Magazine*:

Early on, David Packard was jeered, not cheered, for his views on management. In 1942, at age 29, he attended a Stanford conference on wartime production. Dominated by industrialists from giants like Standard Oil and Westinghouse Electric, it was presided over by business school professor Paul Holden, a major management guru of the day. "Somehow, we got into a discussion of the responsibility of management," Packard later told Peninsula [Times Tribune] *journalist and historian Ward Winslow. "Holden made the point that management's responsibility is to the shareholders—that's the end of it. And I objected. I said, 'I think you're absolutely wrong. Management has a responsibility to its employees, it has a responsibility to its customers, and it has a responsibility to the community at large.' And they almost laughed me out of the room."* [11]

***

Gene Arnold

The GI Bill was very good, but it only paid for your books and tuition. You still had to eat and have a place to live. I worked all kinds of different jobs after I got out of the service. That's what you did in those days, you thought about how you could get a job.

Eventually, I spent twenty-five years with Hewlett Packard, from 1951 through 1975, first at the old property on [375] Page Mill Road and then at the new plant on the Stanford property. Mr. Packard was a personal friend as well as my boss. They were nice people—both of them.

We had a social club called the HP Harmony Plotters, which I was the president of. I coordinated the parties at the company ranch. In the early days, the founders had the idea of buying up an old Spanish land grant south of San Jose. They never did, but they did purchase a large ranch where we had company parties. We would bring in people by the busloads—usually six or seven buses. We would spend the day at the ranch and have dinner, then take the bus home. Dave and Bill would cook. I was the square dance caller. I was not in the HR department; I just kind of became a social leader.

When the sales reps came in, they would go to the ranch in south San Jose for R&R. They came in from all over the U.S. once a year for a conference in the building at Palo Alto, and then we would take them out to the ranch.

We had a softball team, and Dave came to most of the games. Bill came once in a while too. We played at night and on the weekends.

They also bought a parcel of land up in the Santa Cruz Mountains near Big Basin Park and called it Little Basin. Pete Voight ran the place, and I was always part of those events too.

We would have an hour for lunch. Everybody was young, so there was a lot of free time. Both locations in Palo Alto were great. Everything was close. You could go to town during lunch, do your shopping, go to the bank, whatever, and be back to work on time.

We even had square dances at lunchtime at the new building [at 1501 Page Mill Road], when it was being built. We would just go in there and kick a few boards out of the way, sweep up a little, and have the square dances. It was great fun. We played hard and worked hard.

The founders, Hewlett and Packard, did not live extravagant lives; they put it all back into the business. One time, they had some important people call, and between them, the best car they had to show them around in was a '38 Ford. They wanted to impress their guests so they asked my boss, Bill Mullen, if they could borrow his Cadillac.

We also had a lot of gatherings at Ricky's, a restaurant in what used to be Mayfield but is now just south Palo Alto. I remember Mr. Packard coming in one time, just filthy from head to toe. He had been out at the ranch working. As great a man as he was, he was a very humble man. He did things on his own. He did not play the part of a guy who had a lot of money. I never heard him, even in later years, being a smart aleck with his money.

My regular job was in production. In the beginning we worked out of a Quonset hut. We did "bright dipping," which was a process of cleaning aluminum to give it a high luster.

I was a manufacturing manager when we moved up on the hill (to 1501 Page Mill Road) on the Stanford property. We did a lot of things out of doors on sawhorses at the back of the shop. We had a paint shop, but there were things we could do outdoors.

At the time, we mostly made signal generators for the military—a special frequency counter for the Navy. Our model, the HP 524, was designed by Al Bagley and sold in the thousands.

Dave was hands-on in the products. He would come out and see us from time to time.

In those days, Dave wanted us to make as many of our own parts as possible. We also had some parts we bought from others. The idea is that they were components and we could just snap them together to make different products. We had a system of three-by-five cards for keeping track of all "corporate parts," which were front panels, gussets—things like that, that could fit on many instruments. It was a dual system, which was used until computers came out.

When we got our first computer, we put it in the basement.

Life at HP? If you had to work for a living, that was the place to be. 12

Dave Cochran

While in high school, I was a day laborer in the summer and worked digging the foundation for Dave Packard's first home in Los Altos. I started at HP when I ran out of money at Stanford the summer of '56 and switched to full time when I graduated in '58.

Originally, I applied at HP and was accepted on the Wave Analyzer production line in the "saw-tooth" building at 375 Page Mill Road for the summer. I saw a lot of autonomy, people-to-people consideration, and caring. One fellow came down with tuberculosis, but the check kept being delivered to his home. That was before any health insurance. 13

***

IBM

IBM's beginnings in San Jose were quite humble. Since many IBM machines were used in the Bay Area during the war, in 1943 the company began manufacturing computer cards locally.[i] More than one hundred IBMers moved to the Valley from IBM's Endicott, New

---

[i] The idea of using holes punched in paper to program machines was not new. Player pianos had been around since about 1900, and looms in textile mills were run on the same principle even earlier.

York, and Washington State plants and started operations in the former Temple Laundry building at Sixteenth and St. John streets. [14]

IBM's San Jose card plant, 1943. The plant moved to Campbell in 1960.
Courtesy of IBM Archives

Reynold B. Johnson was a high school teacher in Michigan when he invented an electronic test-scoring machine in the early 1930s. The machine used paper cards and a multiple-choice format. Students filled in a box (A-D) corresponding to the correct answer with pencil lead, and the machine sensed the pencil marks on the cards. IBM bought the rights to his invention and hired him to work at its laboratory in Endicott as an engineer. His first assignment there was to develop the technology needed to convert the pencil-marked cards into punch cards. In 1952, IBM put Reynolds in charge of setting up and managing an IBM laboratory in San Jose, California. [15]

Reynold B. Johnson

I was given only two guidelines. . . . "Keep the number of people in the lab to about fifty, and experiment in a technology that no one else in IBM was working on.". . . During those years, I made the two best decisions of my life. . . . First, I decided we should experiment in random-access storage. I soon discovered that several other people around the country were toying with the same thought. They were trying to store randomly accessed information on all kinds of media, such as wire and tape strips. The other decision that I am proudest of was to concentrate on storing information on laminated disks. [16]

***

One technology Reynold Johnson wanted to pursue at the San Jose lab was magnetic recording. Magnetic tape had been around for years, but it was not a commercial success until the late 1940s when a pre-recorded radio show was aired for the first time. The vehicle for the production was a tape recorder built by a six-man company called Ampex in San Carlos, California. The tape was simply a ribbon coated with a thin film of iron oxide, better known as rust. The tape was run past a magnet in a coil of wire through which a signal was sent by means of a current of electricity. This magnetized the tape according to the signal pattern. The next thing you knew you were listening to Bing Crosby on the radio hours after he sang in the studio.

Rey Johnson wanted to record data using the same basic technology. The story that follows is about an early attempt to do just that, as told by an engineer who worked for Johnson.

William "Bill" Crooks

I got an offer to join IBM. One hundred dollars a week. [laughs] And that was a pay cut. I made more money with General Motors, but I thought, "Here's the opportunity to go back to California." So I accepted it and moved to San Jose. It was the best move I ever made. . . .

I was the second engineer. The San Jose lab was going to be a fifty-man R&D lab. That was their limit. I was the second one hired, and everybody couldn't figure out why does a mechanical engineer want to go work for IBM? . . .

I had my first desk in the vault because the back end of the building was previously occupied by bookbinders. . . . There wasn't any room so they put me in the vault. The first thing I did was to make sure they couldn't close that vault door. And from there I helped set up the cubicles for the engineers as they reported.

[Rey Johnson] wanted to pursue magnetic [data] recording. . . . It was proven technology but nobody had really worked on it. The laboratory was turned into what they called [the] Special Products Division. . . .

All the other IBM locations had country clubs for their employees' recreation. So the company arranged for fifteen or twenty memberships at the local YMCA for us. . . . Then, afterwards, we'd go to a little restaurant next to the Y and have dinner. We'd have hamburgers. Al Ewing would play the jukebox. That was the days when they had the 45 [rpm] records in jukeboxes. You'd put your nickel in and select your song. A mechanism would go and retrieve the record from a rack and put it on a turntable. Then the needle would play the song, and at the end the mechanism would put the record back. John Haanstra said, "Well, this doesn't make any sense to me. Why don't they rotate all those records, and when you select one of them, move the needle up and play the music?" And that was a concept that he discussed with Rey Johnson. John was known as "the jukebox genius" with that idea. Rey wanted to pursue that. . . .

I was assigned to research and develop material for the disk. That was my first assignment. . . . Most of the engineers were [against] magnetic recording because they thought it was going to be a boondoggle. Norm Vogel came forth and said he would like to work on the read/write head. . . .

We weren't sophisticated. . . . It was everything by the seat of the pants. We tried all kinds of materials: copper, glass, a material called Zomag, which was aluminum with a corrugated cardboard in between. . . . We tried all kinds of material until we came up with the standard record stock. In other words, you know 78 [rpm] records? That's what we selected; we used record stock. We would cut out the disks and laminate them so we would have a firm disk. . . .

I went to the local paint store to find some sort of material to coat the disk that would accept the magnetic recording. And I said, "Do you have anything with iron particles in it? I've heard of red barn paint and stuff like that." And he said, "Oh, yeah, we have a 3M product that is used in the Midwest. ". . . So I bought a couple of gallons of the red barn paint. And we came back and brushed some paint on a disk, and then they tested it to see if it would record a magnetic spot, and it did. . . . So then it became the problem of how do we apply this to the disk? . . .

Spraying, we just couldn't get a consistent surface on a sizeable disk. And then I thought, "Oh, well, we'll dip them." [chuckles] And it was a big mess. . . it was just a gooey mess running all over the place. And then we decided we had to filter . . . because it did have little particles and bits in it, and you couldn't tolerate that in any of the applications. So we had to filter. And it was pretty viscous paint. And we were having a heck of a time. Gosh, it was taking forever to filter, even with adding some acetones to it. Well, we didn't want to dilute it. We didn't know that we could. We had a secretary that took care of our timesheets and all. . . . She observed this problem we were having filtering this, and she said, "Gee, I don't like your filter paper. Why don't you try a nylon hose?" And we said, "OK." So she takes off one of her nylon hose, and we set it up in our filter apparatus. And, boy, it works fine. And it was timely. We could get the paint filtered right away.

And this was fine, we were proceeding. But Rey Johnson was walking by the area where we were working. And he observed her taking off her other hose. He didn't say anything, he kept walking and went back to his office. Soon I get a call over the loudspeaker, "Would Mr. Crooks please come to the front office?" So I went up. I didn't know what he wanted. So I went into the office and he said, "Shut the door." I did. Rey said, "I don't know if I really want the answer to this question, but I've got to ask it. Why is she taking off her hose back there in the lab?". . .

We'd tried spraying, we'd tried dipping, we tried hand painting and everything. I don't know who thought of the idea, but they said, "Why don't you spin it?" Why don't you take advantage of centrifugal force? And so I built a unit that we could attach a disk to and rotate it, and then apply the magnetic oxide at the center of the disk. And zip, it worked perfectly. We got an even coat. . . . And we tested it and it came out.

So that was our procedure. And the first five hundred-plus disks were made with that process. [17]

***

Top: IBM RAMAC 305 Data Processing Component, about 1955
Bottom: dedication of IBM's new research and manufacturing
center at Monterey and Cottle roads in south San Jose; late 1957
Top: Courtesy of IBM Archives; Bottom: Courtesy of History San Jose

William Shockley, who was raised in Palo Alto, was an American physicist, who, along with two others at Bell Laboratories in New Jersey, invented what was called the point-contact transistor. Their transistor was the first solid-state transistor constructed. A transistor is a device that acts as either an amplifier or a switch for electronic signals. Solid-state means built of solid materials—in this case, that means no vacuum tubes. Between the time of this invention (1947) and the three being awarded the Nobel Prize in Physics in 1956, Shockley published his greatest work, *Electrons and Holes in Semiconductors with Applications to Transistor Electronics*. This book, perhaps as much as anything else, started the semiconductor revolution.

In 1956, because he was frustrated at Bell Labs and also wanted to be close to his ailing mother, Shockley moved to Mountain View, California. He wanted to run his own show, so he started Shockley Semiconductor Laboratory, which was funded by, and a division of, Beckman Instruments.

His work went before him, and to a certain extent he had his pick of young talent, especially Stanford graduates. Brilliant scientist though he was, he was not very good when it came to dealing with people.

James F. Gibbons

I go to Shockley on August 1 [1957], first day of employment, and I didn't know that you had to take an IQ test. I showed up a little before nine and introduced myself to his secretary, whom I later found out was his wife, and she said, "Yes, Dr. Shockley is expecting you." She always referred to him as "Dr. Shockley." I don't know what it was inside their home, but everywhere I was around with her, it was always "Dr. Shockley." I thought, "Well, OK, he's in a meeting and stuff." Some time passed, and finally the buzzer rang, and she said, "Well, Dr. Shockley will see you now." I thought, fine. He didn't come to the door. She opened the door, and I walked in. He said, "Please sit down." It wasn't as if he'd been concentrating on papers or something like that, right? So I began, "So, what was all this fifteen minutes of waiting around?" I found out. He said, "I like to give my new employees some tests." He's got a stopwatch in his hand. And without saying anything more than that, he said, "One hundred and twenty-seven people enter a tennis elimination tournament. Now, because it's an odd number, somebody's going to draw a bye in the first round, and so there'll be a hundred and twenty-six players. That'll be sixty-three matches, sixty-three winners.

Then that guy that drew the bye can come in to make sixty-four players for the next round, so that'll be thirty-two matches. So how many matches to determine a winner? So, let's think about this." And of course, I didn't think about all this stuff at the time, but he's set me up.

Fifteen minutes I've been waiting, I'm wondering what's going on. I go in there, he's sitting there with a stopwatch, and he gives me a problem. He's trying to set conditions to make you nervous. That's part of the test somehow. And I just happened to think about this problem in a particular way. So I said—before he actually had started his stopwatch—"I think it must be one hundred and twenty-six." And he said, what? I said, "I think it's a hundred and twenty-six." And he said, "How did you do that?" I said, " Well, there's only one winner, and you have to eliminate one hundred and twenty-six people. It takes a match to eliminate somebody, so it must be a hundred and twenty-six matches." "That's the way I do it," he said. And I'm just, you know, completely wiped.

So he gives me the second problem. And, you know, I'm everything, nervous and all, and I can't get the problem, and I can't get the problem, and I can't get the problem. And I can see him relaxing and relaxing. And finally he says, "OK, Jim, you're at twice the lab average. Do you want me to tell you how to do this, or do you want to keep fooling around with it?" And I said, "Well, you're the boss." He said, "Let me tell you then." So he did. And this went on for a while, and he said, "OK, the lab's expecting to meet you. Bob Noyce will show you around."

Bob Noyce was known to be a very sharp guy then, but this is long before Fairchild and Intel, and so on. So I go out and Bob's going to be my device coach. I know nothing about this field. I'm a circuit designer. I go out there, and I'm going to learn how to design devices and how to build them using this equipment that I'm going to also learn about and come over here [to Stanford] and set up. Right? So I got to learn the whole thing. And Bob's my device coach, and Gordon Moore is my diffusion coach, and Shockley's thought about all these coaches, and I'm supposed to learn from them. He didn't know, and I didn't know, that six weeks later they would be gone to form Fairchild.

I go out and meet Bob and I must be looking a little shell-shocked, and he said, "So, how was your test?" And I said, "Well, I don't think very well." And he said, "How'd you do on the tennis problem?" I said, "Well, I got the tennis problem." He said, "You what?" He said, "You scared the living daylights out of him," because he was very worried about somebody being as intelligent as he was. . . .

They'd all taken IQ tests. Gordon Moore, at the time when he was hired, was a researcher at the Laboratories of Applied Physics at John Hopkins, and so he went to New York to have his IQ test. Shockley needed to know this because he needed to know who he was working with, and he got an extremely bright group of people. But it was constantly this way. Working with him was a challenge, and these guys had finally had enough of it.

Four weeks along, Bob came up to me and he said, "Nobody knows this, but we're going to go start a company, and we'd like to have you join us." I said, "I'm going to be a faculty member, and I've got to get this done for Stanford."

It's probably the most expensive decision I ever made, but. . . . [18]

***

The following is a comment that most of us who were in the Santa Clara Valley in the early 1950s can relate to very well.

Clarence Robert Tower

None of us suspected that the Valley was about to undergo a major transformation and become a world-renowned center for electronic design and manufacturing. Although occasional references to companies such as Fairchild Semiconductor, Hewlett Packard, and Varian Associates found their way into conversations, not enough was mentioned then to make any of us suspect that a major change was in our future. In fact, I have discussed this with a number of my long-time friends and they unanimously agree that none of us living here during those early years [early to mid-1950s] were aware that our area was losing its identity as the Valley of Heart's Delight and that a new identity, Silicon Valley, was emerging. [19]

***

Next Pages: Lockheed and Hewlett Packard at Stanford Industrial Park; about 1958

Courtesy of Sunnyvale Historical Society

Chapter 6

The Second Wave: Lockheed, 1956 - 1960s

Lockheed Aircraft Corporation began to move its Missiles and Space Division to the Santa Clara Valley in September 1956. The Cold War was on and the sense of urgency was great. Within two months, two thousand people moved up to Palo Alto and San Jose from Van Nuys, in Southern California. By 1965, Lockheed employed twenty-eight thousand people in the Valley, and the build-out of the west side—from Mountain View to Saratoga—had accelerated dramatically. The 275-acre Lockheed site in Sunnyvale was located next to Ames Research Laboratories, which had some of the most sophisticated wind tunnels in the world, and Moffett Field Naval Air Station, from which surveillance of the West Coast was carried out. In 1960, the Air Force purchased nineteen acres from Lockheed and opened Onizuka Air Force Base. That same year, United Technologies began operations on a twenty-five-acre facility about a mile away; it was next to the Westinghouse plant (formerly Hendy Iron Works), and is where rocket sections were built. Suddenly, Sunnyvale was the epicenter for rocket and space development in the country. As such, it also became a prime target for the Soviets.[i] This chapter tells some of the stories from that era. [1]

Glen Christoffersen

I was an Iowa farm boy. There were twenty-three kids in my high school graduating class, I had never been outside of the state except to visit my mother's family in North Dakota, and I was itching to see the world.

I graduated from Iowa State College in 1956 with a degree in aeronautical engineering and took my first job at Lockheed. Engineering graduates were in great demand when I graduated. I had about twenty interviews and only one of them failed to produce a job offer. Lockheed was the only one in Northern California.

We were poor as church mice. We headed west in our 1948 Hudson with only a few dollars that our parents had given us for the trip. Credit cards had not been invented yet, so we stayed in the cheapest motels we

---

[i] Today, in academia especially, many would have us believe the Soviet Union was not a threat to freedom. They willfully ignore the fact that during the Cold War people were not leaving everything they had and risking their lives to escape from the United States, but they were leaving everything they had and risking their lives by the hundreds of thousands to escape from the Soviet bloc countries.

could find. Our dinners consisted of peanut butter sandwiches, or maybe salami sandwiches on a splurge night, and a piece of fruit.

I had specified that I wanted to work in the San Francisco Bay Area, but they weren't ready in Northern California yet, so I hired in at the plant in Van Nuys, on July 6, 1956. This was the newly formed LMSD, Lockheed Missile Systems Division, located in two Butler buildings. On Labor Day weekend of 1956, we moved en masse to Sunnyvale. The new plant was not ready for us, so our first location was on the second floor of an insurance building, located on Lenzen Avenue, just off the Alameda in San Jose, in an office building down the street from the Falstaff brewery. I was twenty-two years old, the youngest engineer in the fold at that time; now I am eighty-two, so I expect there are not many left who experienced those days. I don't remember how long we were at Lenzen Avenue, but it couldn't have been more than a few months. Our first location at the main plant was in building 102. Buildings 102 and 103 were the only buildings on the site at that time. Mountain View—Alviso Road (now Highway 237) and Matilda Avenue were both two-lane country roads then. Highway 101 was a three-lane road; the center lane was for passing in both directions. Mountain View—Alviso traffic got across Highway 101 with a stop sign. (Well, usually they got all the way across.)

Everyone in that first wave from Van Nuys was working on Polaris, the first fleet ballistic missile. Space projects such as Agena and Corona came a few years later, and our name changed to Lockheed Missiles and Space Company.

Construction went on fast and furious. Right after we moved in, construction on building 101 started. We walked by it to get from the parking lot to our work. Every morning we played a game: Who could count the most different state license plates on the way through the parking lot? While we were in 102, construction on the building was continued to the north, and our space was next to a temporary canvas wall that really didn't serve its purpose very well. Every morning, the secretaries would congregate in our conference room while the guys went through all of their desks to flush out all of the field mice that had found a warm place to spend the night. I'm sure that situation didn't last very long, but at the time it seemed very long!

In short order, building 181 was finished. It belonged to the Navy and was labelled NIROP, as in Navy Industrial Reserve Ordnance Plant. That was for the Polaris project, and we moved there right away. The saying was that LMSD stood for "let's move some desks." [2]   ***

Lockheed Missiles and Space, Sunnyvale, 1959

Dean Fisher

My family moved from Illinois to Sunnyvale in 1947. Most of our family—my uncles and aunts and cousins—had moved to California during the latter part of the war. After the war, the war work was shut down, so my father lost his job in Illinois. That's why we moved. I was thirteen at the time.

My first real job was at Westinghouse in Sunnyvale. Some of my aunts and uncles worked there, and they knew when there were openings, so after my stint in the Air Force I got on there.

Among many other things, Westinghouse built electrical transformers, for Pacific Gas and Electric and others. When you look up at a power pole, you see that canister there—that's a transformer. PG&E would put in an order for, say, forty fifty-kilowatt transformers, and it was my responsibility to be sure we had all the materials on hand. At the end of the assembly process, they were filled with oil and then put in stock.

I worked at Westinghouse two years, then got on at Lockheed in 1958. When I first inquired there, in 1957, they were still in Quonset huts. By the time I got in, in late 1958, they had some buildings in and were well into production. I was there to help ship the first rocket engine produced in Sunnyvale. It was sent to the Lockheed facility in the Santa Cruz Mountains for testing.[i] Later I got to go to that facility and meet the people there.

During the Korean "conflict," I was a C-124 aircraft mechanic in the Air Force. I was an engine mechanic, but I knew the other systems of the plane as well and became very interested in aircraft. So that interested me in Lockheed. But in Sunnyvale, Lockheed did missiles and space. Well, I liked that too. And I thought there was a good future in going to work for Lockheed. I was in my twenties at the time and full of visions of grandeur. I felt I could do anything. I was going to go through college...

As it was, I started as a dispatcher, which was one rung up the ladder from cleaning the toilets. It wasn't so great for the first three to six months. I went to college at night and took chemistry, math, and mechanical drawing. I decided I needed to get into those things I liked so I could do more interesting work that paid better. I felt I had much more ability and tried to force the system. Eventually I did. I became an expediter, and that set the tone. Later it was logistics/production /supply.

---

[i] The four-thousand-acre rocket motor testing site was near Bonny Doone.

There was a strike shortly after I started. That was about 1960, and it lasted five to six weeks. It involved only hourly people, and I was hourly at the time. So I had to picket. Soon after the strike I became salaried. I don't think the union ever got the salaried people on board. You had the option when you hired on, whether you wanted to be union or not. I joined. My father had been in the union leadership at Westinghouse. The unions had their place. The unions were trying to get closed shop, but I don't think they ever got it. [3]

Anonymous

I'm a native of Santa Clara and knew the Valley before Lockheed came. After the Depression, my dad would let me go with him and my two brothers to pick fruit. We picked prunes, cut apricots. When Lockheed came to Sunnyvale, they opened up the Valley and my life. Up until then there was not much available as far as employment. All of a sudden, people came from far and wide; job shoppers (engineers who follow contracts) and international people came too.

I first joined Lockheed in '58 and quickly left because of their treatment of me and because I did not understand engineers. They put me through an indoctrination at first. I was so insulted because by that time I was a highly qualified legal secretary. . . . But that was their procedure and I accepted that. After five days, they took me over to building 103, which was one of the few buildings there at that time. They put me in a cage with all these engineers. I had never met an engineer before in my life. I thought they were all crazy.

The cage they put me in was similar to the cyclone fences one sees, except it was fully enclosed, top to bottom. It was a holding area for those people that did not have areas of work yet. Everything was under construction, and this area was separated from the rest of the building area so it would not interfere with other work areas.

In the early days at Lockheed it was almost bedlam. Lockheed needed so many people, but they didn't know what to do with them. They gave me all these manuals that may as well have been in Greek. They certainly did not relate to sound business where I came from. The whole thing was too much. I quit.

I went back again April 1, 1959, and pleaded with their employment gal (who remembered me) to rehire me. She said OK, if I promised I would stay for three years; otherwise she would not hire me. I was faced with supporting my four children alone because of a bad marriage, so I could not go back into legal as it did not pay. By necessity I returned to Lockheed. They were the prime company in the area who had decent wages and benefits.

I had come to Lockheed after four years at Owens-Corning where I was an executive secretary for the controller. Eventually they did not want me back because I was having too many babies on their dollar. They told me that if I wanted to come back, I'd have to go back to the sales force where I started. "Fiberglass" was a terrific company, and I didn't want to leave, but I had four children to feed. So it was a financial decision I had to make, and I went to Lockheed. I stayed on for thirty-three years.

Lockheed was full of great people doing great things, but dealing with them was another thing.

When they re-hired me in 1959, they put me in the Navy building. I said, "You're not going to put me in another cage, are you?" "No, no!" We walked in—the building is huge—and from the mezzanine all I see was a sea of heads. There were no partitions, just desks and a sea of heads.

My first thought was, "How am I going to progress here?" I had four kids to feed and the salary was not much. I knew what I was capable of, but they didn't. How long was it going to take? How will they ever see me? I have to progress fast. All these thoughts were going through my head.

They put me in a bullpen with all these engineers. Everyone was within ten years of the same age. The supervisor thought he was going to have a little fun with me. He put these manuals on my desk, and I thought, "Oh, no, here we go again." He asked me to read the first two chapters and then write out in my own words what I thought it meant. He was really doing a number on me. I walked in the next day and all these men were just hysterical, having read what I wrote. I didn't say anything. I insisted on being a professional.

Shortly thereafter they put me in a division. They knew that with my skills I was going to move quickly.

I was a very beautiful woman. Within a month, the division head, after taking one look at me, wanted me in front of his office. I knew it was not for my skills, but I was determined to show him I was a professional, and did. He was promoted very rapidly and I followed him. So, I was in executive management my whole career at Lockheed. I usually changed bosses only when they were transferred. I was with most of them at least four years, some of them ten years.

I kept confidence and they realized I was trustworthy. They also knew I was a straight shooter. Eventually just about everybody had to flow through my office.

There was an inner core there, just as there is at every company, and the positions I held with the men I worked for put me there. So I knew a lot of people or at least knew of them.

The thing is this: the Valley was like the Garden of Eden—all the fruit trees and everything. But you can't have progress without losing something. When I was a young adult, I wondered, "How am I going to get out of this one-horse town?" Lockheed changed all that. I, and people like me, didn't have to leave; it all came to us. [4]

Lane Pendleton

I grew up on a farm in western Wyoming in Thayne, one of about twelve communities in Star Valley. Our end product was milk, but since the snows started in November and stayed on the ground until April, our biggest effort was to grow grain and alfalfa to feed the cows through the winter.

My father was very progressive. He only had an eighth-grade education but he was on the board of directors of the creamery and soil conservation board. He was one of the first in Thayne to own a tractor. Before that, he used horses to work the ground.

When I was in high school, I was fascinated with everything mechanical. After the war, when the local veterans came home, many wanted to use their GI benefits to learn to fly. Raymond Humphries, a forward-thinking local farmer, purchased J-3 Cub airplanes from Piper Aircraft and started a school to train veterans who wanted to learn to fly.

Every day I saw these planes taking off and landing. There were even impromptu air shows, during and after the war, given by local men who had become Air Force pilots. Watching these airplanes really thrilled me. I bought balsa wood models of World War II airplanes and even nailed pieces of wood together to make play airplanes.

I decided I wanted to be a commercial airline pilot. My cousin, who was older than I and attending BYU at the time, said, "Why don't you study aeronautical engineering in college to give you a good foundation to become an airline pilot?" So, I thought, "Hey, that sounds good." So in high school I concentrated on mathematics, physics, and mechanical drawing. I didn't take biology.

I went to college at Utah State University (which was named Utah State Agricultural College when I started). When I graduated from college, Russia's Sputnik had just gone up and there was a big shortage of engineers. Engineers were getting top dollar, and every aircraft company sent me an offer.

I chose Lockheed Aircraft in Burbank, California. They offered to pay my tuition for a master's degree and allow me to adjust my schedule to attend classes at USC. By the time I completed my master's degree at USC, Lockheed was having trouble because of the crashes of three Electras, which were ninety-eight-passenger turbo-prop planes. About the same time, commercial jets built by Boeing became available, and people preferred to fly in a jet. The airlines couldn't sell tickets for a turbo-prop. So Burbank needed to downsize.

So after two years at Lockheed in Burbank, I went for an interview with a representative from a Lockheed division in Sunnyvale. That was in July of 1958. The fellow that interviewed me wrote across my application: "Hire him." They paid the cost of moving my furniture and gave me extra money to live on for a couple of months while we were getting settled. At the time it was just my wife and me. We didn't have a family yet. We lived in motels and in an apartment until we bought a home, which we moved into in December 1958.

There were two divisions of Lockheed in Sunnyvale. They were called the Missile Systems Division (MSD) supported by the Navy, and the Space Systems Division (SSD) supported by the Air Force. Each division had a president and a similar, but independent, engineering structure. These two divisions were approximately equal in size.

I was immediately put on the Polaris program. They were just about to launch the first submarine missile at that time. The first eight launches of the Polaris AX failed for different reasons.

We developed seven different missile systems during my thirty-four years there: AX, A1, A2, A3, C3, C4, and D5. Each new version increased the range and/or the size and number of warheads. These missiles were sequentially named Polaris, Poseidon, and then Trident.

During this same time, Boeing and TRW were working on the Minuteman missiles, which were the land-based ICBMs. (The submarines were mobile, so range became less of an issue.) During production, we had meetings between the engineers in these two companies. [Lockheed] had all the same problems and found similar solutions. Also, each group had developed its own name for parts of the missile. In England, an elevator is a lift. In the same way, we had different names for the same thing. Everybody (in those meetings) had a security clearance so we could talk freely.

The Navy steadfastly supported Lockheed as prime contractor each time it was agreed that a better missile should be built. In the same way, the Air Force supported Boeing and TRW as the prime contractors for the Minuteman missiles as improved designs were built.

I made several trips to Washington, D.C., to explain why we did certain things. During the early years, Lockheed had a blank check. All they had to do was send the time cards, and they were paid. It was a "cost-plus" contract. Over the years the contract terms changed. The Trident II D5 contract was cost plus an incentive fee, but in actuality it was a fixed-price contract.

Westinghouse, in Sunnyvale, was building the launch tubes, so we worked closely with them. Every time we went to a new missile design, it required a modification of the launch tube as the missiles grew larger to increase range and size of payload. To launch the Trident II missile required the design of a completely new submarine called the Trident submarine. It has twenty-four launch tubes compared with sixteen on the Polaris submarines.

Our final missile design was called the Trident II D5. It carries several independently targeted warheads. Since then there have been 157 successful flights with no failures. I believe my personal efforts contributed to the unusually high success rate.

My thirty-four years working for Lockheed on the submarine-launch missile program have been very happy and rewarding. We felt we were protecting the United States from aggression with a submarine-launch missile that was hard to detect or destroy. The submarine generates freshwater and oxygen and is powered by nuclear power, so it can remain submerged for months. It is a system that cannot be destroyed in a first strike and is therefore available to retaliate as a second strike.

We believe it is still America's best deterrent from war. It has never been used in anger and remains a lethal weapon to protect our nation from aggression. [5]   *******

Polaris launch, 1960, U.S. Navy photo

Jack Balletto

I was off traveling for Lockheed as a twenty-one-year-old hotshot out of college. It was amazing! At Lockheed Aerospace at that time, it was mainly World War II vets and mechanical engineers, civil engineers, heat transfer engineers, very few recent [electrical engineers]. . . .

So Lockheed was the prime contractor to fix up the Polaris missile system because they had decided the bomb—the Russians—could blow this [place] up at pretty much any time. So we had to put countermeasures underneath the nose cone. And I was in the Electronic Countermeasure Group, the ECM Group [clears throat], which was two of us. And my boss would get. . . these gigantic budgets from Washington by describing the entire ECM situation, radar and all that, *in plumbing terms. . . . And he'd come back [laughter] with yet another $5 million. . . .*

It took a long time, but people our age remember—it was touch and go [as to] who was going to run the planet. You know, I mean, the Russians had Sputnik up. They just about had antiballistic missiles in Cuba. That was close. And I was one of those around here who picked my mom up in the car. We headed north. We just got out of Dodge. I thought for sure that they were going to, you know, [that] Khrushchev wasn't going to blink. Lucky for all of us, he did. [i] And, luckily, we had Kennedy there, because I'm not sure anybody else, one of the old-timers—well, anyway, JFK did a good job. [6]   ***

Robert Beasley, who would go on to play a large role in developing the heat protection system for the space shuttle, came to Lockheed in 1960. He had been frustrated by the lack of challenge with his former employer and was ready for a change. One of his friends had recently gone to Lockheed and they kept in touch. It wasn't long before Bob Beasley was at the Lockheed facility in Palo Alto for an interview. He got an offer, took it, and put the house up for sale. His wife, Gloria, picks up the story from there.

Gloria Beasley Lausten

Lockheed was paying for the move, including a place to stay until we found a house in the area that met our needs. Bob decided this was a wonderful opportunity for us to see the country and make the trip west into a real vacation. We bought our first new car, a small Valiant station wagon, for the trip. We would go down the East Coast from Maryland to Florida to say goodbye to relatives, go through the Florida panhandle, on the southern route, with detours to see the Grand Canyon, Bryce Canyon, Flagstaff, and other attractions on the way.

Packing would be left to the movers, but with all the paraphernalia needed for two young girls and a baby, plus clothes, picnic food—those things would crowd all the space we thought we would have, so we bought a luggage rack and located an old gray canvas tarp Bob had acquired during his Navy days to cover it all up.

---

[i] The secret Corona system of satellites was doing polar orbits before and during the Cuban missile crisis of October 16-28, 1962. The Soviets claimed to have bombers in Siberia lined up and ready to go over the pole. That was not true, and Kennedy had the surveillance to know it. Sputnik, the first successful man-made satellite, was launched in October 1957.

But there remained a big problem. Petty[, our cat]. . . found an admirer and had her third set of kittens four weeks before we were to leave. The SPCA said they would have to separate the unweaned kittens from their mother and probably have to destroy them. That was not an option for us. All our friends had large dogs. No one wanted a mother cat and four kittens, no matter how charming. The only recourse was to take them along and hope for the best. So to what we already packed we added a bushel basket for the babies and mother, a cat pan, cat food, and a leash.

There was a little going-away party with the neighbors. Almost everything was packed under the tarp, which loomed almost as high as the car itself.

We had planned to get an early start the next morning, but when Bob went out to the driveway, he saw that someone had written on the side of the car, in red poster paint, "California or Bust." It did look like a covered wagon. It took almost an hour before Bob could get the paint off. And still the words showed palely through the beige enamel of the car. . . .

The car had already turned hot in the August heat, but Bob had to roll up all the windows to about two inches to prevent Petty from squirming out. She stood on his left shoulder, alternately moaning or thrusting her nose into the small opening. Behind him, Amy was blowing on a kazoo and Robin was bouncing up and down. The baby needed another change. We drove down the street to get onto the highway. The light was red. An old, high-bodied truck pulled up beside us, and the driver, a woman, looked down interestedly at the scene and started to smile. Bob smiled balefully back at her. She started to laugh. Bob lowered the window another half inch and yelled that that was nothing—we also had a basket of kittens in the back seat. The light turned green, and, as we pulled away, Bob could see the woman in the rearview mirror, still at the light, uproariously laughing and banging her hands on the steering wheel. After that, it seemed funny to us too. . . .

Bob was to present himself at Lockheed for his physical on August 22, 1960, at 8:00 a.m. He passed the exam and was given employee number 605597. His title was Senior Scientist, and he was thirty-four years old. An orientation meeting with his new boss, Dr. Harvey Crosby, head of the Chemistry and Plastics Department, was scheduled for 1:30 P.M. on September 1, 1960, in building 52-35 in the Palo Alto facility. Bob felt comfortable with his new boss right away. After some "getting to know you" conversation, Harvey told Bob that Lockheed had lost the contract for which he had been hired and asked him, "What are you going to do now?" Bob recalled later to me that he answered, "Hell, I don't even know the way to the men's room. How do I know what I'm going to do?" He felt quite shaken. But he did find his way to the men's room and when he got on the elevator to leave, a sweet young thing made a pass at him. By the time he got back to the children and me at the Flamingo [motel, where we were staying,] he felt better and decided he would hurry up and invent something so he wouldn't be fired. . . .

The Palo Alto Lab was the show place of Lockheed Missiles and Space Company. Most of the company's PhDs and VPs had offices there. It borrowed some of its ambience from Stanford University nearby and one could look out of its windows and see gently rolling hills with cattle and horses grazing under the shadows of wide-spreading oak trees. Here most of the research of the company was carried out by individuals and small groups, and they were well funded. It had an easy-going atmosphere, rather like a well-run club. Most of the money earned by research came from the Palo Alto Lab. If you had an idea you wished to pursue, you had the opportunity to explore it there. The Sunnyvale Plant, on the other hand, was in the flatlands and was composed of boxlike buildings ranging over a large area, a typical industrial landscape, and it was all business. . . .

Harvey probably didn't know what to do with Bob, so he gave him a little room with a small winding machine and then left him alone. Les [a coworker] worked next to this place and began to wonder what that clicking noise was that came through the wall. His curiosity was piqued, so he opened the door and found Bob tap-dancing to the rhythm of the winding machine. That one thing made them instant friends. . . .

Bob meant it when he told me he would have to hurry up and invent something. He ordered small samples of materials from various suppliers, and in his little room in the garage, he mulled over his ideas, writing them down in his logbook—the new ideas that eventually led to the thermal protection system that would keep people and things safe in space. [7]

***

The next story tells a little more about the machinists strike in 1960 that was mentioned earlier. I will preface this story by saying that by 1960 Lockheed, Sunnyvale was a city in itself, and every city brings out the best and the worst in people. Almost all employees I talked to spoke of the company camaraderie and good social times. The strike was an exception.

Anonymous
The strike was the Machinists Union, but it also involved other hourly employees, some of whom were union while some were not. It was brutal. It was the scariest time of my life—by far. People got vicious. People beating each other up. I was terrified.

I went to work one day and couldn't get in. That was before the Bayshore Freeway was widened. The saying was that you had to play Bayshore roulette to get into Lockheed. Getting off the freeway was very difficult and things jammed up on a normal day. But during the strike it was impossible. There were cars parked everywhere blocking the roads in. I had to leave my car in the middle of the road. You couldn't go forward and you couldn't go back.

The women were rioting too. They [the union] brought in people from everywhere. There I was in the middle of it. I attached myself to some [salaried] men who were walking in on the perimeter road. They didn't bother them because they were salaried. All of a sudden, one of the gals spotted me and yelled, "We've got a scab over here!" Somehow they got inside the fence and onto the perimeter road (they were not supposed to be there) and separated me from the men, who just kept walking. These women stood in front of me, blocking my way and shouting profanities at me. This one girl got right in front of me. I weigh ninety-five pounds. I said, "You're going to move. See that black car?" "What black car?" "That one, right there. You're going to go." Eventually she moved. She saw it in my eyes.

When I got into the building, the men said, "Oh, thank God you're here!" I told them, "Yeah, but I almost got killed coming in."

The police were not capable of handling the situation. They called the dogs out. It was horrible, terrifying. The police eventually got help from the surrounding police departments. People got their tires slashed, got their cars beaten up with hammers, had sugar put in their gas tanks. I had my radiator hose slashed one day. People turned into animals. And people who had been friends were no longer friends. The riot lasted about three days. [8]

Al De Ridder
I'm from Michigan, but the Navy brought me to California in 1960. I began working at LMSC on August 12, 1963, as an engine lathe operator. For about three and a half years, I ran all types of lathes. People may remember the guy on the large turret lathe in Building 182,

the guy who made so many chips by running the lathe at very high speeds. I was machining separation rings for the reentry bodies. Then I had the opportunity to be promoted to a machined parts planner trainee. I was promoted to planner after a few months and worked in the reentry machined parts group for about two years. In January of 1969 I was laid off and stayed out until October 1978. I hired right back into the planning group. Soon I was promoted to group lead. In 1989 I transferred to the astronautics' division as the planning department supervisor.

During my nine years of absence, I worked various other mechanical jobs. When I got back, I picked up right where I had left off in 1969. It seemed strange that many of the people I dealt with in 1967-69 were still at the same desk doing the same job in 1978.

During my absence my wife often told me, "I wish you could go back to Lockheed because you were so happy and satisfied with your job." I had a great career at Lockheed and I am very thankful for that.

Oh, payday was Thursday afternoon, if I remember correctly. About the time the checks were handed out, the Brinks men would come into the building with a cash box and stand, and would cash our paychecks right there. [9]

Al Thompson
The largest of the company segments was the Missiles Division, where the Polaris missile was built. After several development flight tests, some of which failed, as expected, design changes ... were made leading to the first official flight that was launched successfully. In the early days, many of us marveled at the ability to send a missile from a submarine up through the ocean into the air, then ignite it to perform an extended range mission. Nevertheless, the Polaris's perfect performance record has continued to the present day in its latest configuration, named the Trident. It still represents America's greatest nuclear defense system.

The other large product division, Space Systems, launched its first satellite in the early 1960s after twelve failed prior attempts. It also became very successful and evolved into the standard Agena, carrying various special payloads. Unlike the Missiles Division, SSD had many programs to meet different customer requirements, many of which were classified. [10]

***

I mentioned at the beginning of this chapter that there were other companies that moved to Sunnyvale about the time Lockheed arrived that were also integral parts of the development of our missile defense system. The following is a United Technologies story.

Charles Chase

My first trip out of Michigan was to California for a job interview. I was completing my master's degree in aeronautical & astronautical engineering at the University of Michigan, and from time to time engineering companies would come to the campus to recruit. One day I happened to meet my faculty adviser in the hall. I had gotten to know him pretty well and in passing asked him what company he had seen that day. He said, "United Technology Corporation" (UTC), a division of United Aircraft (UAC). I had never heard of them but thought I should talk to them anyway and arranged for an interview. The next thing I knew I had a ticket in hand for a flight to California. It was all happenstance. I ran into the guy in the hall and ended up spending my entire career with UTC.

I got there in September of 1962. UTC had just won the contract for the Titan booster program, which became the backbone of the company. The Titan Launch Vehicle used a liquid propulsion core with two large solid rocket strap-on boosters. These strap-ons were ten feet in diameter, about eighty-five feet long, and used 420,000 pounds of propellant. Because this size was too large to build in one piece, the Titan strap-ons were made in segments. One of our key leaders, Barney Adelman (he later became president of UTC), was in his early thirties when he patented the idea of making solid rockets in segments. This idea was later adopted for the space shuttle boosters and for other [rockets] in Europe and Japan.

Initially, I worked in the Grain Design and Performance Analysis section. It primarily involved ballistics calculations and overall motor capability analysis.

During our first year in California we lived in an apartment in Palo Alto. When my wife, Carole, got pregnant, we purchased a starter home in Saratoga. Within two blocks of our home, corn and strawberries were grown, along with other produce. Nearby was a new housing development using an affordable-home building concept of the time, a new tract of Eichlers.

My commute was on a two-lane road called Lawrence Station Road to Sunnyvale, where UTC owned twenty-five acres on Arques Avenue. There was nothing but fields all around the property, and cows grazed across the street. The dominant crop in the area was onions, and the air intakes for our buildings brought in the smell of onions. All our Sunnyvale buildings were windowless (many of our programs were classified), except for the lobby and the cafeteria. Near the back of our property, UTC had a small research building where we tested some small rocket motors. They only had about eight pounds of propellant, but they simulated what would happen with the larger motors. When we first started testing these small motors, it was no big deal—there was no one around and we had no complaints. When the Central Expressway was built, the city rescinded our rights to test-fire our small rocket motors on our Sunnyvale property. From then on, all the testing was done at the fifty-four hundred-acre UTC Coyote Valley facility, just south of San Jose.

At Coyote Valley we test-fired both subscale and full-size rocket motors. Small motors were generally tested horizontally, and the large solid rocket motors (SRMs) nozzle up. Our large SRMs, especially the Titan boosters, were usually fired during the day. On the test day for one of our full-scale Titan booster static firings, we ran into a delay that changed the timing until after sunset. That evening, I was sitting in the family room at my home in Saratoga when the whole house started shaking. I ran to the window and looked out toward Coyote Valley and the whole sky was lit up. This really shook people up. Some thought it was a nuclear attack, and all kinds of calls and reports came in to police and fire stations. Some said there were flames jumping from building to building. There were no such fires, but there was a big panic. We didn't fire at night after that, and the local authorities and the public were always briefed well before conducting subsequent daytime Titan tests.

UTC was awarded the Titan contract in early 1962. By July 1963 we had test-fired the first full-scale rocket at Coyote Valley, and by June 1965 the first Titan was launched from Cape Canaveral. Eventually, UTC's Titan boosters were involved in 106 Titan launches (212 boosters). These launch vehicles were used for communication satellites, U.S. military spy missions, and space research. Space research flights in the early 1970s, using UTC's Titan boosters, included Mars Viking Landers (1 and 2) and Voyagers (1 and 2).

Titan booster static test at UTC's Coyote Valley facility, San Jose, CA

Courtesy of Pratt and Whitney

What is amazing to me, even to this day (2016), is that in the early days all this was done with slide rules, Frieden calculators (which could only add, subtract, multiply, and divide and had no memory), and a very primitive and slow IBM computer. We also used "map readers" and planimeters to determine burnback characteristics of propellant grains. Map readers are small devices with a small wheel you held in your hand and rolled across the blueprints to measure distances. Planimeters are small mechanical devices used to find the area of a shape by tracing around its perimeter on the plans. All these were fairly crude tools. Since sophisticated computer models did not exist in the early days, the engineers had to understand the essence of what they were doing and what the expected results should be.

Eventually, UTC (later called Chemical Systems Division [CSD] and then Pratt & Whitney Space Propulsion Division, San Jose) would be involved in the space shuttle program and many key missile systems. The company had the industry's highest overall demonstrated solid motor reliability history, at 0.999.

I have a great fondness for UTC. We were a family of wonderful and highly creative people who developed an incredible camaraderie. We were always watching each other's backs. [11]

***

The Lockheed and related folks were young and had money, and that changed the social fabric of the Valley dramatically. Those who had been on top no longer were. Our family, and people like us who had moved to the Valley shortly after the war, found ourselves between the farmers and rural feel of the place, and the Lockheed people and the new order of things that came with them. We knew a few of the farmers and in time knew some Lockheed people, but there was an "other-world" transition that took place.

The level of intensity in the Valley increased greatly, and the transient lifestyle of many of these folks upped the tempo in the Valley. There was also Lockheed lingo that no one but Lockheed folks understood.

Along with the great achievements of the Lockheed generation came another phenomenon, and its effect was every bit as intense. Science and science fiction were suddenly the rage, and the two became blended. To a large extent, imagination, in the name of science, took over. In the schools, all of a sudden, everything was about space—and dinosaurs. And it wasn't just the kids. The Valley was suddenly swimming with grandiose statements like, "We have conquered space," "We will colonize the moon shortly," or like this one I heard recently—"We know the universe is 16.3 billion years old."

Well, no, actually you don't know that, there are still no serious plans for a lunar colony, and it is a stretch to say that we have even scratched the surface of space. As Mark Twain so eloquently put it: "Science is fascinating. You can get such wholesale returns on conjecture with such a trifling investment in fact." [12]

Chapter 7

Blitzkrieg: 1950s and 1960s

The term used to describe the German military advances during the first half of World War II was *blitzkrieg*, which means "lightning war." It was devastating to all who stood in its way. By the late 1950s many people in the Valley of Heart's Delight had adopted the term to describe what was happening to the Valley.

Because of the Great Depression, very few homes were built in the Santa Clara Valley in the 1930s. During the war, *almost no* homes were built because of government restrictions on materials. The net result was a fifteen-year housing backlog—and that is without taking into account the needs of the thousands of GIs and others who moved into the Valley shortly after the war.

Add to this scene two additional matters: First, banks were very hesitant to lend money. Second, the state in general, and the Valley in particular, did not yet have the infrastructure in place to allow for much in the way of new building to accommodate the people who were streaming in.

The uncertainty of the times after the end of the war could hardly be exaggerated. No one knew what was going to happen. Would there be more depression? Would the GIs who were new to the Valley go back to where they had come from? Would the Bay Area's wartime industries convert to peacetime production? No one knew the answers, and a wait-and-see approach was taken by most businesses and individuals.

Before the *blitzkrieg* of development could begin in the Valley, several pieces of a puzzle needed to be put into place. To cover them adequately, I need to start with several pages of narrative before I conclude with some oral history from this era.

VA Guaranteed Loans

To help ease the postwar adjustments, in 1944 the Department of Veterans Affairs initiated a loan guarantee program for the veterans of World War II. It was an alternative to a cash bonus that had been proposed in Congress, and it was considerably less expensive for the government. The government did not make the loans; it guaranteed them, "providing the means whereby the veteran could obtain favorable credit which would permit him/her to shelter his/her family or begin a business or farming venture."

The original version of the loan guarantee program and the revisions of 1945 contained many shortcomings, the result being that few of these loans were made. In the spring of 1950, the maximum amount of the guarantee was changed from 50 percent of the loan amount, but not to exceed $4,000, to 60 percent of the loan amount and $7,500. These changes, along with a few others, were more in touch with current economic conditions and more accurately reflected postwar prices, which had inflated. The banks were happy and the vets were happy, but still there was not a great rush to obtain a loan for a new house. People had not forgotten the Depression. But that changed dramatically later in 1950 when the government changed terms again and no down payment was required to obtain a Veterans' Assistance, or VA, loan.[i] All the loan applicant needed to do was prove he or she had served in the military for ninety days during the war and had an income sufficient to make the mortgage payments. It is no wonder that the new neighborhoods that were being built were soon filled with GIs and their families! [1]

It is important to note that these early VA loans were not based upon fanciful idealism but rather on hard facts. First, most of the industrialized world had been destroyed by the war, which gave the United States a tremendous advantage economically for many years. Second, the men and women who received these loans were, by and large, a disciplined group of people. If they were not disciplined before the war, they surely were after their military training and experience.

Infrastructure Development
As the jitters of economic uncertainty began to wear off, the local utility, Pacific Gas and Electric, began an aggressive expansion program and invested $800 million in new infrastructure between 1946 and 1951. In those days that was a lot of money, probably equal to $12 billion or more today.

Expansion was nothing new to PG&E. In a book celebrating the company's centennial in 1952, the company states: "The Pacific Gas

---

[i] Terms for Federal Housing Administration loans for non-GIs were changed to 10 percent down.

and Electric Company of today represents the amalgamation of approximately 520 predecessor companies and miscellaneous properties by a progressive process of consolidation during the past 100 years." Those were not only other gas and electric companies, they also included land, engineering, mining, water, water conveyance, and many other kinds of companies. [2]

Perhaps the biggest infrastructure challenges of the postwar period were water conveyance and electricity generation and conveyance. By overpumping water from the aquifer that lies beneath the Valley, the farmers had already caused significant land subsidence in some places and made not a few wells go dry. In Alviso, the effect of the land sinking was disastrous. The ground level there fell thirteen feet, and flooding from the bay and from runoff caused big problems. By the 1930s the subsidence was severe enough that percolation ponds were built along the creeks in an attempt to recharge the aquifer. The pond projects, begun in 1938, proved successful and slowed the rate of subsidence. But those efforts did not bring in new water, which the Valley desperately needed. [i]

Water
The Hetch Hetchy Aqueduct, built to supply water to San Francisco, was started in 1914 and after much legal wrangling was finally completed in 1934. Since San Francisco would not need all the water from that source, a turnout was designed in the aqueduct for supplying the Santa Clara Valley. Water from it flows through a pipeline to Calaveras Reservoir, just east of Milpitas. The water from this source, however helpful, was far from adequate for the thirsty valley.

Spurred by a six-year drought, in 1947 voters approved a bond issue to build Lexington Reservoir on Los Gatos Creek. Before the dam could be constructed, however, Highway 17 had to be rerouted and the towns of Alma and Lexington relocated. Construction was further delayed by legal challenges, as the safety of the proposed dam was called into question. As it was, the delay probably slowed development of the west side of the Valley for a few years. The dam and reservoir were finally completed in 1952, and the remains of the

---

[i] Land subsidence in the Valley was not halted until 1969 through ongoing imported water deliveries from the California State Water Project and the Central Valley Project. Due to the compaction of the aquifer, however, storage capacity was lost forever. I don't know the subsidence record after that time.

small town of Alma can be seen from Highway 17 when the water is low.

While Lexington was delayed, Anderson Dam, to the east of Morgan Hill, was completed in 1950. These two new reservoirs were much larger than those built in the mid-1930s at Almaden, Calero, Coyote, Stevens Creek, and Vasona and nearly tripled the local reservoir capacity. The result of the construction of Lexington and Anderson Reservoirs was a green light for development, and the floodgates, not only of water, but also of new homes opened. Those floodgates remained open later in the decade with the completion of the Chesbro and Uvas dams and reservoirs in 1955 and 1957, respectively. [3]

The approval for construction of the San Luis Dam and Reservoir in 1960 kept construction in the Santa Clara Valley going at an unrestrained rate until the end of the 1960s. [i]

Electrical Power

To provide electrical power to the Bay Area, nine hydroelectric plants were built on the Feather River in the three decades following the war. The first two came on line in 1949 and 1950. Dozens of other hydroelectric plants would be built on other California rivers during the 1950s and 1960s, some connected by miles of tunnels that carried the water from reservoir to reservoir. During the 1950s about 60 percent of the state's electricity was generated from hydroelectric power, most of it coming from new dams on the Sierra Nevada's rivers. [ii]

In addition to hydroelectric power, two large oil-fired steam-generation plants were built near the Valley: one at Moss Landing, near Watsonville, the other near the town of Antioch. They came on line in 1950 and 1951.

An interesting note: by 1952 Pacific Gas and Electric, the company that served an area populated by five million people, had 118,463 stockholders, the majority of whom owned fewer than a hundred shares. [4]

---

[i] Ground was broken for the construction of San Luis Dam and Reservoir in 1962. It was completed in 1967.

[ii] The building, ownership, and management of the dams in Northern California vary considerably but are usually a joint government and industry venture—the industry usually being PG&E. The 60 percent figure is from "Facts on California's Use of Hydroelectricity," State of California Energy Commission, April, 2014.

Natural Gas
Natural gas was a challenge. San Francisco, tired of manufacturing its natural gas from Australian coal, and later from fuel oil from the refinery in Richmond, had placed a new pipeline in service in 1929. The pipeline was from the newly discovered Elk Hills oil field, which is west of Bakersfield. But wartime needs drained those reserves greatly, so a new source was needed. It was found in two places. Los Angeles had completed a huge (34-inch diameter) one thousand mile long pipeline from West Texas and PG&E made an agreement to tap into it. In addition, abundant natural gas was found in the Kettleman Hills of central California. Pipelines were constructed from these two sources beginning in 1949. [5]

The investment of putting in all that infrastructure was a commitment to build-out. No private company would be foolish enough to spend anything close to $12 billion without some assurances of seeing a good return on the investment. So before PG&E would start spending the money, it needed assurances that state and local governments would back its efforts.

Blitzkrieg
Although other civic leaders and jurisdictions cooperated, PG&E found a champion in San Jose's general manager, Dutch Hamann. His goal? To make San Jose "the Los Angeles of the north."

In the 102 years before Hamann's tenure, the city of San Jose made forty-two land annexations. During Haman's tenure, from 1950 to 1969, it made 1,377, and Hamann's era became known as the *blitzkrieg*. During that time, the city expanded from 17 to about 150 square miles and the population increased from 95,000 to 446,000. On Hamann's watch, the policy was, "Annex, annex, then annex some more. We'll worry about a plan later." The city had no General Plan until the 1960s.[6] The result was not only an endless landscape of housing tracts and strip malls, but also severely strained city and county services.

To understand San Jose's ambitions, one must realize that from time to time, beginning with a short stint as the state capital and continuing today as the self-proclaimed "Capital of Silicon Valley," the city has suffered greatly from Scuffy the Tugboat Syndrome.

If you want to understand San Jose, read the children's book, *Scuffy the Tugboat*. Scuffy was a little toy tugboat that the man with the polka dot tie brought home for his little boy to play with in the bathtub. Scuffy felt being in the tub was beneath him and complained, "I was meant for bigger things!" Even after the man with the polka dot tie and his little boy took Scuffy out to float in the little brook near their house, Scuffy was cross and said, "I was meant for bigger things!" So Scuffy ran away down the brook, which flowed into a larger stream, and then into a river, which became a bigger river, which flowed into the mighty ocean. Poor Scuffy got in way over his head! The story has a happy ending because Scuffy was eventually rescued by the man with the polka dot tie.

As for San Jose, the city is still striving to get out of the mess it got into by expanding too fast without planning.

Reaction to the Blitz
The mid-1950s were unsettling times, as many of the Valley's new residents (to say nothing of those who were here before the war) tried to maintain at least some of the "rural feel" of their communities.

Alarmed by San Jose's expansion, the residents of neighboring unincorporated towns voted to incorporate: Campbell in 1952, Milpitas in 1954, Cupertino in 1955, and Saratoga in 1956. For the most part, the initial boundaries of these new cities followed the lines of existing postal districts. At the time, Cupertino, unlike the others, was really more of a wide spot in the road than it was a town.

Other neighboring cities and towns had incorporated earlier. Santa Clara in 1852, and Alviso and Los Gatos in 1852 and 1887 respectively.

The City of Santa Clara, which since mission days had at times been a bitter rival of San Jose's, caught Hamann and San Jose's other expansionist leaders by surprise when they annexed county land at the northwest corner of Winchester and Stevens Creek roads with the intent of developing a major department store there. This was 1951, and to say that the land was in the boonies is an understatement. Hamann's troops quickly grabbed the land on the other side of Winchester. The Emporium Department Store, on Santa Clara's turf, and the Valley Fair Shopping Center, on San Jose's, both opened in 1956. People on the west side of the Valley (where the initial growth was greatest) went there to shop instead of driving all the way into downtown San Jose. That sealed the doom of downtown San Jose. Even the big department stores—Harts and Hales—folded up and blight took over for decades. It was not merely a matter that businesses failed. The bigger issue was that the city no longer had a strong center. [7]

While all this was going on, the town of Los Gatos went on an annexation binge of its own, to the north and to the east. The mayor of Los Gatos, Colonel A. E. Merrill, was of the mind that the town would die without additional tax revenue and therefore needed more retail businesses. So he led the expansion charge. While the town leaders were knee-deep in the process of expansion, residents on the west side of the town, repulsed by that expansion effort, rebelled, and the battle for Peaceful Mountain ensued. Retired Vice Admiral Thomas Inglis wanted to maintain the rural nature of the area and so did a lot of his neighbors. Inglis led the march to the ballot box, and the residents of Peaceful Mountain, or Monte Sereno, incorporated in 1957. [8]

Residents of Los Altos, wanting to maintain the character of their town, and afraid of being annexed by Palo Alto or Mountain View, incorporated in 1952. The residents of the Los Altos Hills area, where there was no town, wanted to keep their community rural and incorporated in 1957.

In spite of not wanting to be swallowed up by San Jose, most of the new cities built out just as fast.

Two interesting side notes: Willow Glen residents, who had incorporated in 1927, opted to be annexed by San Jose in 1936. The move was due to the fact that they could not afford a sewer system, and had to build one. Alviso, an important shallow-water port in the early days of California, was annexed by San Jose in 1968. Alviso's importance as a port was diminished by two factors. First, the bay silted up greatly due to hydraulic mining in the Sierras, which made it less accessible, and, second, the arrival of the railroad eliminated the need for a port.

Production-style Housing

The scope of the wartime projects set the pace and scale for the development of the Santa Clara Valley. Prior to World War II, new subdivisions typically consisted of surveyed lots with streets and utilities. People bought the lots and hired a local builder to build their house. Nearly all the builders of these homes were small-scale contractors who built four to ten houses a year. Some people built their house themselves. This practice led to a variety of design and construction in the neighborhoods and not a few lots that remained vacant for years. But this approach was inefficient, and the need for inexpensive housing was tremendous.

Construction methods learned during the war years—mass production, speed, and efficiency—were applied in full force in the postwar era. There was no going back. Inexpensive custom-built homes, vacant lots in the middle of subdivisions, and the typical five-year mortgage all but disappeared in the Valley and elsewhere. Back alleys were also eliminated, and the garage door became the predominant architectural feature of most homes. Many of these changes lowered the cost of building and helped meet the enormous demand for affordable housing.

The astounding success of Levittown, on New York's Long Island, which opened in October 1947, took everyone but Mr. Levitt by surprise. And it lit a fire under builders everywhere. Mass-produced single-family housing would sell. [i]

There was a fly in the ointment, however. The lease agreement (which included an option to buy) stated that the properties could not be used or rented by any individuals other than those of the Caucasian race. The company explained that it could not tackle both the housing shortage and racial segregation at the same time, and the Federal Housing Administration agreed. The U.S. Supreme Court, ruling on another case, found that such limitations were not enforceable by law. That was good as far as it went, but it did not strike down the practice altogether. In the meantime, by 1951 Levitt had built 17,447 homes in or near the initial development. [9]

---

[i] The initial 2,000 homes in Levittown were rented—half of them within two days of the announcement of their availability. Homes built thereafter were sold.

Production-style housing. Top photo is of a tract in Mountain View.

Top: Courtesy of Mountain View Historical Association and Library
Bottom: Los Angeles Times Photographic Archive, Library Special Collections, Charles E. Young
Library, UCLA

When my parents closed escrow on their home in Saratoga in 1950, they received papers including one titled "Declaration Imposing Covenants, Restrictions, Reservations, Servitudes, Easements and Agreements." Clause 8 states, "No persons except those of the White Caucasian race shall use, occupy or reside upon any lot or plot in this Subdivision, except when employed as a servant or domestic in the household of a White Caucasian tenant or owner." The paper was unsigned, and there was no place for a signature.

Although this practice of segregation was not enforceable by law, it was widespread during the 1950s and left its mark after that. During the 1950s and into the 1960s, the new housing tracts—at least those on the west side—were almost entirely Caucasian.

The architectural design of our neighborhood was typical of those being built at the time. The 220 homes in El Quito Park all had the same floor plan. Some of the houses were reversed floor plans, there were three different roof styles, and some lots were ten feet wider to accommodate a two-car, instead of a one-car, garage. Otherwise, they were all the same house. Later tracts added one or two additional floor plans and had more options, which were mostly cosmetic variations of the same basic house.

I suppose economy of scale did not allow for development any other way. The cost of extending utilities to only one or two houses at a time made the prewar approach to growth impractical. Builders needed to construct large subdivisions to spread out those costs. As a result, the development of the Valley's housing during this era consisted almost entirely of large tracts of homes.

Before any of this could take place, the farmers had to go. The mechanism used to evict them was the state property tax system, which, until Proposition 13 passed in 1978, called for a reassessment of property values every year. Some farmers got out before high taxes forced them out; many did not. But taxes were not everything, as Annette Elissagaray relates.

Annette Elissagaray
My granpa, Gioacchino Tuso, was from Santa Flavia, a small village outside of Palermo, Sicily. In 1907, he left his wife, Beatrice, and their three children and came to America, headed for the Santa Clara Valley.

When he arrived in San Jose, he bunked with other men—some related, some from the same or nearby villages, one as young as twelve, but all with the same hope for a better way of life. Here they joined other Sicilian immigrants who were already established with their families.

Granpa Tuso was a very strong man. Before coming to America, he had shoveled coal in Tunisia for fifty cents a day. In the Valley, even though wages were very low, by 1910 he had accumulated enough money to buy a small farm with a house and at the age of thirty-three sent for his wife and children. It was not much—just a small orchard and a house that, in my father's words, "was nothing more than standing boards."

My father, Sam, was born in San Jose, and he and his brothers, Charlie and Roy, like their father, farmed here. During the Depression, they leased orchards from banks, and eventually the young, strong, and ambitious brothers acquired about 250 acres of prune, apricot, peach, cherry, and walnut orchards. They did their own [prune] dipping and had their own dry yard for the prunes and apricots.

In 1948, with the influx of people coming into the Santa Clara Valley after the war, my dad and his brothers realized they would not be able to continue farming here for long. They could already feel that a housing boom was going to take place, and in fact it had already started in a small way.

When I was born in the mid-1950s, we lived off of Graves Avenue in Cupertino at the home ranch, but the parcels the family farmed were spread out. There were thirty acres here, another twenty there, five or ten over there, and so on. All were referred to by name—that of the previous owner.

My father and his brothers wanted to continue to raise their children in a rural setting, so they started buying property in Tracy. The Delta-Mendota Canal was under construction, which created a water source for a place that up until then was only good for dry farming. They purchased over one thousand acres of property, on both sides of the canal, and had a long-term contract for inexpensive water. There, on both sides of the canal, was this land that no one had farmed with irrigation before, and my dad and uncles had the foresight and were intrigued by the prospect. As they bought property in Tracy, they began to shut down their farming operation in the Santa Clara Valley.

The transition didn't happen all at once. My uncle Roy and aunt Margaret moved first, then Uncle Charlie and Aunt Vickie. In 1958, my father and mother moved. I was three at the time and remember it was raining hard that day. The other thing I remember is that the moving van got stuck in the mud in our driveway, and my dad had to get the D-4 tractor and pull the moving van out and onto the paved road.

The land my dad and uncles purchased was mostly bare land. They had to do everything—prepare the land, put in the irrigation system, plant the orchards, build the structures—everything.

So between 1948 and 1958, my dad was one of the first Tracy commuters—but in the reverse direction.

On a summer day in 1948, my dad and his parents left for a trip to Tracy to visit the newly acquired properties. They left the Santa Clara Valley on a calm, crisp day and arrived in Tracy. When they stepped out of the car, it was 110 degrees with the wind blowing. His father told him: "I think you are moving to hell." It is hot over there, and windy and dry—very different from the beautiful and cool Santa Clara Valley.

In Tracy, we grew 'cots, cherries, almonds, and walnuts. My dad often compared how the crops did in Tracy with how they had done in the Santa Clara Valley. Nothing compared! Everything was inferior to what the Santa Clara Valley produced. Even the wild mustard that grows in the orchards in the winter is sickly compared to that of the Valley.

The move from the Santa Clara Valley to Tracy was rooted in continuing the family lifestyle they knew. The property values and taxes were not much of an issue, and I don't really remember them talking about it. They wanted a rural environment for their family and children. By that time, other Sicilian families had moved to Tracy. My father and mother, my uncles and aunts—all of them—were wonderful, hardworking people. They loved and were dedicated to the families they were born into and the families they raised. [10]   ***

After I told Allen Fox I was writing this book he recorded some interviews with his mother and sent me the files. She is such a sweet lady, is very articulate, and was pleased to share some of her story. Please remember she is talking to her son in this next story.

Joan Fox
We came in the summer of 1958. We were living in Ann Arbor, Michigan, where your dad was finishing up his master's degree in engineering.

Why did we come here? Well, the weather was the most important thing.

What were the other people like who were moving here? They were like us. In many cases, they had the same backgrounds. Bruce's friends, the engineers, were from the Midwest. They were in the same spot we were—starting to make a new life and being able to do stuff that they wanted to do. The people who became our close social friends initially were from the antenna lab at Lockheed where your dad was.

Before we moved to California, both of us had jobs to come to. They were so desperate for teachers at that time in Sunnyvale that they were interviewing for teachers in Michigan. So I actually had a full-time teaching job in Sunnyvale before we ever got out here.

There was a real shortage then; the people moved in so fast. They went back east for engineers, for teachers. There were all these things attracting young people out of college to come out to California. But it was a specific group—it was the young educated people. There were jobs for them and you could make a life [here].

All of a sudden you had this demand for people. I turned down five teaching jobs when I came out of college. Your dad had job offers. There was a period of years where our life was very easy because we were in such demand.

There was a freedom out here for people like us. One of the things I have always felt about the people of my age, of our group who moved here— we were a little more adventurous than those who stayed near their families. I think there was a personality difference.

After we moved out here, one of our friends and his wife came out to visit us. While they were here, Sunnyvale offered him a job as an assistant principal, and he really wanted to take it and move out here, but his wife wanted to be in Michigan near her family. I saw that pattern in a lot of people.

It was the ones who had that little extra "go" and were willing to leave their families—and I think that affected the whole culture out here.

Shortly after we came, we went looking for houses. We were driving down Highway 101 and there were all these billboards. Then suddenly there were all these tracts of houses everywhere. There was one advertisement that always came on the radio [with a little jingle,]— *"Live in Tropicana Village—only $99 moves you in." They were south of Santa Clara. They were tiny houses.*

So buying a house was fairly easy. We were lucky. I had a teaching job, so we were able to save money.

The old schoolhouse that was still at the end of the street was built in the 1880s. Otherwise, everything was very new. There was development at different stages going on everywhere. [11]

***

Tropicana Village brochure
Courtesy of History San Jose

I should say something about the transient nature of the new housing tracts. For most of the people moving in from out of state, their loyalty was to their employer, not to the place. Lockheed took this to new heights as many of its people moved in and out of the Valley more than once. From what I observed, the turnover rate in the new housing tracts was probably close to 15 percent per year during the blitz. How that compares with prewar times, I don't know. What I do know is that the house became much more of a commodity than it had been before. People spoke in terms of buying a new or used house in the same way they spoke of buying a car.

In the next story, a prominent architect summarizes how the Santa Clara Valley ended up being developed during the blitz.

Goodwin Steinberg
An early tenant [at Stanford Research Park] was Levinthal Electronics, founded by Elliott Levinthal, a former director of Varian Associates. Among his electronic devices were the defibrillator and the pacemaker, which are still in use for emergency heart therapy. Levinthal was no-nonsense: he favored good-quality construction for his utilitarian building, and he wanted ample parking for his employees. I was his architect, and I designed for mood and quality of life as well as quality of construction. I wanted to include landscaping as part of the design, to soften the parking lot and to screen the driveway. Such landscaping, however, took up space that could otherwise be used for parking.

Demonstrating the difference between an engineer and an architect, we walked the grounds together, blueprints in hand, Levinthal crossing out the trees in the parking lots as fast as I could draw them, and both of us learning from each other. Levinthal was mentally calculating his annual income per employee, each of whom needed a parking spot. Fewer spots meant fewer employees, which meant less income. Multiplied over several years, Levinthal calculated that each parking spot was worth a substantial amount of money.

I blinked when I learned how much money he thought I would cost him with my trees. [12]

Peter Gillies
I grew up in San Jose in the 1960s, and even though the urbanization of the Santa Clara Valley was in full swing, there were still plenty of orchards and fields that had yet to be gobbled up by pavement. As a kid, I had an appreciation for the beauty of the valley I lived in. I dare say

that few landscapes on Earth could rival the color and fragrance that God gifted the Santa Clara Valley with in the springtime. [13]

***

All the development of the Valley was done in the name of progress. We heard this term all the time, just like we hear the word progressive today, as if it were the positive justification for any and all change that was being imposed by a few people on the many. It was not until the end of this era that the effects of this so-called progress—including choking smog, greatly strained p services, and the blight from lack of planning—finally brought the blitz to an end.

Those who had lived in the Valley before World War II were the most shaken by the development blitz that swept over the Valley, but nearly all who saw it would later agree: "It all happened so fast."

Aerial photographs on the next (6) pages:

The new Ford plant at Milpitas, 1955
Courtesy of San Jose Public Library, California Room

Saratoga and Campbell avenues, 1959. The open space at left-center is the grading work for Westgate Shopping Center. Bucknall School at lower right.
Courtesy of History San Jose

Lockheed and Moffett, 1969, with widened Bayshore Freeway   >>>
Courtesy of Sunnyvale Historical Society

Chapter 8

Growing Up in the Valley in the 1950s and '60s

Skip Hazen

In 1955, at the age of fifteen, I had an early morning paper route for the San Jose Mercury News. We would get up at 5 a.m. each day, pedal our bikes to Fifteenth and E. Santa Clara streets, and fold, or "box," our newspapers on the porch area of a medical professional building. Four paperboys would meet there each morning. Many times we would challenge each other on how fast we could box our bundle of papers and then deliver them. This stirred our competitive nature.

One early morning in 1955, as I was pedaling my bike to get my newspapers, nothing was stirring in the neighborhood except for a few cats and an occasional barking dog. I arrived at the newspaper drop-off, got my four bundles of papers, and started boxing them so I could deliver them to my customers. As I sat there folding the papers, I could hear a banging noise coming down the hallway on the first floor of the medical building. Thinking it was a janitor cleaning and knocking the walls with a broom handle as he swept, I began throwing my papers against the glass door to get his attention. I wanted to let him know that someone was on the front porch.

Approximately fifteen minutes later, John Chaffin arrived on his bike to begin the same task. As he ran over to where I was, he yelled that he saw two men through a side door who were breaking into the pharmacy. We both ran across the street as fast as we could to Mel's Drive Inn and asked them to call the police. We waited anxiously for what seemed an eternity for the police to arrive.

They surrounded the building and then arrested two men for burglary and possession of burglary tools. The men were attempting to steal drugs and narcotics. Much to our surprise, the headlines for the next day's newspaper was "Mercury News Carriers Thwart Burglary in Progress." We were heroes for a while. Little did I know this deed would be a forerunner to a thirty-year career as a police officer with the San Jose Police Department. [1]

***

The next three stories are from letters I received from people who read and enjoyed *The Last of the Prune Pickers.*

Bill Sleight

I lived in the Cambrian Park area and went to Union School and Camden and Leigh high schools (first graduating class at Leigh in 1963). My first work was cutting 'cots at the Murphy's on Shannon Road off Blossom Hill. Eventually, I was a 'cot picker using one of those three-legged ladders. Then I worked many jobs on the Mirassou's properties in the vineyards and orchards where the Good Samaritan Hospital is today. Clovis and Mitch Mirassou were my classmates. Afterwards, for three consecutive summers during high school, I worked in their Beret prune orchard on south Branham Lane driving two old trucks, the "Georgia B" and the "Gutless Wonder." We put flames on the side with chalk and picked up the full prune crates that the braceros left in groups. We threw them onto the truck and left empty ones behind for them. Then we unloaded them with an old forklift onto an old covered wooden dock, where they waited for the big semi to take them to the dehydrator.

My friend and I certainly picked millions of prunes too. I even picked pears at the Amado's on Saratoga Avenue near Fruitvale. My dear old friend and I also rode our bikes before school (about two miles each way) to lay irrigation pipe for the orchard and then rode there again in the late afternoon to lay them again, two rows over. Muddy. We also propped up the heavy-laden tree branches and had our share of prop fights—in addition to some memorable prune fights. They are so perfect for throwing!

We ate our lunches on the covered wooden dock with three prune boxes: two to sit and stretch our legs on, and the third box placed at an angle against something as a backrest, so it was like a lounge chair. After our lunch and recuperating from the before-lunch work, we listened to our portable radios (I remember the Four Seasons' "Sherry," for some reason). We drank the cold water—the best tasting water I have ever had—from the artesian well near the pump house. Later, while I was going to San Jose State, I worked for two summers at the old Sunsweet dehydrator in Campbell. I was the guy who controlled the shaker. Older kids on forklifts unloaded the boxes of fruit being brought in on pallets by the farmers and dumped the fruit into the bin at one end, where the prunes were washed and then rolled onto a conveyor belt, where the machine shook them. They came out onto the large wooden trays that would be fed into the machine by other kids. From there the trays were stacked on a multi-tiered cart that was rolled into the dehydrator. That smell of fruit is special and comes closest for me when I visit the Napa Valley during the [grape] crush.

Anyway, I thank you for writing the book! It was really enjoyable and reminded me again, how lucky I was. The lessons I learned have always served me well, and the physical work that built my body in those formative years has served me well. And your description of Mr. Pitman as a mentor and model in your life mirrors my experiences with special people I have been lucky enough to know and appreciate beyond words.[2]

Thomas Hauber, Bill's "dear old friend"
My family came to California from Chicago—first to Marin in 1957 and later, in 1959, to the Santa Clara Valley. Dad thought California would be a better place to raise children.

The South Side of Chicago was a pretty edgy place, race and crime-wise. Kids were in and out of "juvie" at an early age, and I was already getting into trouble as a grade-schooler with schoolyard fights, petty theft, and other forms of malicious mischief, including smoking and so on. Kids already carried knives. High schoolers had gun and gang affiliations. What a place, Chicago. . . .

In San Jose, we lived on Branham Lane near Union Avenue. The place was later excavated for Highway 85.

My first job in the orchards was at Mirassou's, laying irrigation pipe on their Blossom Hill and Branham Lane prune orchards. We'd lay thirty-foot sections of pipe twice a day in the spring, slogging through eight inches of good mud in high boots, moving the lines over two rows at a time at 6 a.m., before school, and again after school.

During the hot summer months, beginning in June, I cut 'cots at Murphy's. Later, with my fingers in shreds, I decided to pick 'cots for better money. We had a ladder and a punch card from Orchard Supply to tally the pails. What a joy to pick the fresh 'cots in the Fourth of July hot sun and eat a warm juicy one every now and then!

We graduated from pipe layers at Mirassou's prune property to full-time orchard hands at age sixteen, driving ancient compound-gear trucks through the orchards and loading forty-pound prune crates. Boy we were in good shape!

Those long days of summer were full of hard work and we loved every hour of it. I think we made seventy-five cents an hour and as much as $75 every two weeks.

Those days in the orchard as a young man were among the most formative of my life. The combination of hard work and the reward of earning one's own money so early in life is lost on today's young people. Those days of good solid manual labor are gone, but not the memories. Ah, the smells and tastes of California in the summer: ripe cherries plucked off trees drive-by style from old orchard trucks, festoons of warm apricots on the tips of 'cot trees, and the sweet dusty smell of prunes lying on the ground under a heavily laden and propped French prune tree.

Another angle to the story is the explosion of housing tracts in the south valley in the early 1960s. The Campbell Union High School District was building a new high school every one to three years. I went to Camden High in 1961. When Leigh High School was built, the then-to-become senior class at Camden was split geographically and half of us went to Leigh, where we became the Class of 1963, which was the first graduating class at Leigh High School. The first stone pebble at Leigh bears "The Class of '63."

Other schools followed: Branham High School and Westmont. Of the original four schools, Campbell, Camden, Del Mar, and Blackford, none remain. [3]   ***

Cuttin' 'cots   Courtesy of Peter Wolfe

Floyd Frederickson

I was born in Redwood City (1956) and my family moved to Sunnyvale a year later. I grew up trudging around the Sunnyvale/Santa Clara fields and orchards and knew nothing about borders and fences. There were many times my buddies and I would pick whatever we could in the morning and spend our wages at the movie theater downtown or get a Greyhound bus ticket to Santa Cruz for the day. Other summer activities included hanging out at the local dairy or cleaning up the stalls at the horse stable (for a quarter) before riding our bikes to Stevens Creek Reservoir for a swim. [4]

***

I am at least somewhat qualified to comment on the effect on kids of working on the farms during this period. Since *The Last of the Prune Pickers* came out, I have talked to thousands of people about this subject and heard hundreds of their stories. In addition to giving book talks at a variety of venues, I sold the books at some local festivals, most of which attracted tens of thousands of people.

At the festivals, I had a banner with the book title above my table. People walking by had a few specific responses to the banner. Most of the young people, and not a few others, did not react at all and walked on by. Others came over to investigate or to tell me their story. Some saw the sign and broke into a big, knowing grin. (These folks almost always purchased a book.) Another common response was usually subtle, but not always. For some people, the banner brought to mind unpleasant memories. You could see it in their body language. One man was with his wife, who by her body language must have said something to him like, "Oh, look honey. . . ." But he stiffened, set his jaw, and make a "forget it, get it away from me" gesture with his hands. He obviously had had a bad experience with picking prunes. Most were not that dramatic, but not a few bristled at the memories.

From my experience, one thing became exceptionally clear: about a third of those who grew up working on the fruit farms really appreciated the experience, about a third were neutral, and about a third hated it or were bitter about it. These three responses were consistent across economic backgrounds. Some of the landowners' kids were bitter about their growing-up years, although they were often among the most privileged. And some of the Mexican American kids who had been fieldhands during that era greatly appreciated how they grew up, although they may have been the least privileged by economic standards.

One farm family I knew quite well had three children, all of whom felt differently about growing up on the farm. One told me it was a wonderful way to grow up; another said, "It was just life," and the third was bitter about it. And all were from the same loving family. This kind of varied reaction to the same outward circumstances I found to be typical.

The following short stories and comments are representative of many I heard from Mexican American men and women who had grown up working the crops in the Valley. Had I known I would write this book, I would have gotten their names and more of their stories.

- *We picked everything—tomatoes, cucumbers, green beans, corn, melons—you name it, we picked it!* [laughs] *Pears, apricots, peaches, plums—walnuts were the worst. Your fingers would be stained black for weeks afterwards. I tried to hide my hands when school started because they were all black.*

- *I was one of sixteen children. We worked the crops—all of us—from the youngest to the oldest. In the mornings, my mother would get a switch from a tree and then we would go out to work. We were expected to work. If we didn't—whack! But that's how we ate. We needed to work. To tell you the truth, it was a good way to grow up. We learned that nothing good comes easy. You have to work for it. I worry about my grandchildren. They expect everything to be given to them. They don't know how to work. They never had to. It's not good.*

- *My father told me it would build character, so I guess I got a lot of it* [shakes head and laughs].

Of course, it wasn't all work; kids knew how to play too. In the 1950s and '60s the Valley was full of kids riding bikes everywhere, exploring in the creeks; collecting pollywogs, salamanders, and crawdads; going down to the railroad tracks and placing pennies on the rails before the train went by to flatten them; flying kites, selling lemonade, and making homemade slingshots.

But the Valley was changing during the late 1950s and 1960s, and organized activities for kids that were not work or school related increased greatly. I suppose the best-known evidence of this shift was when the Moreland Little League won the Little League World Series in 1962. There was a lot of excitement over that!

Before the Valley was built out, the bookmobile—a library on wheels—made weekend stops of about two hours at various locations.
Photo Copyright © San Jose Public Library

Debbie Hall

I was a Lockheed kid, born in Burbank in the early 1950s. Like military families, we moved often as Dad advanced his career. My parents purchased their two-bedroom starter home in Sherman Oaks, Los Angeles, in 1950. After nine years, they bought into a new housing tract in Woodland Hills, then on to Saratoga eighteen months later. We lived in an apartment while a house in one of Saratoga's new tracts was being built. Many evenings our parents would walk through the house, and my sister and I would pick up "nickels" (popped-out metal circles from the electrical outlet boxes that were being installed). We were rich in our own currency! Then we moved to Yucaipa (southeast of Los Angeles), to Redlands, and then back to Saratoga again.

As an incentive to relocate, Lockheed would sell the homes directly if the market was slow. Dad moved and started his new job right away; Mom stayed to sell the house, handle the movers, and then settle us again. Those were stressful times for parents and kids alike. Although Mom tried to make it an adventure for us, it got old, making new curtains and planting new landscapes. It was also very awkward being the new kid again and again—always the odd one, different, and feeling dumb.

Dad worked classified projects. When my sister was three and I was five, he was sent on a company mission and told Mom, "I can't tell you where I'm going, why, or for how long." He was gone for three months. Communication was restored when he was on his way back home and in South America. Mom and many other Lockheed wives were courageous, confident, solid women. Twenty to thirty years later, we found out that Dad had been in the South Pacific to test the Polaris missile, which was launched from a submerged submarine. The Polaris was a very meaningful project for the United States and was huge for Lockheed.

Mom and Dad befriended other young Lockheed couples, many of whom became lifelong friends, aunties, and uncles. They all came from somewhere else—most from the South. We shared holidays and the adventures of life away from home.

My mother loved to roller skate and made sure we learned to skate from an early age. Mom, Dad holding my baby sister, and I skated together from the time I was four. We all had metal skates that clamped onto our shoes with a special key. Later we experienced shoe skates at the local roller rink—grand fun!

When skateboards came out, my sister and I each got one for Christmas, but I was never as comfortable on a board as on skates. We also "motorized" our bicycles by attaching playing cards to the wheel spokes with Mom's clothespins. We "gassed up" our bike-vehicles with Mom's old vacuum cleaner that had a curved handle and accessories.

At fourteen, my sister drove a motorized minibike. They had become popular and she loved the independence it gave her. Unfortunately, after a summer of fun, while riding on a gravel road she lost control of the bike and rolled it. She arrived home with raw, cut and scraped knees, and was treated at Los Gatos El Camino Hospital. That ended the minibike fun.

From a young age, I have lived up to my name's meaning: Busy Bee. Accomplishments and being productive have always been important to me. At ten years old, I began sewing on Mom's Necchi sewing machine. Soon afterward, I was given a used sewing machine for Christmas. From doll clothes I advanced to making my own clothes. I loved experimenting with style and fabric choice, and consistently simplified the pattern directions with success, and a few disasters. I made my skirts, blouses, and dresses for school, and made A-line skirts for my many bowling events at Saratoga Lanes.

For the work I did for dinner chores and cleaning our house, my parents gave me $5 per week. I used this for clothes and sporting events. I also earned money by babysitting, ironing, and cleaning houses.

In addition to play and work, my folks wanted to give us cultural experiences for character building. We went to both fancy and informal restaurants. As a young teen, we attended Man of La Mancha *on Broadway in San Francisco with fancy dining before the show, and dessert at an outdoor cafe afterwards. It was quite a memorable outing. The training succeeded. By my mid-teens, I was able to handle myself confidently in very formal situations and in casual ones.* [5]

Doug McNeil
My parents moved to Sunnyvale in 1958 and my wife's parents in 1966—both to join the space race. One father was at Lockheed Missiles and Space, the other at NASA Ames. As soon as I was old enough, I asked my parents to wake me up for every Mercury, Gemini, and Apollo launch. I grew up in a place where there were lots of conversations about the space program, as our neighborhood in West San Jose was made up of NASA, Lockheed, Philco Ford, and UTC solid rocket engineers.

My dream to become part of the space program was set in stone the day I watched Neil Armstrong set foot on the moon. I was only nine at the time, but I can still feel the excitement of that moment. [6]

Anonymous
Junior high was a trip. I went to Castro in the early 1960s. I think it was harder on the boys. Some of them were using the classroom as their stage; others were just bent on getting into trouble. The men teachers would paddle them right there in the classroom. Usually, that would

achieve the intended result. If Mr. Howard was doing the paddling, it sure did! The preferred instrument was a cello board, which was a wide wood board with a hole in it for the tip of a cello—to hold it in place. The women teachers sent the unruly boys to Mr. Tomichek, the vice principal. If you were in Mrs. Goolsby's English class across the hall, you could hear them getting whacked. It was muffled, but sometimes you could hear what was going on. Without the discipline, it could have turned into The Lord of the Flies. [7]

High school typing class, early 1960s
Courtesy of San Jose State University

T.S.

When I was sixteen, I worked after school and on weekends for Carl and "Short" Alford at their Shell station. In those days a gas station was a service station. We pumped the gas for the customers, washed their windshields, checked the oil, and checked the water level in the radiator. [i] *If the customer needed air in their tires, we put that in too. To total the day's receipts, we had an adding machine that had number*

---

[i] At the time pressurized cooling systems were only on new cars.

keys on its face and a crank handle at the side. You entered the amount of a sale and pulled down the handle to have it register in the machine. When you finished entering the receipts, you punched the Total key, pulled down the handle, and got your total—automatically!

Sometime in the mid-sixties, the auto manufacturers got the idea that it was groovy to place the gas filler pipe behind the license plate. The license plate was mounted on a hinge, and you pulled it down to access the filler cap. This probably wasn't the best idea because gravity works pretty well, and when these cars left the station and turned onto the street, they dipped down into the gutter and while coming out of it deposited a pint or more of gasoline into the gutter and on the street from the overflow on the filler pipe. Since the cars of the day were rear-wheel drive, when the light turned green and they accelerated, the front of the car reared up, the back went down, and they frequently deposited more gasoline in the intersection. And of course, this happened at every gas station. We tried to stop filling the tank before it was completely full but often were unsuccessful. Also, a lot of customers, regardless of what we told them, insisted that we fill it up all the way.

Another not-so-good idea of the day was expressed eloquently by a Corvair owner who would tell us, "Fill it up with oil and check the gas." Those cars, which made Ralph Nader a household name, burned and leaked a lot of oil.

Those were the days not only of 32.9-cent gasoline, but of promotional gifts as well. For a while, if you purchased more than ten gallons of gas, you got a free drinking glass or a steak knife. Yes, a steak knife.

The promotional after the steak knives was a game in which the customer received a sealed envelope; inside were five little stamps with letters printed on them. All five stamps were on one piece of paper with perforations so you could separate them easily. The letters were saved and torn off to spell words on a separate playing card. If you spelled certain words you received a prize of $5, $10, $20, or up to, I think it was, $500. It didn't take long to find out what the winning, and rare, letters were. That was all well and good, but one night as my buddy Jeff and I were closing the station, another one of the regular night shift workers drove in and parked right in front of the office. He got out of his car and had a very serious look on his face. "Let's go in the back—I need to show you something."

We went into the back room, which was shielded from outside view. He pulled a game envelope from his shirt pocket and said, "This is a winner. I don't know for how much, but it's a winner. Open it." We looked at him in amazement and hesitated, saying nothing. After a moment or two of silence, Jeff opened it. Sure enough, it was a winner. Then he said, "I can find the winners in all the boxes of envelopes." It turned out the perforations between the stamps for the winning letters were more accentuated than the others, and, by running your thumb and finger across the envelope you could feel the difference. He told the boss, and the game was discontinued shortly thereafter.

On a more serious note, we began coming up short in the tally of cash from the cash boxes that were kept out at the islands where the gas pumps were. (We all had a key for the cash boxes and used it when we had a cash transaction.) When we arrived at work in the afternoon, we would find a note for the night crew from the owners advising us we were short $60 or $80 or so the night before.

We had not had the problem previously, and this kept happening, not every night but perhaps once or twice a week. We all figured we had a thief among us, and that was hard to take because we were a pretty tight bunch and respected each other. This went on for months. Then one night, when we were very busy, I happened to look around a tall truck I was servicing at just the right time to see a kid my age, who did not work there, with his hand in one of the cash boxes. The surprising thing was that I knew him. I grew up with him and he was a regular customer. I stopped what I was doing and went over to him, called him by name, and said, "Now I know." He responded by pulling a knife on me. I called his bluff and told him, "Go ahead and stick it, _____, but I know." By this time one of his friends, who I also knew, came running over and excitedly told him not to do it. The tension of the moment was pretty high—for them. I was surprisingly calm, I suppose just greatly relieved to know what had been going on.

It turned out that a number of these kids, all close to my age, were working together in a theft ring. They had figured out they could open the cash boxes with a specially bent wire inserted into a slot for the credit card receipts. They had tall vehicles, always used two of them, and they would come in when we were very busy, parking in a way to obstruct the view to one of the cash boxes. We told the owner, he filed a police report, and I told the investigator what had happened, but the police did not have enough to press charges. The kids were drug users and were stealing to pay for the habit. They had also hit other gas stations in the area.

To talk about young people becoming addicted to drugs is not the most pleasant topic, but if I did not say something about it, I would not have told the story of growing up here during that time. The situation was very unlike that in earlier days when drug abuse was uncommon. By 1968 it was rampant. Uptown Saratoga had become a hangout for young kids plastered out of their minds. I knew some of those kids. Not a few kids in my high school cared for nothing other than the next time they would get high. Many came from wealthy families—the sons and daughters of stockbrokers, engineers, and civic leaders. A lot of young people gave in to this temptation and really messed up their lives. Thank God, some of them eventually came to their senses and turned their backs on that form of slavery.

Chapter 9

The Third Wave: The Chip Makers (1960s to Early 1980s)

In the late 1870s, three technologies came together at about the same time and completely transformed the Santa Clara Valley. The technologies were: rolled steel, pressure cookers, and refined sugar. All three had been invented some time before, but they were not perfected until the 1870s. The perfection of these processes and products gave birth to the canning industry, and the Valley was quickly transformed from a wheat-growing region to a fruit-growing region.

In the same way in the late 1950s and early 1960s three technologies came together at about the same time that transformed the Valley once again. The first was a process for making pure, single-crystal silicon ingots that could be sliced into wafers that would provide the substrate for integrated circuits; the second was improvements in the photolithography process for making circuit patterns on a substrate; and the third was the planar manufacturing process. The first two processes were worked out elsewhere at an earlier time but were further developed in the Santa Clara Valley. The third was conceived here in the Valley. Out of the perfection of these processes came the integrated circuit and Silicon Valley.

Pure silicon proved to be a perfect substrate, or foundation, upon which to build electronic circuitry because, depending on which chemicals are added to it, silicon can be either a conductor of electricity or an insulator, blocking the flow of electricity. Hence the term *semiconductor*.

The silicon substrate is simply a flat piece of highly purified sand, on which the image of an electrical circuit can be applied through the lithographic process. Add a little secret sauce here, and expose the image of your circuit to light, and you have made conductors; by keeping the secret sauce away from other areas, you have made insulators; put them together, and you have fabricated transistors, or on-off switches.

The planar process allows multiple circuits made in this way to be stacked on top of one another, the way you build a sandwich. In the process, a layer of oxide is placed over each layer (or circuit image) to protect the electrical junctions in the layer below. Puncture the layer of oxide in precise locations, fill the holes with liquefied copper, squeegee off the excess, and you essentially have wires connecting the two circuits. Voila! An integrated circuit!

All this is done using a high-powered lens to shrink the size of the circuits so that several integrated circuits can fit onto one wafer. The wafer is then cut up to separate the integrated circuits; hence the term *microchips*.

Near the end of chapter 5, James Gibbons gives an account of his first day at Shockley Semiconductor. The stories in this chapter pick up from there the overall story of the semiconductor industry in what became Silicon Valley. All are from the perspective of some of the people, famous and unknown, who were involved in it. I will begin with some stories about the business side of the early microchip industry and conclude the chapter with stories that describe the physical process of making the integrated circuits in the early days of the industry.

First, I must say something about the Traitorous Eight, who left Shockley in late 1957 after he decided to shift research focus away from silicon-based transistors.[1] Here is a little of that story.

Richard Hodgson
I was born in northern British Columbia in a town that doesn't exist anymore. It was a mining camp. . . . [Later] the family moved to Palo Alto, and I went to Palo Alto High School and Stanford University. I couldn't get a job in 1937 around here so I managed to get a scholarship to Harvard Business School and graduated from there and came back out here and worked for Standard Oil Company in San Francisco for a couple of years. Then the war came along and I was recruited by Fred Terman to go back to work at MIT in the radiation laboratory. And I worked there through 1945. Late '45. Then the opportunity came, and I thought I wanted to stay in science and went to work for the Atomic Energy Commission as the general manager and engineering manager at Brookhaven Laboratories out on Long Island.

But I decided I was not cut out to be a physicist and ended up starting a company that turned out to develop a color tube, which we ultimately sold to Sony. The tube's concept originated with Ernest Lawrence from Berkeley in Lawrence Laboratories—it was a sideline and a hobby of his.

And about that time, Sherman Fairchild. . . a very wealthy man in New York. . . was enthusiastic about new developments and things of that sort. He wanted to get this small company, Fairchild Camera and Instrument, into the electronics world. And he came across my background and hired me in 1955. And for immediate work with him, I worked on developing satellite cameras that were used in the early days in the satellite reconnaissance business. . . .

But I was continually looking for an opportunity in the electronics field, and through a set of odd circumstances, Sherman heard about the group out here in California through some contacts at Hadyn Stone, which was a small but successful investment banking firm in New York. So I came out to San Francisco and met with Bob Noyce and Gordon [Moore] and I think Gene Kleiner. We talked about what they wanted to do and eventually hammered out an agreement where [Fairchild Camera and Instrument] would advance up to $3 million and buy them out if it were successful. And we set up this small laboratory in Palo Alto. . . .

I think the larger companies—they all thought they knew more than [our] group did. I mean the GEs and the Westinghouses and companies who were in the component business, the tube business, . . . they had all the answers at Bell Labs. We at Fairchild were looking for an opportunity and recognized the talent that was there—just if you looked at the pedigrees, at least the top four of five of them from a technical point of view. And I had, some years before, been able to attend one of the Bell Labs seminars on the early transistor and was intrigued by what this could do.

You know, I saw a television set that was run completely with transistors in the early fifties and this seemed to me an opportunity for Fairchild to get into a new business without any preconceived ideas as to how to run it or how to go about it. [2]

Floyd Kvamme

[I] grew up in San Francisco in the Sunset [District]. . . . Starting with my high school years, I worked as a carpenter to work my way through school. . . . An English teacher took a real interest in me because no one in my family had ever gone to college. That was not something that was done. And he approached me one day, and I don't remember what started the conversation but he said, "Floyd what are you going to do?" I said "I'd like to be a math teacher." He said, "You know what an engineer is?" And I said, "No. What is an engineer?" He said, "That's

applied mathematics, using mathematics to build things." And I said, "Boy, that really sounds interesting." And so I decided I was going to go to college. . . .

My goal was to see if I liked engineering at all. And I really enjoyed it, but what I really liked was these transistors, and we were starting to use a few integrated circuits. They were very, very simple in 1960. So I said, "Ah-ha, now I know what I want to get a master's degree in. I want to get a master's degree associated with silicon, with transistors, et cetera." And I wrote to some twenty-five or twenty-eight—I can't remember the exact number—colleges in America asking if they had a master's program featuring semiconductors. Only two came back with a positive answer. Most people would not guess who the two were, but they were Syracuse, backed by GE Semiconductor, which was in town, and Purdue in Indiana.

The reason for Purdue is—most people don't know that the transistor effect was at Crane Naval Air Development Center three weeks after Shockley [invented it]. And [that is] the tragedy of being second. But [Syracuse] had a transistor program.

Well, by this time I was married, of course, and so it worked out that I could go to work for GE Semiconductor in Syracuse and work during the days and go to school at night. And so that's what we did for the next two years, '61 into '62.

Well, at GE I got my first taste of marketing because there was a book that we wrote there every year that was very, very popular. It was called the GE Transistor Manual. *And, in fact, my master's thesis is in the last issue of the manual. I wrote about six chapters of that because I was placed into a section that interfaced with the users in the application side, because if you think about it, in those days particularly, the chemists built the semiconductors. The electronics guys designed them into things because they really weren't—I mean, the making of a semiconductor has nothing to do with electronics. It has to do with the fusion processes and all those kinds of things. So there was that translation necessary from how does this amount of boron, or whatever, develop a certain amount of capacitance in the device, et cetera. . . .*

I tried to get into a formal marketing position at GE, and they wouldn't allow it because I didn't have the proper academic credentials for marketing. I was an engineer. And I wasn't very happy with that, and so

I decided, well, I want to get back to the West Coast then. I mean, Syracuse was neat, but the winters were ugly. . . .

I joined Fairchild [in Mountain View]. . . . April of '63. . . . My job was in product marketing, working for Mel Phelps, who ran product marketing, and I was the integrated circuits product marketing guy. And integrated circuits, like I said, were in their infancy at that time. . . .

Fairchild, by this time, had introduced the family of logic called RTL, resistor transistor logic, and they had a backlog for the "S" element, which was the most complex element at that time. It was a half of one bit, a half-shift register, if you can imagine that. They had a backlog of about two thousand parts. That week's production was thirteen pieces. And they were trying to figure out who to give the thirteen that they had built to. A company on Long Island had the biggest order with them, so they decided to give them two of them.

I mean, the yields were terrible. They got one good chip per five wafers started that week.[i] I still remember these numbers because I said to myself, "Holy mackerel, this isn't as clear as I had thought. Is this—I mean, can we really build anything?" But they waged on. And, of course, very shortly thereafter, epitaxy was discovered as the way to isolate things. Don't do the back side diffusions, which were the early days of those early wafers. And it changed the world. I mean, suddenly the wafers—the yields on that "S" element—went from one [chip] per five wafers to five per one wafer and higher. And the whole thing changed. [3]

Charlie Sporck

I'm from a little town called Saranac Lake in upstate New York, and I went to school in New York State—Cornell University—mechanical engineering, even though I never really worked at mechanical engineering. After graduating, I went to work for General Electric. . . .

I worked some nine years at GE and really, in a strange way, the reason I got into the semiconductor business is because of General Electric. . . .

It turns out that the last assignment I had at GE was a job called supervisor of shop operations. I had the production people as well as methodology people working for me. And in those days, you know, GE

---

[i] A wafer is a thin slice of silicon ingot on which the microchips are produced. At the time there were about sixty-four chips per wafer. (I explain the process later.)

was very strongly unionized in that particular place and in the capacity department by the UEW, United Electrical Workers, which was an outfit that was suspected of being communistic in those days. Anyway, the contract was written such that in order for you to change the price in any way in terms of building a product, you know, the labor price per part, you had to significantly change the method.

So I had worked something like a year and a half to two years, coming up with a new method to assemble these power factor capacitors, and when we started to install it, the union started to object to this because they recognized that it was going to represent a change in price. And there was a fight for some time. And actually it was a friendly fight because I had a very good relationship with the guys. However, the company chose to back down, so there was two years of work down the drain. And I decided then, when they finally made that decision, that I was going to change jobs, and I bought a New York Times *on the way home. In the* Times *was an ad for a production manager for this company called Fairchild, in August of 1959. So GE is basically the reason why I ended up in the semiconductor business. . . .*

We have been very successful in keeping unions out. As a matter of fact, there's only been a couple real threats—one in the early days at Fairchild, at the diode plant. There was a real threat, and we actually had an election. It turned out that we were fortunate. We found [out] the business manager at the local [who] was trying to unionize the plant up there was making more money than Bob Noyce was making as a general manager of the company. We spread that around like crazy, and we won big there. And then there was one other election that happened at Raytheon in later years. But other than that there has been no progress by the unions. . . .

You know, a lot of us came from the East Coast and worked in conventional companies. You know, Bob Noyce worked at Philco—very unionized. I worked at GE—heavily unionized. We had experience in those environments where there was a restriction on your ability to be flexible. I worked for a short time in the steam power plant of GE, a steam turbine plant rather, of GE, and the chief shop steward could walk in and turn the main power off and just shut the whole place down and go into discussions. I mean it was an entirely different environment. Now, can you imagine somebody turning the power off in a semiconductor wafer fab facility? . . .

The problem, really, was that the bulk of our product was going into the military, and to a much lesser extent to [the] computer business. But there was this vast consumer market out there and the bulk of the computer market. But [Fairchild] didn't have prices low enough to participate [in it] because of our assembly cost. You are building one-at-a time transistors, and these things were not heavily automated at the time. [So] we looked at this issue. Labor cost was the predominant item for our cost of building transistors. And the availability and the cost in the Bay Area was a problem.

So first we started looking (I started looking) elsewhere in the country. That's why we located a plant in Portland, Maine; but that didn't really solve the problem.[i] So one of the guys had been traveling around the world and he happened to have stopped in Hong Kong. And Bob [Noyce] and I had an investment in a radio company in Hong Kong. This was like 1962, a failing radio company, it was, and this guy came back and he says, "You know, we got to look at Hong Kong." So I, and Julie Blank, went over to Hong Kong and we became convinced that. . . we could assemble these devices there, especially now that we had planar chips, which excused a lot of problems. . . . So we set up a factory there, and that's where that all started. . . . It was originally driven by labor cost, and then, secondly, it turns out, overhead costs. It's just that it was a mad rush into Southeast Asia by all companies eventually. [4]

***

Here is the story of an Iowa farm boy who moved to Sunnyvale to become production manager at Fairchild in the early 1960s.

Tom Maher

Fairchild was a company that was vertically integrated, for they had to design and manufacture all of their own equipment. They even grew their own silicon that they used to make the wafers. There were at least four hundred mechanical and electrical design engineers on board designing not only product—integrated circuits—but the equipment to make the product, such as mask aligners, diffusing furnaces, all the

---

[i] Fairchild also opened a plant in Shiprock, New Mexico, on Navajo land, in 1969. It was a joint effort between The Bureau of Indian Affairs, the Navajos, and Fairchild. The idea was to keep jobs in the United States. A nice thought, but it turned out to be a very bad idea. "We were really screwing up the whole societal structure at the Indian tribe. You know, the women were making money, and the guys were drinking it up. . . . We had a very major negative impact upon the Navajo tribe." (Quote is from Charlie Sporck in Silicon Genesis interview, February 21, 2000.)

assembly equipment and the product testers. This group was always inventing new and better equipment. . . .

It wasn't long before we heard that some of these designers were going out to start their own [integrated circuit] equipment business. . . . It was strange to suddenly start buying equipment outside the company from people we used to work with inside, but their equipment was better. Also, this was the beginning of Silicon Valley that we all know about.

With all the new company start-ups happening, Milt Meyers and I were constantly getting calls from venture capital firms and the new company founders to run their "would-be" production process. We knew a lot of the founders because they either worked at Fairchild or were related somehow to some of the Fairchild employees.

Most of the founders of the new companies were developers and/or designers of the new integrated circuits or new processes. They were brilliant high tech engineers and only they could design the new circuits. Unfortunately, most. . . didn't really know what producing or manufacturing was all about. Some thought that manufacturing was a simple task and could be done by idiots.

Anyway, Milt and I went with a start-up as general foremen of the manufacturing of the new company called GME. . . . By this time (1964), there were many start-ups happening in the Valley and [General Microelectonics], which was shipping good MOS [metal oxide semiconductor] product, was getting some attention from investors. There were several attempts to buy out the company. Then, suddenly, Ford Motor owned us. . . .

We soon learned that functioning with a large company owner was very different than working with a small Silicon Valley company. A purchase order request for anything—including raw materials— required twenty-five signatures in Dearborn, Michigan, if the value exceeded $500. Due to this sign-off delay of five weeks or better, we soon ran out of raw materials and the factory stopped. . . .

So, as the raw materials ran out, we started laying off people until there was nothing left. . . . I went next door to a new start-up called National Semiconductor. I did not even have to park my car in a different parking lot. [5]

***

An early wafer, containing about two hundred memory chips

James Downey

I graduated from Santa Clara University in 1962 with a bachelor's of science in electrical engineering, and went down to the University of Arizona for a master's degree. [I] thought about going on for a PhD for a while but decided that would take too long. And so in 1964 I came back to the Valley. First job was at General Electric. In those days, GE was still in the computer business and they had an advanced peripheral equipment laboratory, they called it, in Sunnyvale. I was put onto an optical character recognition project early on. That's where I met Bob Shriner and Bill David Alan and some other guys. So that was a good experience. But in 1966, or maybe late '65, GE decided that they couldn't compete in the computer business, even though they had been the first to develop an all solid-state commercial computer, the Erma

System for the Bank of America. But [GE] had this saying in those days that a GE manager could manage anything, and they brought these guys in from [places] like the small DC motor division and [places] like that, and they just couldn't, couldn't, manage the computer business. And so they finally sold out to Honeywell. They tried to get all of us in the lab to go down to either Phoenix or Oklahoma City as part of Honeywell, and nobody went. Harold Bytel went for a few months and came back. And at that time, Fairchild was doing very well, and I was impressed with Fairchild because I had used their products in some of the discrete amplifiers and that sort of thing that I'd built up. They were hiring at the R&D facility in Palo Alto, so some of us went up that way, and that's how I got into Fairchild. [6]   ***

I introduced you to Jack Balletto in chapter 6. Here is another part of his story. You'll need to hang on to your hardhat—this one is quite a ride, but it tells you something of the times.

Jack Balletto
I did three years at Lockheed in that [Electronic Countermeasures] project, and then I realized I wasn't using any of the engineering classes I took, so I quit. I took a pay cut and went to a company called Western Microwave Labs as one of a two-man band. We were the solid-state design group for Western Micro, whose basic skill was ferrite switches. They had contracts [to supply] the communications system. So, my boss and I had the solid-state group. We were using 709 [and] 711 op amps (operational amplifiers) from Fairchild and designing these things, and the kick was that we were both taking our master's degree at the time. We needed the classes we were taking. The boss went out and booked this big contract, which we never would have said, "Yeah, we can do it." [He] comes back from Washington: "OK, we got the next level up. It's all integrated. You know, you guys, you solid-state guys, you're going to have to—you have to step up." [laughter] So, we're reading our books to figure out how to get this thing done—and talk about learning! It was a hoot.

The thing worked and they sent it into outer space. But then I noticed... the next data sheet that came out. Everything I was doing was on the new, improved 709A, or whatever they called it, and so [I was] pretty clear where the engineering content was going. It was going on the chip. . . . And, of course, later on everything went on the chip. All the digital stuff basically got sucked into a chip. So, when I got a phone call to join [General Microelectronics], I was a pretty easy target. . . . I just [thought], "Hey, I've got to go see what these guys are doing. This is interesting.". . . So, I went over to GME in '66. . . . I just wanted to get into the chip business. . . .

So I quit Western Micro, [and] went over [to GME]. I show up. I'm now an employee of Philco Ford. They hadn't told me they were selling it to Philco Ford, [laughter]. . . . So, I was part of Philco Ford Microelectronics, which reported to the Tractor Division of Ford. . . . And, sure enough, one time this little old guy from the tractor group came out for a sales meeting. What a scream. I mean, this is the whole Midwest, East Coast versus California [culture clash]. Very proper chap, and sold [clears throat] electronics, I guess, to the tractor guys. And, of course, at the sales meeting everybody put their expense accounts on his room. Oh, he went ballistic. . . . So they shut the whole thing down, and they figured probably ten or twenty key people would move out to [their other locations], and of course nobody went; not a single person went. [laughter]. . . [They] didn't quite get it. . . .

A lot of the team. . . went to work at Fairchild. . . . When I was getting hired, they said, "Well, look, you're a design guy, why don't you go in that design group?" And I said, "Yeah, OK; well what else do you do?" And they had a big opening. They couldn't make anything. I said, "Where's the action?" He said, "Well, product engineering, if you could ever figure out [how to] get the yields up." I said, "Oh, well, fine, let's start out there." So I spent a year in wafer fab[rication], and testing wafers and shift registers, [which] were the easy ones to test, trying to figure that out. . . .

It was a tough year, and their yields were horrible. I was an instant hero because they had barrels full of rejected shift registers with slow rise times on the output. The specs at that time were all ten picaferit load, ten pF load, so these things were slower than molasses. I just went around and measured some of the test jigs, and they were all, like, 80 pF or 400 pF, and [I] just spruced them up, you know, got them back to— they all worked. So, it was like, "Wow, it's lucky we hired that guy from the microwave world." . . .

I got to Fairchild in '69. I remember there was a period—and I left in '72—where we had a new fabrication manager every thirteen weeks. [laughter] At least I got time for one [fabrication] run. . . . That was frustrating. That's a shame. They handed the market to—I mean, without much of a fight—to Intel. [Intel] would have won anyway.

[Interviewer: "And there was no intellectual protection for functions. There was for process."]

Well, boy, the times have changed on that front! All the advice used to be: "Don't worry about the patent; you gotta outrun 'em" [laughter]. [7]

John East

We got married in June of '68, and I needed to finish my master's as soon as I could and then get a job because we needed the money. So I finished the master's in September. But I hadn't gone through the college on-campus recruiting thing, so to get a job I had to write just a whole bunch of letters. I remember Pam and I—she typed for me, and we probably sent out forty or fifty letters, and I got hardly any responses back. I think I got one really interested one, that was Fairchild, and then one from HP and one from IBM, but they were just sort of kicking the tires.

So I went down to interview at Fairchild and the story I'll never forget. I talked to an operations guy named Gene Flath, who I was very impressed with. He just blew me away. He seemed to be young and energetic and smart. And then there was a human resources guy named Jerry Briggs, and we hit it off, and they asked me to come back, I don't remember, maybe a month later. And a month later when I came back, . . . they offered me a job. That was probably in May of '68. But I wasn't ready to come out of school until September. So they told me not to worry about it. They gave me their cards and said, "OK, a couple of days before you're ready to come, just give either one of us a call, and we'll tell you what to do—you're on." So we shook hands; I had the offer there.

[I] went back and didn't check in with them, didn't do anything with them, until the day after Labor Day, which is when I finished my last test. And I picked up the phone and called Jerry Briggs, who's the HR guy. (Gene Flath—I was maybe a little scared of him, he was going to be my boss's boss.) So I called on Jerry Briggs—asked for him, and the lady that answered the phone said, "There is no Jerry Briggs that works here." "Well, what happened to him?" "I don't know. There's never been a Jerry Briggs here in all the time I've been here." "Well, how long have you been there?" "Well, I've been here a month now."

Well, OK, maybe I'll call the other guy. So I hung up and called Gene Flath—asked the lady who answered for Gene Flath, and she said, "There's no Gene Flath that works here." "Well, what happened to him?"

"I don't know; there's never been a Gene Flath here in all the time I've worked here and I've been here a long time now." "Well, how long have you been there?" "Oh, about six weeks now, it's longer than anybody."

Now I was starting to think I was caught in The Twilight Zone. *But after a while, I figured out, well, I should call back the human resources; they'll know how to handle the problem. And they put some guy on the phone, I don't remember who it was, and the guy said, "Oh, yeah, there has been a little bit of turnover. Let me get your file." And he came back and said, "Actually, Mr. East, we don't have a file on you. Are you sure we offered you a job?" And I needed that job. Boy, we were broke. We were really broke. So I offered to drive down there and show him the offer letter, and he said, "No, no, I'll take your word for it. Just show up in a couple days and we'll figure something out."* [8]

***

Jerry Sanders grew up on the South Side of Chicago and, like many others, got some breaks along the way. He joined Fairchild in 1961 and was politely fired in late 1968. Here is some of his story.

Jerry Sanders
[Fairchild] was a wonderful place to work, but it had a character flaw. And the character flaw was called Syosset, Long Island. That's where Fairchild Camera and Instrument was headquartered, and they were the owner of Fairchild Semiconductor. All the cash flow and all the money that was being made was flowing into their pockets and being dissipated on not-such-great other activities. Meanwhile the contributors at Fairchild weren't making very much money particularly, but, worse than that, as I got to the end of my time there, the company was being starved for capital investment. And so we couldn't even afford to buy the testers to ensure that we were meeting the specifications. . . . We couldn't guarantee the quality because we didn't have enough testers to test all the parts. It was grim. I thought this was a tragic situation for a company. And I'd remind you that, at the time, Texas Instruments was already a giant company when Fairchild got started. Fairchild got started in '57, as I recall. In '58 Bob Noyce invented the integrated circuit, the [silicon based] monolithic integrated circuit.

I joined in '61, but by '67 and '68, we were in a serious retreat. . . . So it was a sad time, and Fairchild began to decline and people started to leave. And it was about that time, of course, that Bob Noyce and Gordon Moore left to found Intel. That was in 1968. . . . [9]   ***

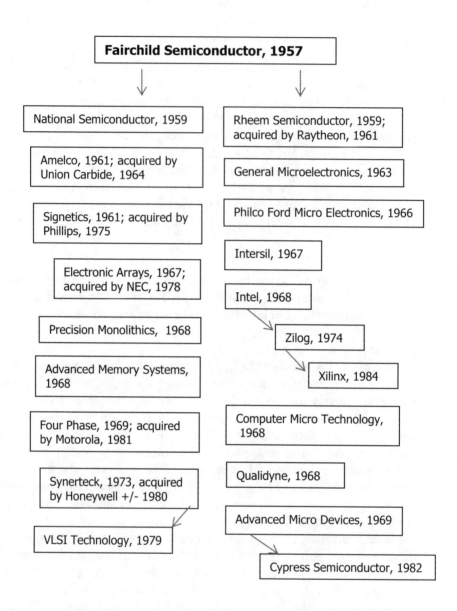

"Fairchildren," or some of the major semiconductor
companies that had their roots in Fairchild Semiconductor.
There were many more. Spin-offs are designated by arrows.

Jim Reynolds

I'm from Syracuse, New York, and graduated from Williams College in Massachusetts with a degree in physics. Immediately after graduating, I accepted an offer from Westinghouse because it was a management-training program which promised to expose me to several engineering opportunities and allow me to choose the one I liked best.

So I went to work at Westinghouse in Youngwood, Pennsylvania, in the semiconductor business. In that job, I was setting up a wafer fab operation and making simple semiconductor products like transistors and diodes.

A friend of mine came out to California a year before I did. He told his girlfriend's roommate, "I've got the perfect guy for you." So I came out to California in October of 1962.

I had no intention of joining Fairchild when I came out. From my imprecise research, I had determined that Mountain View was in Southern California and I wasn't interested. We were staying in Sausalito and one day we decided to drive to Santa Cruz. I was asleep in the car and woke up just as we came to the Mountain View sign and Fairchild. So I found out where Mountain View was. Some people plan their whole career out very carefully. I guess mine was determined by waking up at the right time.

Coming to California was a big cultural shock, but I just loved it out here. All of a sudden, I was free of the many social constraints of the East Coast and could fashion my life in the way I saw fit. Within nine months, I had a new house, wife, job, car, and child on the way. I refer to it as my early career epiphany. Westinghouse had been full of structure, and I could see my career unfolding slowly before me, one agonizing preprogrammed promotion at a time. At Fairchild, my progress was limited only by my talents and ability to work hard. It was a complete meritocracy. It was intimidating, but I survived, even if it was scary at first.

I was from a fairly well-to-do family, went to prep school, and grew up with all the social formalities. But I really didn't fit in that lifestyle, and California was a perfect solution for me.

There is a California stigma back east. My family thought I was nuts for coming out here where all the hippies and liberals were. There was, and still is, a feeling among many people on the East Coast that that is where the country started and that is where all important activity takes place. They feel like anyone from west of the Hudson River is just a pretender trying to participate in the action but not really able to contribute much.

There were two hundred people at Fairchild when I arrived, so I worked with everybody—Noyce, Moore, Sporck, Grove, and others.

I started as a production supervisor and worked in the "donut room," so called because of the layout of the equipment. Around the outside were diffusion furnaces, predeposition furnaces, and wafer-cleaning stations. It was this area where the oxides were grown and the doping of silicon was done. [He explains this later.] *The important things here were careful cleaning and drying of the wafers plus the ability to properly load them into furnaces, open the valves that allowed the correct gases to flow, and run the clock to time the operation. Flow meters measured the rate of oxygen or other gases delivered. A timer buzzed when the set time was up.*

As production supervisor, I monitored the product going through. There were six to eight ladies working for me who performed these tasks. They were really skilled and took a lot of pride in their work.

In the center of the donut was a room that was bathed in yellow light to avoid exposure of the ultraviolet-sensitive photoresist material that was being processed. It was here that the photographic and etching operations were done to open the small holes where the dopants were to go. The key equipment there was the aligner.

At that time the images were made using a contact printing process. The wafers were placed on the stage of the aligner beneath a "mask," which was the photographic negative of the new layer to be printed. There was an optical microscope with which an operator could see the pattern that was already on the wafer and the new pattern which was on the mask. The operator would move the wafer until the two patterns were aligned, whereupon the mask would be clamped together and an exposure light would go on.

I was responsible for a six-transistor device, a dual three-input gate, I think it was. It was a six-week process to manufacture the integrated circuits (ICs). Now there are billions of transistors on integrated circuit chips, and the process takes even longer.

Fairchild manufactured their own silicon ingots and built most of the equipment required to manufacture ICs. The industry was so young that the many suppliers that offer all that equipment today did not exist. Fairchild made everything from diffusion furnaces, aligners, and test equipment to the polished wafers on which the circuits were built.

What we were doing in the donut room was a process that was determined by R&D. We were executing the process they came up with. I kept notations when the wafers came out of the furnaces and would suggest to R&D that a certain process change might increase the yield. They would investigate and approve or disapprove.

I'll tell you a little more about the process. An integrated circuit consists of individual components, mostly transistors and resistors on a common silicon substrate. The transistors are fabricated by replacing a small number of silicon atoms with, for example, boron and/or phosphorus atoms. The location of these so-called doped regions is such that transistors (small electronic switches) are created. Roughly the first third of the process is involved in creating these transistors. The second two-thirds are involved in depositing multiple layers of metal and etching it back to form the conductors that interconnect the transistors so they can do the intended job. In a modern IC, some thirty layers (masks that define the doped and metal regions) are required. In my Fairchild days, it was more like ten layers.

Any contaminant (dust, dirt, skin flakes et cetera), that lands in the wrong place (interfering with the light in the aligner or contaminating the high-temperature doping furnaces) would cause a catastrophic failure of the chip on which it landed. The clean rooms were not very clean. You could see dirt in the photoresist and in the image. The clean rooms and dressing regimens that allow today's multibillion transistors and ten nanometer cutouts were not known. We fought giant dust particles and our yields were quite low. For the circuits we considered complicated (one hundred to a thousand transistors!), our yields could go as low as 15 percent. If they did, the product engineer (me) would have to analyze the rejects and act to eliminate their cause as quickly as possible.

Later I became an engineer, and then my responsibility was "womb to tomb" for the entire process. I knew a little bit about a lot of things. Now each process engineer is highly specialized but not at that time.

Some people got to California but just didn't like it and went back. For me, the lack of structure and the freewheeling California lifestyle was just the thing.

During that era we worked hard, and long hours too. But we kind of had the feeling we were doing something spectacular. We knew that what we were doing could take off.

And yes, I married the girl. We raised two boys and a girl who in turn married, stayed nearby, and raised our six grandchildren. That match made in San Francisco was a good one and we are still together. [10]

H.P.S.

In June of 1972, I was hired by a temporary agency that sent me to a small electronics company to do final testing on a large microcircuit they produced. I think the company was called CMI, for short. It was on Pastoria Avenue in Sunnyvale and had maybe thirty to fifty employees. I tested thousands of microcircuits and then the company hired me directly to do a process called wafer sorting.

They had two shifts, and a woman named Gloria and I were the wafer sorters on the swing shift.

The company bought blank silicon wafers and built integrated circuits (Ics) on them. I never saw the fabrication process there, though I did see the wafer fab at a large Sunnyvale company where I worked later.

The job involved looking through a microscope to examine the wafers. The "run" (lot) came in a black slotted box. It was of paramount importance that the wafers stay in the same order in which they were received. Also, you had to make sure you had set the machine up correctly so it would step from one integrated circuit on the wafer to the next. The ICs were about one-sixteenth of an inch square. Toward the end of my time we were testing four-inch wafers; originally it was three-inch wafers.

There could be a hundred ICs on one wafer. Without magnification you could see that there was something on one side of the wafer. As I looked through the microscope, I had to find the proper edge of the wafer to start on. Each product required a different setup of the machine. The machine would move the focal point from one IC to the next, left to right, then it would step right to left for the next row, until it finished at *the bottom row of the wafer. It took several minutes to test each wafer. I filled out the paperwork while the machine was doing the testing and finalized it after all the wafers in the box had been tested.*

While testing each IC, it dropped a blob of red ink on a bad circuit. The machine made the decision if it was a good circuit or not. My job was to get the wafer on the platform correctly. You had to be quite precise, as there were also electrical wires with very small probes at the tip that had to be aligned. All this was done under the microscope. After the testing of a wafer was completed, there was some kind of indicator that the testing was done, and I would take that wafer off with tweezers and put it carefully in the wafer box for that job, then get the next wafer from the box and set it up.

One had to be very precise how they were going to cut the wafer up. I don't know if the company did the cutting or not. I never saw the entire operation.

So I did this for about six months. Then the company was taken over, and they laid people off and had a skeleton crew left. They gave us severance pay, I believe for two weeks, which I considered a very generous thing to do. That job was pretty intense for me, as we were expected to do a certain number of wafers per hour.

About ten days later I was hired by Precision Monolithics, Inc., as a final test operator. PMI was in Santa Clara, in a new industrial park near San Thomas Expressway, south of the 101. There were vacant lots next door and across the street. They employed maybe two to three hundred people at the time.

Once the silicon chip was assembled into a case, the many-legged item [a microprocessor] had to be electronically tested. The ones I tested were an inch long. I was doing the final testing on them and was much happier doing this testing than I was sorting wafers. I was also glad to be working swing shift. The day shift always had engineers looking over their shoulders.

These were high-end ICs (also called microcircuits). The least expensive was about $10. Most were much more expensive. The units were so costly they were kept in a secured cage—a cyclone fence type of enclosure. Only one woman, named Carol, had a key to it. She worked in that cage doing inventory control. All the ICs were checked in and out of that locked enclosure.

In the same room as final test, we had assembly, where these products were soldered and whatever else was necessary to give the chip its casing.

We had a good supervisor, Chuck, and a good team of hard workers. My coworkers were nice ladies. There were about eight of us and we all got along very well. Chuck was my supervisor the whole time I was there, which was three years. I enjoyed it there. A big part of it was that we had a good crew and we had fun together. And Chuck knew he could trust me to do a good job.

One time I was sent to the assembly row to do a test in a bath of some sort. I had to put a probe on the IC and get a reading on an oscilloscope. Some ICs only required room temperature testing, and we all did that.

I did the testing using the Fairchild 5000C machine. It was about 12-15 feet long and was entirely enclosed. All you could see on the outside were the tape readers. It did testing at different temperatures. The greatest temperature extremes were minus 55 degrees and plus 125 degrees Celsius. We also tested at 25 degrees, which is room temperature. You had to wait for the chamber to be cooled by liquid nitrogen and then for it to heat up to the temperature required for the test for a particular lot.

I would load a paper-punched tape program into the 5000C, and it would produce another paper-punched tape with the test results on it. The units tested and the tape readout, which I labeled, would then be placed in a plastic bag.

A lot of time had gone into these units, so the "burn-in," when it was required, was crucial. I ran the burn-in room, which is where we put electrical power to them. I would load the ICs onto a board that was about ten to twelve inches by three feet, then load the boards with the ICs on them into racks in an oven. They were subjected to heat and electrical power at the same time. The process could take a couple of days or up to a week, depending on the product. After burn-in, the ICs were tested again.

The process of making integrated circuits had not been perfected and quality control could be a problem. Sometimes there was a high percentage of rejects. The engineers were working to solve the problems. One time, they were looking for three good units out of a hundred. Another time I was given three units and we needed one good one out of the lot. It was going into a rocket.

It could get boring loading the units on the boards! Eventually, I wanted something more mentally stimulating. [11]

***

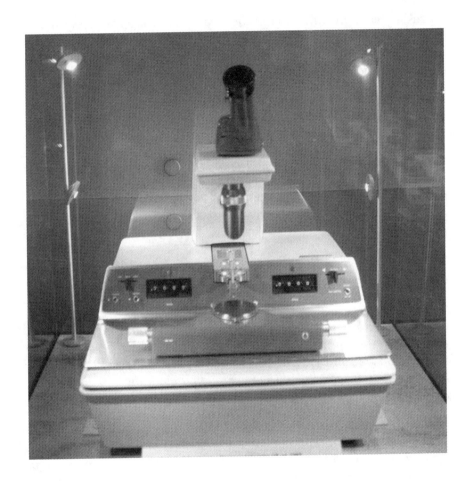

Wafer-scribing machine, circa 1965

Here is a story from a Sacramento native who moved to the Valley and became a circuit layout designer and chip floor-planner.

Todd Gilman

My part in the process was in floor planning the engineers' schematic drawings—retooling them into a physical concept and conceiving them with interconnections so that everything fits into a nice solid rectangle with no empty real estate. Then I go about to physically lay it out, dealing with all the problems and engineering changes along the way.

When I entered layout design in the late 1970s, there was no school or class for this. There was no prerequisite degree or course of study. It was mostly OJT, on the job training. You learned from other layout designers by doing—the same way they had learned.

I designed my first two chips on Mylar [a transparent plastic sheet], on a draft board with colored pencils and a T-square. That was before chips were designed on computers.

The processing department would set up "design rules" for each process that fabrication ran. For example, how close two metal lines could be before they interfered with each other, and how large or small a contact/via could be to reliably send a signal between a wafer's layer of conductivity.

We floor-planned and designed all the processing layers at the same time. It is like looking down on a ten to fifteen tiered layered cake, with each layer being a layer we designed on. Imagine fifteen-layer chess.

All the time throughout the design process, we made sure our layout matched the fab-processing design rules and checked it against the schematic. (We call that LVS, or layout versus schematic.) Both had to be error free to continue. These were first done over a light-table, manually, and then later done solely on a computer.

Layout designers were often working on three chips at a time. They could be chips being laid out for the first time or chips coming back from fabrication for required changes. These chips were often of different processes with different layer compositions and design rules. I may be working on a chip for one to two years; others two to three years. Often the experience is so intimate I would actually dream of a solution to a problem or dream of something I forgot clear across the chip.

My first chip measured less than a quarter- inch on a side. The chips just got bigger while layout designer responsibilities and tasks became smaller. I retired in 2006, still in love with, and in awe of, my art and craft. Today I look at it as a lost art. I still have old four-inch glass-processing reticle plates (one was used for each layer while processing a wafer) as well as old clear acetate sheets—each with a single layer of process on them. These are treasured. [12]

***

The devices and tools we used in our daily lives were changing, but at the beginning few people had any idea how sweeping the changes would be. They came upon us gradually.

Transistor radios came out in the mid-1960s, and that really got people's attention. The electronics folks were indeed up to something. Then came handheld calculators. I will never forget holding a Texas Instruments calculator in my hand and using it for the first time. That was probably in the fall of 1969. After a few minutes of using the calculator, I looked over at my slide rule, then back at the calculator. Unbelievable!

The electronics industry was dominant in the Valley by the late 1960s and early 1970s. By that time, the semiconductor folks had begun marketing their chips to manufacturers for just about every application. The head of National Advanced Systems, Floyd Kvamme, put it this way: "We had a slogan at National that anything that used springs, levers, stepping motors, or gears was performing logic and it was better done in silicon. And we just looked for applications." [13]

By the early 1970s, nearly everyone in the Valley knew plenty of people in the business. The Santa Clara Valley had become Silicon Valley.

For the most part, young women were the production and assembly workers. By then, typically, large production runs were manufactured overseas; development and short runs stayed local.

The personal accounts in this chapter testify not only of the brilliant intellect involved in producing these early integrated circuits, but also to the precision required in the entire manufacturing process.

First, there are the intricate processes of manufacturing the silicon ingots, slicing them up into wafers, and polishing them. Then, the individual circuits must be designed so that they stack on one another correctly and function as one integrated circuit—a daunting task in itself with no room for error.

The manufacture of the integrated circuits themselves involves meticulous processes of dispersing the chemicals, several steps of the lithography process, alignment of the layers, correctly burning in the wafers, and cutting them up—all of which must be done in an ultraclean environment free of contamination. After the silicon ingots are manufactured and the circuits are designed, there are more than one hundred specific processes involved in manufacturing an integrated circuit. During the five or six weeks required to perform these processes, if there is one mistake made by one person, on one shift, the yield will be garbage.

The physics, chemistry, and engineering departments at major universities teach these things in great detail. The most amazing thing to me, however, is that right across the quad, in the biological sciences building, educated people teach that a redwood tree, a robin's song, and the function of your eyes and brain while you read this page all came into being randomly and without thought.

Chapter 10

A Valley Reinvented: 1960s and 1970s

The basic change in the Valley during this period can be summarized by something my brother, who is thirteen years younger than I, said when he was about ten years old: "Moss grows on the north side of the buildings." I had always thought it grew on the north side of the trees.

Another big change, perhaps as telling as any that took place in the Valley, was the near disappearance of the local dialect. As more and more newcomers arrived, you started to hear people refer to San José instead of Sanazay, Lōs Gătos instead of Lasgadus, and San Francisco instead of The City.

I will start this chapter off with two stories, which are representative of the changing times. The first is from one of the old farm families that was fortunate to be able to hang on to some of their land in the hills of Saratoga and adapted well; the second is from a couple who arrived during the mid-1960s.

Vince S. Garrod

During the 1950s it became apparent that prunes and apricots as a money-making operation in the hills would not survive and some changes had to be made. Dick and Vince [Garrod] reviewed many options, including selling the land and subdividing the property, building a large trailer court, closing the farming operation entirely and just using the land to graze cattle on, or board horses. . . .

So in 1961 serious [family] discussions were held regarding the use of the property for stables. Gene Pezzollo, a neighbor, talked Vince into trying a dude string and boarding and training horses. [i] *Other land-use options were discarded. . . .*

This was not entirely a Garrod decision. The total infrastructure for the fruit industry in the Valley had changed, and in order to get prunes dried by Sunsweet they had to be delivered to the east side of the Valley. The canneries were closing or going bankrupt—including California

---

[i] A dude string is group of horses that work well together and can be relied upon to handle inexperienced riders on excursions into the hills.

Canners and Growers! [In about 1968] Sunsweet moved out of San Jose to Stockton. [1]

Liz Iverson

Jim and I fell in love with the Bay Area when he was stationed at the Presidio in San Francisco for about seven months before being sent to Vietnam. We lived on Funston Avenue. Bliss. Winter, but no snow, waking to foghorns, and the bay right next to the commissary. We had our first child at the old Letterman Hospital, which was full of dark tramways. After Jim returned from his tour, we could not wait to get back to California from the Midwest but had no money.

In 1966 Jim began sending out resumes to technology companies and getting responses—more than one! He finally accepted a job with United Technology Center in Sunnyvale, who took total care of our move, paying for our meals and temporary residence here. That turned out to be the Holiday Inn in Santa Clara, which we thought was high living. UTC even sent [to California] all the goods we had collected back in our student home at Purdue, including our bookshelf boards and the bricks that propped them up.

Vern Lovelace, president of American Realty, was wonderful, driving the three of us through neighborhoods in the Santa Clara Valley, always teaching the old adage, "Location, location, location." He sold us our first home, which was obtained using the GI bill, with no money down. We could not have purchased one otherwise. The house was on Stephen Way, near Lynbrook High School, situated in a neighborhood with young families like ours.

We had our second child soon after we moved in and were settled in the suburbs. The radio played, "Do You Know the Way to San Jose?" as we wondered what the valley had looked like when it was full of orchards. There were small plots of fruit trees here and there, plus a larger orchard on Rainbow Avenue, but a few years later a park appeared where the orchard had been. Of course, that was very popular with moms who had toddlers and strollers. We called it Rainbow Park. It was just a small green park with some swings and slides. Now it has baseball diamonds and soccer fields as well as a toddlers' playground.

Along with the parks, stores appeared, plus other services that made life a lot easier for young parents. There was a fantastic nursery/florist/gift shop on Saratoga-Sunnyvale Road, which was a fantasy of delights at

Christmastime. It was located about where Outback Steakhouse is today, which in turn replaced an appealing A-frame structure that was called Any Mountain. Westgate, on Saratoga Avenue, was a small strip mall which had a department store called J.M. McDonald's. No hamburgers, but I could always find a beautiful pair of shoes in narrow sizes. There was no El Paseo center at that time.

Soon after the birth of our second son, the four of us drove up to San Francisco to check out what was going on. This was the Summer of Love, with so much activity going on in the Haight that there were long lines of cars with passengers craning their necks to catch sight of some flower children. We were astonished at the large throng of unkempt-looking young people who were our age, the language used in the various tracts and newspapers, and the good quality in some of the poetry, the street music, and the artwork. We still have two sepia-toned watercolors of California Avenue and Telegraph Hill. Back in the suburbs, all was quiet—a different country than that area of San Francisco.

Meanwhile, as our family was growing, Jim was undergoing a metamorphosis. He had come out here, to United Technology Center, with an MS in structural engineering to work on the booster rockets for the Titan 3M, and soon became captivated by using the computer to do slide rule work. From UTC he was employed at Stanford Research Institute in Menlo Park, writing computer programs relating to nuclear blast effects for the Office of Civil Defense. That was during the Cold War era, when relationships with Russia were tense.

Next, Jim moved to the time-sharing division of IBM to enhance his computing skills. At the time, IBM was the foremost provider of hardware and computer services and offered internal software development classes and marketing skills. The IBM 360-50 computers filled an entire floor on Watson Court in Palo Alto with blinking lights and whirring sounds. At home, Jim used a Selectric typewriter called a terminal with a modem to connect by telephone to the mainframe. By 1984, Jim had started his own company developing software related to the stock market. [2]

***

Another big change in the Valley was the constant presence of patrol aircraft flying in and out of Moffett Field. Here is part of that story.

Tom Spink

I am originally from Kansas City, Missouri, and graduated from the University of Kansas in 1968. In the fall of 1970, I arrived at Moffett Field fresh with my new naval flight officer wings of gold. NFOs are the navigators and tactical coordinators on P-3 Orion aircraft. You start out as the navigator. It is your responsibility to get the aircraft to the assigned point in the ocean and record on paper charts and logs what transpires. Later, you work your way up to tactical coordinator. It is now your responsibility to coordinate the information from all of the sensors into tactics that will result in the successful completion of your mission.

While I was in Patrol Squadron 46 (VP-46) at Naval Air Station, Moffett Field, California, in the early '70s, we were tasked to go out to YEMPA (Yankee Eastern Missile Patrol Area) and find the Soviet Yankee class ballistic missile submarine, currently on station 1,000 miles off the West Coast of the United States. It was the height of the Cold War, and both the United States and the Soviet Union had ballistic missile submarines off the coast of their adversary. The term used to describe the strategy then was MAD, mutual assured destruction. It is based on the theory of deterrence, which holds that the threat of using strong weapons against the enemy prevents the enemy's use of those same weapons. Neither side was willing to accept total annihilation.

We flew out west for four hours and dropped sixteen sonobuoys in a pattern from high altitude, as directed by the Tactical Support Center (TSC). While you wait for contact with the submarine, you monitor the sonobuoys, identify surface contacts, perform plot stabilization, take LORAN fixes, and shoot celestial lines of position (sun during the day) or a fix at night (using three stars), and made hourly Ops Normal reports back to the TSC.

If you gain contact on the submarine, it is then that the intensity inside the aircraft rises to a palpable level. For once you have contact, you better not lose it. Every operational mission is graded, and if you gain contact and then lose it, your grade is an F on the scale used at school when I grew up. Depending on whether your contact is close in or far away, you perform the appropriate tactic and drop more sonobuoys to hopefully get closer and closer to the submarine. The plan is to covertly track the submarine for as long as possible. We are not at war, and we carry no weapons. The challenge is to track the submarine and know its position well enough that if we were at war, and we did have a weapon, we could drop it and prevent the submarine from killing millions of Americans. The patrol community was the only aviation community that exercised against their Soviet counterparts on a routine basis.

While at Moffett Field, the majority of the flights were for training. After the squadron returns from a six-month deployment to the western Pacific (WESTPAC), many people rotate out of the squadron and go on to their next assignment. New people come in, and most crews have to start the process of qualifications all over. There is a series of qualifications that a crew has to successfully accomplish in order to attain the highest readiness status. It is expected that all the crews will get this completed in the twelve months that the squadron is at "home."

In addition to patrols, there are many different types of training flights. The most exciting one involves working with the fleet off of San Diego in an exercise. Ships and aircraft are challenged to protect the carrier and prevent a "hostile" submarine from getting close enough to the carrier for a simulated weapon release. These flights are always graded so everyone has to do their very best.

Other training flights consist of flying off the coast and finding a merchant ship that is alone. Multiple merchant ships put a lot of noise in the water, and it makes it easier if you have just one target. The crew uses its electronic sensors to track the ship. This allows the crew to exercise basic tactics and to work as a crew without the stress of the flight being graded.

After my first squadron, I was selected to be an instructor. Patrol Squadron 31 was in Hangar One. I did that from 1974 to 1977. At that point, I got off active duty and joined the Naval Air Reserve at Moffett Field in Patrol Squadron 91. I flew all types of missions for eleven years. We deployed for a month during the summer, and I would regularly find myself in some dangerous place tracking a Soviet submarine. I was commanding officer of VP-91 from 1986 to 1988.

Aside from the squadron, the reserves only have staff jobs or billets, which are not nearly as exciting but still satisfying because you know you are helping your active-duty counterparts.

I retired as a captain with thirty years of service—nine active duty and twenty-one reserve. [3]

***

US Navy P-3 Orion
US Navy

The local aerospace and electronics industries spawned many smaller businesses that directly supplied them. One of the chief categories of those businesses were machine shops. Hundreds, if not thousands, of them opened during this period. Most were small specialty shops, although there were large production shops as well. Here is a story from our neighbors who started a machine shop in their garage. They were originally from Minnesota and moved to the Valley in 1952.

Harold Voshage

My first job in California was at a company the founders of Hewlett Packard created for eight of their key employees, called Palo Alto Engineering. They manufactured small transformers for HP instruments. It turned out the manager and I didn't get along particularly well, so I left.

Almost immediately I was hired at Western Gear Works in Belmont, fifteen miles north of Mountain View where we lived. In the early fifties, Highway 101 (Bayshore Highway) was three lanes. The center lane was a passing lane and there were some signal lights. This was the main drag between San Francisco and San Jose. When I commuted to Belmont, sometimes there were accidents at intersections.

My years at Western Gear Works were very rewarding. The company manufactured large planetary transmissions for government personnel carriers and I learned a lot about machining and its various facets.

In 1959, Varian Associates in Palo Alto hired me. My first job was in the radiation division. This division manufactured and marketed linear accelerators that universities used in their labs. The devices were so difficult to manufacture that for years the division was unprofitable. Today they use the linear accelerator as the heart of a cancer treatment medical device, and it is the most successful device to radiate cancer cells.

[Later] I was transferred to the Super-Power Klystron division, [then to] the Central Research Labs. These were interesting years. . . . The first project I was assigned to, I was to assist several scientists and engineers in building an electron microscope. . . . [During the] several years I worked at the Central Research Lab, I attended San Jose City College, taking evening classes in Vacuum Technology. I will always remember these rewarding classes. They were fascinating and related well to my responsibilities at Varian.

After thirteen years, I terminated my employment at Varian Associates and decided to take my part-time contract machine shop to a full-time basis. I had begun the shop in 1966 in my garage with a lathe and a milling machine and several drill presses and ancillary tools. All indications were that it could be an opportune time to go for it.

When Carol and I developed our manufacturing business, we employed a number of high school boys, and they worked for us part time most of the time. Every single fellow showed us much potential, and it was an excellent opportunity to learn how to become an employer and a mentor to young men.

In the late 1970s, we purchased a new Hardinge computer-controlled lathe with automatic stock bar feed. I could run errands, and the machine would make parts while I was away.

Since the garage was full of machines, we needed to move in order to expand the operation. In 1980 we rented and moved into a 3,300 square foot facility in Campbell, purchased another Hardinge computer-controlled lathe, and hired full-time employees.

That was an eye-opening experience for me. Frankly, until I had been in business a few years, particularly after we moved and became "legitimate" in a rented facility, I had never really faced the issues and vicissitudes of the business world. Paying rent for a building space, paying all the necessary benefits of full-time employees, dealing with government regulations, fire department rules, etc. were all new experiences. Last, but not least, was the need to develop more customers and accounts, and deal with the customers' purchasing agents and personnel. I had a lot to learn and occasionally had to deal with surprises.

A neighbor boy we hired when he was still in high school made the most of his opportunity with us. He was bright, hardworking, and stayed with us seven years. When we moved [the shop] in 1980, he graduated from high school and worked full time. We taught him to program computer-controlled machines and he was soon better at it than I was.

By this time we had hired programmer-machinists. One was very good at setting up and operating Hardinge lathes. These are high-precision lathes and we had several manual and the two computer-controlled lathes. . . . The only fly in the ointment is that after he left our company, we hadn't trained a backup programmer. One of our young men was learning, but he had a way to go. Programming is not my strong suit, so we couldn't continue our operation without another experienced programmer. I saw "the handwriting on the wall" and prepared to exit the business. In retrospect, what I remember the most are my outstanding employees and excellent customers and buyers. [4]

***

The west side of the Valley was developed first and was almost entirely built out by the end of the 1960s, during the blitz. A large part of the southeast, however, was not developed until ten to twenty years later, after the blitz. That is why the stories that follow are not contradictory.

After the *blitzkrieg*, development in the Valley became comparatively sporadic, as the next story describes.

John Giacomazzi
Around 1958 the California Highway Department did planning that showed a new [West-side] freeway that was to connect Highway 101 at Mountain View with the 101 near Monterey Road in south San Jose. The plans showed this freeway would cut our property into two pieces. Of

course, there was nothing we could do to change those plans, so we had to plan that sometime in the future we would most likely discontinue the farm operation. As a result, we did not replant prune trees when old trees were no longer productive, since we assumed the freeway would be started at about the same time the trees would become productive. We later realized that was not the case.

In 1966, we sold eight acres that would be cut from our property by the freeway to a shopping center developer. This sale enabled my mother to receive additional nonfarm income, which was needed since property tax increases were reducing income that could be generated from farming. Also, the prune trees were not producing as much when they got older, and prune prices were not increasing. This property was held by the developer for many years and finally developed into the Almaden Costco twenty years later.

I continued to operate the ranch until 1973, when a golf course operator proposed developing a driving range on about eight acres fronting Almaden Expressway. Since this was in the planned right-of-way for the freeway, and the operator was willing to lease the land, it seemed to be a good way to get income until it was determined whether the freeway would ever be built.

In 1990, thirty-two years after the first plans were made to have a freeway, the state acquired ten acres of land from our family, which included the driving range. [5]

Anonymous
When I was eighteen, I went to work at one of the new electronics plants soldering parts onto circuit boards. That was in '72, and that was the kind of job that was available in Sunnyvale for kids just out of high school. It was an assembly area with long rows of women, mostly young, soldering those parts on. It was not hard work, but it was tough on the neck, and you needed to get up and stretch frequently. More so later in the day. The smoke from the soldering was not the most pleasant thing. I quit after about a year—figured I'd better go back to school. [6]

***

Students and faculty work in early computer lab
Courtesy of Santa Clara University

Paul McJones

I started working in Silicon Valley in 1974. There were still quite a few orchards. In those days, Silicon Valley was mostly silicon semiconductors, only a small fraction of which were DRAM[i] or microprocessors. There were also a few companies that made computers, including IBM, HP, Varian, and Four-Phase.[ii]

I went to work for IBM Research—what is now the Almaden Lab but was then part of the main plant site in southeast San Jose. I worked with John Backus on functional programming (before his Turing award), and with the System R group, building the first relational database system to use SQL (it was called SEQUEL originally).

---

[i] DRAM, or dynamic random access memory, stores each bit of data in a separate capacitor.
[ii] Four-Phase was sold to Motorola in 1982. The former location of the company became the Apple headquarters on Infinite Loop, in Cupertino.

*When I heard the January 1975 issue of Popular Electronics featured
the Altair 8800, [i] I ran out to purchase a copy, but I had to drive all the
way downtown to a tobacco and magazine shop near San Jose State to
find a copy. Computers and electronics still were not of interest to most
people in the Valley. [7]*

I told Paul he was right, that "computers and electronics still were not
of interest to most people in the Valley," and went on to tell him the
nickname the locals gave one of the IBM facilities. Way out of town,
off Guadalupe Mines Road, near Hicks Road, on the way to the dump,
IBM had a facility the locals dubbed "the nuthouse." Rumor had it that
the people who worked there just sat around all day playing with toys
and thinking stuff up. I assured Paul that I was not making that up,
but that is how ignorant many locals (me included) were about what
was going on out there. He told me he believed I was referring to the
Los Gatos Laboratory of IBM's Advanced Systems Development
Division, or ASDD. Hardly a "nuthouse."

So the Valley had changed forever, from orchards to vast industrial
parks and housing tracts with expressways running between them.
Most of the canneries had shut down by the mid-1970s, although Del
Monte #3, off San Carlos Street, hung on until 1999. By the early
1970s "junior" colleges had sprouted up everywhere: West Valley in
Saratoga, DeAnza in Cupertino, Foothill in Los Altos, and Evergreen in
south San Jose. And Orchard Supply, though it added several new
stores, was probably selling more barbeques and ice-chests than it
was orchard supplies.

Perhaps my aunt put it best, when she said of San Jose, "The town I
grew up in no longer exists."

---

[i] An early home computer kit.

Chapter 11

Out and About in the 1950s to 1970s

I will begin this chapter with a couple of comments from Joan Fox, who arrived in the Valley from Michigan in 1958.

Joan Fox
It was so exciting to go and see all the produce stands, with all this fresh fruit and stuff, up and along Stevens Creek Road and what is now De Anza Boulevard. To be able to buy all that fresh produce was something!

That was in the days when the ladies got dressed up to go shopping. I would go to San Francisco to meet my aunt, and she always directed me that when you went to the city, you always wore hat and gloves. [1]

Geoff Goble
When we were kids, my dad would take us over to Los Gatos to ride the Billy Jones Railroad. It's the miniature train that is at Vasona Park now, but then it ran around a prune orchard on Winchester at Daves Avenue. There were always a lot of kids.

In the summers we spent a lot of time at Alum Rock Park. There was a little zoo and an indoor swimming pool with a slide. It had a deep end, a shallow end, and diving boards.

Other family outings were miniature golf and drive-in movies. The El Rancho Drive-in was one of several drive-ins. It was on Alma Avenue and what is now Almaden Expressway. The Spartan Drive-in was nearby and there was the Winchester Drive-in in Campbell.

At the El Rancho, next to the big screen there was a pole sticking up high with a chair on top of it. One of the AM radio stations had a contest for who could sit on the chair the longest.

In the 1960s there was a trampoline phase. Places opened up where a large trampoline was placed in a pit. For fifty cents you could wear yourself out pretty good. [2]

Deborah Stanley
Sports car performance and racing are very popular among mechanical engineers, and as a propulsion guy at Lockheed, my dad was all over it.

He loved drag racing and putting a car through its paces. I remember being about four years old when he stopped at a signal next to a sporty-sounding car and revved the engine—a signal to race—and off we went. Standing behind, and hanging on to the front seat, I yelled, "Go, Daddy, go!" My mother followed with, "Grady, slow down!" which in turn solicited my "NO, Daddy. Go!"

From the time I could stand, I was going to car races. Dad's favorites were the drag strip and oval racing. We also went as a family on at least one rally. Dad drove, Mom navigated. Riverside Raceway (a drag strip), San Jose Speedway (an oval), and the Laguna Seca road course were well-attended favorites for our family.

In grade school, a family evening of fun was going to the races at San Jose Speedway, which was an oval track. "Popcorn, Cracker Jacks, sodas!" shouted the snack-man. We got Cracker Jacks most times. "Al Mombo Pombo, starting in the first car position!" echoed from the loudspeaker. I always rooted for Al and he won most of the time. The quarter-mile track was narrow for the crowd of cars racing. The dents along the sides of the cars told the story. But cars in the 1960s were made of steel, not steel and plastic, and they handled the sideswiping well.

The craziest, "over the top," event I saw at the speedway was the destruction derby held in the dirt infield of the track. Dad loved it. His side clutching, loud, rolling-in-the-aisles laughter was hilarious in itself, though embarrassing too. The drivers pressed down hard on the accelerator until they hit something—forward or backward, whether they could see or not. Soon wrecked cars were positioned at all angles, some with the hood up, giving the driver a narrow slit at the hinge of the hood to see forward. The winner was the driver of the last car with an engine still running—maybe smoking billows, but still running. Amazingly, after being knocked around by multiple collisions, the drivers climbed out of the wrecked cars at the final horn. I'm sure most were very sore the next day, but off they would go to make ready for the next time. [3]

T.S.

We lived near Westgate before the shopping center was built. Campbell was the closest thing to a town for us in many ways: the high school football games, which were played at night; the lighted tennis courts, where we rarely had to wait for a court; the A&W Root Beer stand, where we filled up our one-gallon glass jugs on many a summer Saturday; the Hudson station, where you could get regular gas for 24.9 cents a gallon; Campbell Lumber Company where they had a bin of scrap wood free for the taking and with which we built all kinds of things—all good memories of fun family outings.

In San Jose, there was the Alameda Skate Rink, off Race Street, that was always packed with kids and adults who came from everywhere. The Carnation Creamery had the best milkshakes, although I don't remember ever leaving there without a bellyache. We enjoyed the Rose Garden, and I remember driving by the Star and Bar gas station on San Carlos, which claimed to be "The World's Longest Gas Station." It may have been—the street frontage was very long. It looked like a carnival with just about every kind of merchandise you could imagine hung up on display all along its length. Oh, and there was the Ferris wheel on the roof of Macy's and the Karmelkorn store at Valley Fair.

But San Jose had the same problem back then that it still has. Typically, when people wanted to go somewhere or do something special, they headed out of town. If you wanted to be in a city, you went to San Francisco; if you wanted the country, you headed for the southern hills.

A trip to Santa Cruz was always a treat—lunch or dinner at the Miramar on the wharf was a family favorite. Highway 17 was much more dangerous than it is today. There was no middle divider, just a double yellow line, and many people drove it much too fast, which unfortunately resulted in horrific accidents. For that reason, there were fake cop cars placed in selected areas at the side of the road to deter speeders and hopefully prevent accidents. They were often retired highway patrol cruisers, although sometimes they were billboards that were cut out and painted to look like a cruiser. This was a constantly changing display. At times there were badly wrecked cars left in those locations to send a sobering message. A mile below the summit was a large turnout with a water trough for cars that overheated. On hot summer weekends the place was always crowded with cars with their hoods up and steam billowing out.

Going up to Saratoga summit when it snowed was always fun, but we never did find a safe place to use the toboggan. Fishing at Uvas Reservoir was short lived—the signs warning not to eat the fish put a damper on that one. So if we wanted to go fishing or play in the snow, like so many others we went to the Sierras.

Speaking of going out of town, there were two types of county fairs: the type featuring cotton candy, arcades, and a demolition derby; and the type featuring cows, chickens, and strawberry preserves. We were more the cows, chickens, and strawberry preserves type of people, so we went to the San Benito County Fair instead of the Santa Clara County one.

Top: Rock bridge at Alum Rock Park
Bottom: Vasona Reservoir

Top: My sister, Susan, and brother, John, at Saratoga summit
Bottom: Santa Clara County Fairgrounds, late 1950s
Bottom courtesy of History San Jose

Top: Villa Montalvo, Saratoga

Bottom: The Paul Masson champagne cellars on Saratoga Avenue in Saratoga were built by the railroad tracks in the late 1950s and torn down in the mid-1990s. Its design followed the space-age mind-set of the time.

Sometimes the show came home—literally. That was surely the case one winter when Dick Comeford, our next-door-neighbor, brought a war-surplus searchlight home and fired it up on a Friday evening. We had a continual parade of cars driving slowly down the street, the people in them wondering what the attraction was in the middle of a housing tract far from town. They probably didn't realize *they* were the attraction—the puzzled looks on their faces were priceless. The show also came home when the Navy's Blue Angels came to Moffett Field, which I think was every year until the early 1990s.

Anonymous

They would fly right over our house. The windows would rattle, and it sounded like they were going to tear the roof right off the house. You were sure glad they were on our side! What a show of force! A lot of people in our neighborhood were up on their roofs watching. Some who had flat roofs took their lawn chairs up there to watch the show. There were crowds of people on some of the overpasses. When it was over, it seemed eerily quiet. After an hour or two you calmed down a bit and maybe could get something done at home, but your nerves were shot for the rest of the day. [4]

Anonymous

Cars were a big deal in the 1950s and '60s. To customize a car was considerably different then. In those days regulations were almost nonexistent, and you could make a car into whatever you wanted it to be. Cars were "chopped and channeled," or modified in almost any way. There were "Bucket T's," which were Model T's with V8 engines in them and an extra helping of chrome plating. There were '48 Mercuries with the roof lowered so far there were just slits for windows. Volkswagen beetles were made into "dune buggies" of many variations. And, as now, there were lowered cars, which were favored by the guys on the east side. There were cars built for speed, cars built for show, and cars made into pickup trucks for work. You could do just about anything you wanted to do to your car and still drive it on the street. A fellow named Joe dropped a huge V8 engine into his '57 Chevy. The engine was too big for the engine compartment so he took out the front seat, extended the steering wheel shaft, and drove from the backseat.

In downtown San Jose, cruising was big. Friday nights were a continuous parade on some streets. If it wasn't for the strong machismo attitude that was prevalent on that side of town, you could have stood on a street corner and watched the show. But it wasn't safe there, so you kept moving and didn't make eye contact. Too many guys there were obviously just hanging around looking for a fight.

It's a real pity what happened to downtown and the east side. The old-timers all say that that was the preferred place to live. The stores were close, public transportation was good (streetcars and buses), the streets were clean, and the houses were in good repair. That had all changed dramatically by the 1960s.

As for cruising, it was not conducive for a peaceful city or for people who actually wanted to get somewhere, so after a while the police started writing tickets for small violations, like driving with only your parking lights on, or driving too slow. Later, they designated "No Cruising Zones."

Chapter 12

Mountain People

When you leave Los Gatos or Saratoga and head up the hill, you are in the hills. When you arrive at Summit Road or Skyline Boulevard, you are in the mountains. There is no sign that says where the hills stop and the mountains begin, and I suppose that is why, among the locals, there is some confusion about this, just as there was in the Valley about the terms *farm* and *ranch*. In both cases, the words refer to the same thing, but that has never stopped some folks from arguing about which term is appropriate.

Regardless, Valley dwellers have been flocking to the Santa Cruz Mountains since before the Spanish arrived. In the early days of Mission Santa Clara, the padres noted that sometimes the Indians just took off for the hills or to the ocean. In that regard not much has changed. There is a solace found there that is not found in the Valley. For this reason, after the logging days of the middle to late 1800s, many San Francisco and Santa Clara Valley residents bought property in the mountains. Tracts of logged land that had available water were subdivided into lots, and people bought the lots and built summer homes or weekend cabins on them. When the automobile came along, this became a well-established trend.

This logged-off land was inexpensive. During the Depression, it was so inexpensive that some land in Boulder Creek was subdivided and the lots were given away in exchange for subscriptions to one of the San Francisco newspapers.

Loggers had also built some cabins along the creeks during the logging days, and some old loggers or logging families remained after the timber played out. Not long ago you could drive up any gulch on either side of the Santa Clara-Santa Cruz Divide and see cabins, or what was left of them, along the creeks. Many of these earlier cabins remain, although in modified form.

Gulch is an interesting word. I have never seen it used other than to refer to a location in the Santa Cruz Mountains. If you look on the maps of any other place with similar geography, you see the words *ravine*, *canyon*, or *gully*. Elsewhere, it is Trabuco Canyon Road, Chavez Ravine, or Smith's Gully. But in the local hills, it is always Moody Gulch, Lockhart Gulch, or some other gulch.

When the Santa Clara Valley began to fill up with tract homes in the 1950s, the number of weekend cabins and summer homes increased dramatically. People in the Valley, especially those of us who had known something of open spaces, felt the pressures that came with urbanization. By the early 1960s, the Valley was congested and the smog was terrible. Not only in the summer but for most of the year a yellow-brown haze blocked the view of the hills and often caused shortness of breath. Some people couldn't take it and headed for the hills. We were among them.

Living in the mountains was quite different from living in the low foothills and driving down paved roads to go to work in the Valley. In the mountains, dirt roads, falling tree branches, overgrown brush, water quality and supply problems, septic tanks, and the challenges of dealing with trash without a trash collection service were a way of life. The combination of these things led to a different kind of lifestyle. If you wanted to live in the mountains, you paid a price.

Since we were mountain people ourselves for a while, and have relatives who were mountain people, I have more than enough material from our own experiences to paint the picture for this chapter. So I'll claim author's privilege and include only one story in this chapter—ours.

T.S.
When my wife, Deborah, and I were married, for our honeymoon I took her home. That is because there was no more beautiful and serene place we could have gone. At the time, I was living in a charming cabin in the Santa Cruz Mountains, the last cabin off a mile-long dirt road secluded in the redwoods. It had a fine view of the hills across the creek from which I pumped our water. Deer routinely came through the property, which, along with the redwoods, had an abundance of bay, madrone, and oak trees, and when it rained the fragrance of the forest was heavenly.

Due to increased age, my aunt's mother was no longer able to stay in the cabin, and since this was 1971, when the hippie movement was in full bloom, I was invited to live there to watch over and take care of the place. This was necessary because hippies were roaming the hills looking for a place to live off the land, or, more accurately, on the cheap. Since there were many seldom-used cabins in the more remote places in the hills, some of these folks availed themselves not only to the shelter, but also to whatever provisions were in the cabins. Sometimes after all the food had been eaten, they stripped the cabins of whatever they could sell.

Anyway, that is why I was living in the hills, and it was to this beautiful place, and into these circumstances, that I brought my bride and carried her over the threshold.

As a couple of young kids who had grown up in typical California housing tracts, we had a lot to learn about living in the mountains.

The first challenge was the trash. We could burn paper in the fireplace, but not if it was soiled with food—the residue would stick to the chimney lining, and that is the cause of many a burned-down cabin in the woods. We buried garbage—less bones, eggshells, and grease—in the garden. What we could not bury, we stored in sealed containers, carried down the hill along with any plastic, and deposited in the dumpsters at our places of work.

As I mentioned earlier, I pumped our water from the creek. We were fortunate to have good water in the creek. Many creeks in the flatter areas had had fuel oil sprayed on them to control mosquitos, and the oil residue remains for a long time after the last spraying. Other creeks, especially in the densely populated areas, have septic overflow in them, and septic springs are commonly seen in the summer months.

While we were living there, we were in the middle of a drought and the creek was low, so before setting the "foot" of the pump-hose into the little pool dug out for that purpose, I had to clean out any leaves or other debris that had collected there. As the level of the creek continued to drop, I could pump for shorter and shorter periods of time.

On my way down to the pump house, I would walk by the Radcliff place. As the drought grew worse, one day Mr. Radcliff told me he had plenty of water from his deep well and I was welcome to it. He said that a water line had been run from his well to my aunt's parents' water tank, and he had filled their tank whenever they needed water while they were living there. From then on, and for the duration of the drought, he filled our tank every three weeks.

They were nice people, the Radcliffs, and they enjoyed having us as neighbors too. We not only kept a watchful eye on the area around us, we were young and in love, and who does not like to be around that?

They were retired and had built a new home (as opposed to a cabin) on the slope down below us.

Mr. Stephanie, across from them, had an old cabin, that was probably built around the turn of the century. It was built in a whichever-way-it-went-together manner, which was typical of many of the cabins in the hills going back to the logging days. Mr. Stephanie made his livelihood in San Francisco with his catering truck, but on the weekends he always retreated to his cabin in the hills.

Across the creek was "Old Henry," who was well into his eighties. Mr. Radcliff told me that Old Henry had kept a water supply during the last drought, when the creek ran dry, by driving a pipe into the hillside behind his cabin. He said Old Henry had water the size of a pencil coming out of that pipe and it kept him going. [i] *Some people had to have water trucked in.*

In some places in the hills, the stream or well water contains a high amount of iron or sulphur. That means rust-colored or rotten-egg-smelling water. Before modern filters, and before bottled water was commonly available in grocery stores, one man, whose water was slightly rust colored from iron, told me, "We drink a lot of juice." People who had less than desirable water often loaded their cars with every container they could get their hands on and took them to a public spring off one of the highways. I remember a few of these public springs, one on Highway 17 just before the summit, and one on Highway 9 just after the summit. I also remember a public spring on the road into Half Moon Bay. In that area people had trouble with saltwater intrusion in their wells, and cars were almost always lined up along the road while people waited their turn to fill their containers with drinkable water.

Down the road from Old Henry and built on—and sometimes over—the creek were several abandoned treehouses. All had been partially disassembled—perhaps salvaged for building materials. From the looks of what remained of those dwellings, they had probably been built not too long before. My guess is that the county had come in a few years before our time there and evicted the people, who probably were squatters.

---

[i] A horizontal well. These are common today in the southern hills for bleeding excess moisture out of a hillside.

Building right on the creeks and even over them was common in the hills until the late 1950s or so. Just about anywhere a road could go next to a creek there was this kind of impromptu development. Apparently, county governments did not address the unhealthfulness of that building practice until the mid-1960s.

Speaking of unhealthful conditions, one day I decided to try to walk up the creek from our place. The creek is narrow, the slopes on either side are steep, and the vegetation is prolific, so the going was tough. I didn't get very far, but when I paused to rest, I noticed something was different on the bank on the left side of the creek. Looking closer I saw what it was—hundreds of rusted-out tin cans of various sizes. Someone had thrown trash down that bank for years. I was thankful that by then Mr. Radcliff was supplying our water.

The roads to most of the cabins in the hills were narrow, bulldozed just wide enough for a Model T to pass, and over the years, as the trees alongside the road grew, many of the roads had some pretty tight spots. If you met another car coming the other way, etiquette dictated that the uphill car was to back up to a spot wide enough to allow the downhill car to pass.

In the early 1970s, almost all of the roads that were off the main roads were dirt. In some areas, if most of the neighbors chipped in, they were graveled, which not only fortified the road base but also greatly reduced the dust in the dry season.

Today most of these private roads are paved, and how they came to be paved is often an interesting story. Years ago, the people who lived up in the hills were not highly endowed with cash. Of course, not all of them are now, but in decades past it was another thing altogether. Anyway, as the Valley became wealthier, that wealth spread up into the hills, and the people who were buying places up there needed to have a reliable road so they could get down to work in the Valley. To address this, these newer landowners began forming road associations. The typical association would have many meetings, but after all was said, little was done. Only half the people who lived on the road would help maintain it, or were willing or able to pay to improve it. I know one case where paving the road was talked into the ground for years and nothing happened. Then, one day when people got home from work the road was paved—probably a half-mile of it—all the way up to the place owned by a fellow, who, according to the scuttlebutt, was a drug dealer.

As for us, on our road, Mr. Radcliff and Mr. Stephanie, both of whom were probably in their mid-sixties, were sure glad to have me—a strong young guy in his twenties—help them with road repairs. We would go out to the highway in a pickup truck with shovels and get a load of gravel from a large overgrown pile. After we were loaded up, we filled the holes and crevices in our road. We were fortunate that we did not have the major culvert problems that many of the roads had. Roads often washed out due the lack of a culvert in the right place or one that got blocked up because no-one tended to it. On a private road there is no county road crew. You and your neighbors are the road crew. And it was not uncommon, during a wet winter, for people to be stranded for weeks after their road washed out.

While driving down our road I frequently had to stop and remove tree branches to be able to pass, especially during or after a storm. During a storm, dead redwood tree branches make a lot of racket as they ricochet down from high above. So if you are out there clearing the road in a rainstorm, you do your work quickly.

Speaking of storms, they provided some of the most pleasant experiences we have ever had. When it rained, the aroma of the forest was wonderful. If it wasn't too cold, we would throw open all the windows and let the wind roar through the house.

Another effect of the storms is downed power and telephone lines. If you live up there, outages are a part of life.

When we lived up in the hills, there were three ways of heating your home—burning wood, fuel oil, or propane. Those three represent three different eras. Burning wood is labor intensive and can really smoke up a neighborhood, so people were happy to have fuel oil heaters when they came out, which was probably in the 1920s. That is what we used in the cabin—a fuel oil heater.

With the exception of small cabins, a fireplace, no matter how well designed, has the net effect of taking the heat right out of the house and up the chimney. An oil heater is much better. Ours was basically just a large can with a fuel line at the bottom and a stovepipe on the top. You turn on the valve and the fuel oil flows into the bottom of the can. Then you light a scrap of paper and drop it in to light the oil.

One winter night I woke up and it was very cold. Obviously the fire in the heater had gone out. So I, still half asleep, opened the top of the heater and dropped in a piece of burning paper. Bad idea. Oil had continued to flow into the heater, lit or not. I was fortunate I wasn't burned or didn't burn the place down. The inferno that came out the top of that heater woke me up the rest of the way, and my wife stayed home from work that day to clean up the soot that had settled on everything in every room.

Although there was, and is, a wide mix of people in the mountains, I found that nearly everyone who moves up there "improves" their land. Practically speaking, that usually means they do something that takes away from the beauty of the setting, which is the reason they moved there in the first place. One of those so-called improvements is planting English ivy for erosion control. It works very well for that purpose, but it also chokes out all the other plants, is nearly impossible to control, and is impossible to get rid of. It spreads fast, does not care about property lines, and the person who planted it typically just cannot understand why anyone would think it is objectionable.

There are also many dedicated gardeners in the mountains, although for some reason a significant number of them are only interested in growing only one kind of plant.

You can always tell a mountain person, though. The woman in your office who wears the four-inch heels? She's not a mountain person. The one with the sturdy shoes, sunburn, and scratched-up arms? She is. She was clearing brush all last weekend.

The commute down the hill and into the Valley in the early 1970s was exhausting. My wife and I both worked in the Valley so we "drove the hill" over Highway 17 five days a week. We rode together, and since I worked closer, I drove her to her car, which we had left in a shopping center parking lot at our rendezvous point the evening before. It took us about an hour to get home, and after an abbreviated dinner, we were ready for bed. Now I see the cars at the freeway onramps lined up to go over the hill on weekday afternoons and I wonder how the people make it.

Highway 17, with its continuous curves and elevation changes, is no leisurely drive during commuting hours. The cars move as a pack and there is a pace and rhythm to be kept. Any deviation causes disruption and is dangerous. Newbies and out-of-towners who do not know this often do foolish things that endanger themselves and others. The whole pack moves as one quite well, but if someone drives slower or faster than the pack, the potential for a mishap is increased. When someone drives too slowly, they encourage someone else, who may be impatient, to make a quick move. That quick move will start a chain reaction and it takes a while for things to settle into a rhythm again. Too often, someone cuts in front of a sand truck and then slows down. Those trucks can't respond very fast, especially when they have forty tons of sand pushing them down a hill. The accidents are always ugly: the truck is on its side, broken into several pieces, there is sand everywhere, and often one or more cars are involved. And in all those vehicles there are real people with real families.

If you live up that way, being snowed out every once in a while is a real possibility. We didn't make it over the summit one evening before a snowstorm hit and had to stay with my folks down in the Valley that night.

The good part about living in the mountains was that we didn't want to go anywhere on the weekends. We were already there.

That being said, I would be remiss not to tell you the rest of the story. There I was, in my early twenties, with everything I could have wanted—a lovely bride whom I admired and loved, and who loved me too, a most beautiful place to live, interesting work that paid well— everything was all that I could desire. Yet within me was an emptiness I could not shake off. All those things, however good, could not fill that void.

I continued in that state of distress for a year and a half, and I caused my bride not a little grief. It would not be until we left the mountains that I found what was missing. Through a series of circumstances, I was led to the point where late one night I opened my heart to God and told Him everything that was on that heavy heart. I knew He heard me and I found my heart strangely desirous to give myself completely to Him and to follow Him in His way. At last I said, "OK, I'll go this way, but first I need You to answer every question I have ever asked."

That prayer surprised me. It was as if it did not originate with me. It seemed so bold, yet at the same time it was a humble request, and I sensed even while praying that my request was granted.

Over the next month, I was answered far beyond all I could ask or think. Everything was made new. The burden of vanity left me and has not returned in what is now more than forty years. The Bible became an open book to me, and the Person hidden within its pages, Himself the answer to every question, came to live in this earthen vessel. Like millions of others down through the centuries, I can testify to the truth of the words spoken by Jesus, "The one who comes to Me, I will certainly not cast out." [1]

I hope the reader, regardless of his or her persuasions, will be happy that someone as pitiful as me was delivered from my own misery.

Chapter 13

Convulsions: Late 1960s to Mid-1970s

The late 1960s and early 1970s were trying times, both nationally and locally. The Vietnam War became increasingly unpopular and both Stanford University and San Jose State became anything but peaceful. Unfair racial discrimination came to a head locally. The war against the Valley of Heart's Delight had been won, but the result had left a bitter taste in the mouths of most Valley residents as they took stock of what had been lost and determined not to lose the remaining natural beauty of the place. Sexual harassment in the workplace came to the forefront. The Cold War abated some, and with that, Lockheed Missiles and Space had massive layoffs. The semiconductor industry was having a credibility crisis, and chip manufacturers were moving their operations overseas for cheaper labor at a blistering pace. Inflation came in a big way, and construction stopped. The build-out of the Valley had strained water resources in multiple ways, and for the first time the powers of the Middle East flexed their muscles and the country was out of gasoline.

A professor of engineering at Stanford, who later became dean of engineering, had the following to say about that time on campus.

James F. Gibbons
Times of turbulence arise, I think, not so much because of anything that's going on at Stanford but because of things that are external to Stanford of which we are a part. The things that pop to my mind most quickly about turbulent years are the years that surround Vietnam and the years that surround our "overhead crisis," and what we had to do to respond to those issues and find our way through them without destroying the place or doing serious damage to it.

The parties that were involved weren't thinking about the potential damage to Stanford. If you brought that up then, they would think it was an excuse, a way to just stop them from doing what they wanted to do. And when you've got students who are as opposed to Vietnam as the student community generally across the U.S. was toward the end of it, they're already accustomed to saying, "Yes, you're part of the military-industrial complex, so don't tell me what to do."

Engineering and science [were more heavily affected in those difficult times than other parts of the university], largely because the military-industrial complex can't run without science and technology. The DOD (Department of Defense) supported me, through the Office of Naval Research, when I was a young faculty member, and particularly the Defense Advanced Research Projects Agency (DARPA). They were agencies inside the government, inside the Defense Department, that were responsible for funding a lot of research. If you look at the list of major accomplishments of DARPA, one of the things they'll tell you is, well, we created the Internet. As a matter of fact, they did.

It's a curious thing, because the man who invented packet switching, on which all of this depends, is not nearly as well known as the people who started companies and who did research at Stanford and places like that. His name is Paul Baran, and he thought of this [while] working with the RAND Corporation. He was worried about how we will communicate when our communication infrastructure was completely destroyed, but you have paths that open up here and there for a moment or two. [i] *He had to think of a way to communicate reliably between point A and point B when the path could go anywhere; or you might even choose to break up your information and send a piece of it this way and a piece of it that way for security reasons or to be sure that part of it got there. So he invented essentially structuring the information in a series of packets with an address. It's just like a letter, basically. There's an address of where it's going, and there's the address of where it came from, and inside is a packet of information, a string of ones and zeros, basically, that gets the pieces of information from the source to the receiver. The receiver collects the information and puts it back together, and you get what you think is a message.*

In order for Stanford to make a contribution, somebody had to invent the process to make the packet system work. It was computer science and electrical engineering [that] developed the home of the Internet fundamentally. One of the businesses that spun out of here to start with was Cisco, with a multiprotocol router, routing the packets between source and destination. So you have this work going on, and you can't deny that there are practical, commercial applications for stuff that starts out being a military piece of research. . . . And then there's the question, Can you actually do the research without the support of the military? Well, it's kind of hard to do because you need a lot of money.

---

[i] The threat of nuclear war was very real at the time.

You don't go in there saying I know how to do this. You don't even start thinking about that.

The efficiency of research output is not a good measure—the efficiency toward a particular objective is very poor. But if you're educating students, you don't care about that. It's the educated student that is the product, the basic product. If a faculty member and a student are working on some interesting problems, and he or she is getting a degree, and knowledge is being extended, expanded, et cetera, that is what we're supposed to be doing. It's irrelevant, or not immediately important, where the money came from as long as there's enough of it. That's the baseline. But when you get to a critical situation like Vietnam, now you've got the students saying you're part of the military-industrial complex. . . . [But] if somebody hadn't done it for DOD at RAND in L.A., somebody else would have done it someplace else. When it's time, it's time. And you can't debate that. It's a philosophical debate, and, meantime, they're throwing bricks through windows and so on. So you've got an issue. . . .

But, in that general time, there was a point where the university was at the edge of having something like what happened at Kent [State] happen here. . . .

There are a series of houses that have themes on the Stanford campus... Grove House was filled with people who were in the special studies programs and very well-to-do, as many Stanford students are. My wife and I were faculty associates, so we went there for dinner once a week, and I would go over a couple times during the week for lunch, just to be available. These students were amongst the ringleaders in this confrontation. At one point, they decided to occupy Encina [Hall, an administration building.]. . .[i]

About two o'clock in the morning, I was awakened from a deep sleep. . . [by another professor and told,] "There's something happening here, and I hope you'll be able to join us to help us think it through.". . .

So I came, and I was the fresh face at two-thirty in the morning. . . . These guys were just disconsolate, just sitting on the floor, slouched over. . . not knowing what to do, having tried what they could do, believing that, sooner or later, this was going to blow up. . . . We kept getting reports from the students which were worse and worse as

---

[i] This was in 1969.

people would go into Encina. So finally [a faculty member] called the police and came out and announced to the group that he'd done that. And, you know, everybody was, "Well, that's what you have to do." And I thought, "Well, this is really going to be bad." So around about four, maybe it was four-thirty, or five. . . . I began to argue for, "Let's go back in there and tell [the students occupying Encina] what's happened, so at least we give them a chance." . . .

[At] first there was the issue about, "No, we've given enough chance," and there began to be a feeling of, "Well, they'll get arrested. So what?" You know. Well, when you grow up where I did, and you see people who have the means of force—nightsticks—which are extremely destructive things, especially in the hands of somebody who knows how to use [them], and guns and gas masks, and everything else, those guys are set to do a particular thing. They'd like to not have to use that stuff, but they're prepared to. And there's a tipping point in there somewhere when fifty students and five police—you're going to get this "who's outnumbering who?" here. That may not have been what the data, or what the actual numbers were. But there's a lot of fear and there's a lot of additional courage, or fool-heartedness, or a combination, that keeps you there in a conflict.

So we finally got the approval to go in. I go in, and there are a fair number of students from the Grove House. And of course, I was their friend until I showed up there (at Encina). And they said, "What are you doing here? You don't like Vietnam. We know you're an engineer, but we know you're not like all the other engineers because we've talked to you, and we've talked to them. We know you're different. And what are you here for?" And I told them, "You know, the police have been called, and they're going to get here in a half an hour, and they're going to be ready for battle, and you guys need to leave now. You've made your point, the police will show up, there'll be plenty of photographs, and if you stay, you're going to get hurt, and the university is going to get hurt, and no good purpose is going to be served for your cause or for anybody else's."

And the police did show up. . . . And you know, I got a fair number of those kids to leave. The last guy out the door, the back door, was a guy whose father was a very famous ophthalmologist in Chicago. This student is now a venture capitalist, has done very, very well, and laughs about this now. But at the time, you know, I had lost all credibility with him, except that he realized that I was right, and left. [1]

John McGowan
I chose Stanford even though we lived in Pittsburgh, Pennsylvania. This was partly because the family had lived in Los Angeles in the 1940s, and my father, who had worked with the aircraft industry in L.A., had visited Stanford on recruiting trips in the early 1950s, before the family moved east. He strongly urged/pressed me to pursue a degree in engineering. I applied to Stanford, Cornell, and Lehigh universities, and was accepted by all three in the early spring of 1964. My dad agreed to take me to visit Cornell and Lehigh in early March, with snow and slush and sleet still hitting the campuses. On the drive home to Pittsburgh in the snow, I declared my choice to go to the sunshine and palm trees at Stanford.

I started with aeronautical engineering as a major but soon discovered that calculus was not as much fun as I imagined. So I changed to mechanical engineering, and then as a junior switched to industrial engineering, which is what I received my degree in in 1969. I was on the Stanford campus during the massive transition between 1964 and 1969, when the protest movements and the Vietnam War changed college campuses nationwide. When I arrived, Stanford was peaceful and bucolic, with campus picnics, recreation on the lake, and homecoming dances. By 1968, buildings had been vandalized and burned down (Navy ROTC), and there was a great deal of anger and tension on campus. After a bout with double viral pneumonia and some problem courses, I graduated in June of 1969 after five years on campus and was eager to leave and find a job. [2]

San Jose State
San Jose State had its share of upsets during this time as well. At the end of the 1967-1968 school year, the college president, Robert D. Clark sent a letter to college administrators titled "Student Unrest at San Jose State college, 1967-1968." Part of that letter is below.

With headlines of the nation's press predicting the new academic year to be one of greater turmoil than 1967-1968, with the intelligence activities of college administrations indicating that the press is not crying "wolf," I think that all of us concerned with the educational enterprise must pause for a sobering view of the academic year. . . .

On opening day of classes in September 1967, the full drama of racial discrimination was brought to the attention of San Jose State College and the community. Charges of discrimination, later translated into demands by Black students, was precipitated against Blacks in various areas of the college and the community.

Four days of open forum hearings on the campus revealed that a number of complaints registered by Black students were just. The college moved vigorously to redress these wrongs.

- *The Athletics Department, after an intensive self-study, determined the discrimination charged was largely unconscious and not malicious, [and] took immediate corrective steps.*
- *Fraternities and sororities were placed on Presidential probation until they guaranteed in a written plan that discrimination would not be practiced; all fraternities and sororities complied and were later taken off probation.*
- *An Ombudsman was appointed to search out instances of discrimination and to alleviate the frustration of Black students trapped in the racial problem.*

The most frequent criticism of action taken during the weeklong investigation into racial discrimination was the cancellation of a scheduled football game. The cancellation was not at the insistence or request of the Black students, but because of threats of violence from the external community, both Black and White militants. Recommending the cancellation were the Director of Athletics and the acting chief of the San Jose Police department. [i]

Campus ROTC training sessions became fodder for antiwar protesters. Then came the Dow Chemical protests. Dow had sent recruiters to the school, a normal practice for companies seeking new talent in their fields. Dow, however, manufactured napalm, which was being heavily used in Vietnam, and that was not appreciated by the antiwar folks. So they protested Dow's presence on the campus and disrupted the recruiting as much as they could. It was a rough school year as some, including many who were not enrolled at the campus, made San Jose State their theater. The year ended in much the same fashion as it started according to the June 1968 letter from Dr. Clark.

Mexican-American (Chicano) involvement in campus unrest began in October with the announcement of the showing of an educational

---

[i] According to the *San Jose Mercury* (September 26, 1967) about one hundred African American students were enrolled at San Jose State at the time, out of total enrollment of twenty-three thousand.

television program, entitled "Day of Concern," designed to acquaint faculty members with local racial discrimination.

An active Chicano dissenting group, called the Student Initiative Committee, charged that the Chicano minority position had been de-emphasized in the televised show because 11 Black students and only four Mexican-American students had been included. On the strength of their claim that the Chicano minority constitutes 20 percent of the society and the Blacks only a 2 percent minority, the SIC representatives threatened to disrupt the showing.

The President, in an effort to engage the Mexican-American students in a cooperative effort with the college to combat all vestiges of racial discrimination, agreed to meet with SIC representatives and to postpone the showing for three weeks. Through the office of the Ombudsman, the Mexican-American students were drawn into the college effort to alleviate racial injustice.

In a later reaction to the dissatisfaction with the discriminatory treatment of Mexican-Americans in the American higher education system, the Chicanos presented in May a list of six demands to college officials threatening a massive demonstration of 4,000 Chicanos and sympathizers at the June commencement unless their demands were met.

The college, while trying to be sympathetic and understanding of the Chicano demands, continued its stance of rejecting coercive threats as an atmosphere for working out a compromise. To ensure safety and order, the college requested San Jose Police support. [3]

The demonstration lost its steam when Robert Kennedy was assassinated on June 5. In light of that, the public was in no mood to put up with angry people, and most of the organizers recognized that. It seems both sides wanted to keep it peaceful, and there was only a minor disturbance "when six faculty members, 14 graduating students, and 200-300 people in the stands staged a walkout during the graduation ceremonies." [i]

---

[i] According to an open letter to the college, titled "Concerning the MASC Demonstration," dated June 14, 1968, President Clark stated there were on campus, "Some four or five hundred students with Spanish surnames whom we believe to be chiefly of Mexican descent."

And on and on it went for several years. One cause after another—some were just, some were not, but all were disruptive. Eventually, it seems that everything became a cause to protest about. Certainly, there was merit behind some of the complaints and protests, even if there was not in the way they were presented or carried out. But the protests also had a large element of rebellion for rebellion's sake, and the whole thing got old pretty fast. It was not a fun time for those who were actually trying to get an education in something other than the art of protesting, and Stanford and San Jose State were classic examples of that. Peace was taken away from the campuses and in its place came what was accurately called "bad vibes" (vibrations). Those who had worked, and were working, to pay their way through college—and there were a lot of us—had little appreciation for what was going on.

T.S.
I don't know that the local "junior" colleges had much trouble, but the spirit of hypertension and of calling everything a social injustice became pervasive. I remember a young man in my political science class at West Valley College giving an impassioned speech to the class and telling us, "There are slums right here in Saratoga!" and "We have to help these people!" At first I didn't know what he was talking about. After a while, I realized he was referring to the older neighborhood behind Wildwood Park. I was quite familiar with that neighborhood. As a matter of fact, I intended to buy a house in that neighborhood as soon as I could. I suppose we had a different view of things. I saw a great location that, minus some weeds and a few dead vehicles in some yards, would be a great place to live. He saw a slum. It was my first exposure to the passion of (some) privileged people who think the way they grew up was normal, then came to realize that not everybody grew up that way, and then set themselves to right the "injustices."

The "Slow Growth Movement" and Open Space
Another kind of protest was going on too, this one not on the college campuses by people who were making the campuses their stage, but by residents who took their concerns to the voting booth. By the late 1960s, nearly all Valley dwellers except for the most recent arrivals had had enough of the unbridled development of the Valley. And therein was the problem—those who arrived after the end of World War II only understood what they saw when they came on the scene.

They did not see, and, by the early 1960s could not fathom, what had been there before they arrived. All they knew was that the Valley was nicer than Detroit or Pittsburgh or Chicago or wherever else they came from. The way things looked upon their arrival was their reference point. So it was not until the Valley had become an endless landscape of housing tracts, strip malls, and paving with little or no visual relief—and smog so bad in some places that it made you sick—that voters finally moved to stop the "progress."

What had been called *progress* was not working out very well, so the citizens of San Jose finally elected a "slow growth" city council in the late 1960s. As I mentioned in chapter 7, the city of 17 square miles and 90,000 residents in 1950 had become a city of about 150 square miles and more than 446,000 residents by 1970. City services were spread over a wide geographic area and were severely strained, downtown had been decaying for more than a decade, and the city needed a workable general plan.

The other cities in the Valley also slowed development at about the same time, although most were already nearly built out. Voters made it clear to city and county elected officials that they wanted them to focus on quality of life, not more development.

Saratoga is a good example. City government finally put a plan together to develop parks in 1969. For two decades El Quito Park, which my dad dubbed "Gopher Hole Stadium," was a field of dirt with a couple of baseball backstops in it. It, Wildwood Park (uptown), and a couple of others were finally developed in the early 1970s.

The "slow growth movement," I suppose had its roots in the Sempervirens Club, which was formed in 1900 by a group of influential people from San Francisco, San Jose, and Santa Cruz. These folks went on a camping outing together at Big Basin and determined then and there to do something together to save the redwoods, most of which had already been logged off. Photos from that era of the hills above Los Gatos and Saratoga tell the logging story.

Following in the long-faded footsteps of the Sempervirens Club, the Peninsula Open Space Trust and the Mid-Peninsula Open Space District were formed. The idea for the trust originated with a Palo Alto native, a piano teacher named Nonette Hanko, who loved nature and was alarmed by the spread of development into her beloved hills above Stanford. She rallied some like-minded folks, including a couple of attorneys, and out of a lot of hard work and some donations came the Peninsula Open Space Trust.

In Saratoga, some locals did not want to see their beautiful hillsides covered with houses either and rallied in much the same way.

In both cases, the saving grace was that city consultants determined the development of the foothills would result in infrastructure so costly to maintain that developing it could not be offset by the increased tax revenue. With the backdrop of already strained resources due to the existing widely spread out development already in place, the cities along the hills put further development of the hillsides on hold. That gave the Open Space organizers time to get Measure R on the Santa Clara County ballot in 1972. The initiative called for a ten-cent tax per every one hundred dollars of tax liability and needed a two-thirds vote to pass. It passed overwhelmingly. San Mateo County voters had to override their county supervisors' veto and did not get the initiative on the ballot until 1976. It also passed.

The Mid-Peninsula Open Space District followed the pattern of the East Bay Regional Park District, founded in 1934, which had saved some of the Oakland and Berkeley hills from development and eventually resulted in a string of parks in Alameda and Contra Costa counties.

When a property was targeted for purchase, a few different things could happen: the owners could sell at the offered price, they could be threatened that the land would be taken by eminent domain and then sell, or they could fight it. Not many landowners had the deep pockets to fight it. That's the rough way of putting it. Thankfully, some of the owners wanted to see their land preserved from development and were glad to sell to the Mid-Peninsula Open Space District.

The Peninsula Open Space *Trust* was funded primarily by donations and bought its first land in Portola Valley. The district is still adding properties, but purchasing property that people may not want to sell has never been a walk in the park. Over the past decades, some owners have made serious challenges to some of the agency's moves, and sometimes it has overstepped, but walking through some of the places that have been preserved, well, that would take a chapter to describe. It is interesting to note, however, that at the same time land was being taken by eminent domain for roads and freeways, it was also being taken for relief from those roads and freeways. [4]

The effect of the city of Saratoga's slow growth movement can be seen in this 2016 photograph of Quito Road. The widening of the road during the build-out years was abruptly halted and it has remained as-is for more than forty years. I think almost everyone is thankful to be able to drive the south end of Quito Road or to drive into Saratoga from the north by way of Saratoga Avenue's Heritage Lane, which was also saved from widening.

Sexual Harassment
Women in the workforce were commonly targets of men devoid of character, and practically speaking were unprotected by law from being sexually harassed at work until the mid-1970s. If you were in the workplace in the late 1960s and early 1970s, you know that.

Anonymous
In the 1970s, when affirmative action hit, I was working for this one VP. A group of VPs had a meeting and I was there taking notes. They got to talking about sexual harassment. They were all saying, "I don't know of any," or "I've never seen that." Eventually someone said to me, "You train all the VPs—you haven't been exposed to sexual demands here, have you?" The room went absolutely silent. You could have heard a pin drop.

Then I told them about the first person I worked for there, who, after a few months walked me out to my car and said, "I need to tell you one of the prerequisites for working for me." I said, "And what would that be?" He said, "You have to sleep with me from time to time." That was on a Friday evening. I addressed him by name and told him to have my pink slip on my desk on Monday morning. I suppose he figured I would collapse and cry. I didn't until I got home.

That is what really started my career at Lockheed. They respected me from that day forward. The word spread like wildfire.

Women had a hard time in those days. It wasn't a Lockheed thing. Women were very subservient in the culture. Those in authority sometimes wielded it in an improper way, especially if they thought you were vulnerable. There was no HR department. You had to stand up for yourself. Some of the women didn't. [5]

Lockheed Layoffs
In the early 1970s Lockheed Missiles and Space entered a new era. Most importantly, the Cold War eased up, and beginning in the late 1960s, Lockheed would have to learn to deal with fixed-price contracts. Secondly, its new L1011 airliner, scheduled to roll out in September 1970, was delayed almost two years because Rolls Royce, which built the engines, was on the verge of insolvency. Third, the C-5 cargo plane fell considerably short of meeting expectations, which eventually became the central issue in a contract dispute. Lockheed

settled, but the reputation of the company was damaged. Even though these two airplanes were not in the Missiles and Space Division, they hurt the parent company greatly, at least initially. Fourth, the company did not win big contracts for the space shuttle. Fifth, the Trident submarines were nearly completed, so that income would evaporate. All these events happened at roughly the same time, and only government-backed loans kept the company from going under. In May 1971 Lockheed ordered salary reductions from the top down. Eventually, in January 1973, a 10 to 15 percent workforce reduction was ordered. For now, the gravy train was over.

Anonymous

By the early 1970s the Cold War had eased up some. In addition, most of Lockheed's contracts had been changed earlier from cost plus to a fixed fee. That time was intense. There were massive layoffs. [Previously, under cost-plus contracts] Lockheed made money by bodies. I even heard someone say we were flesh peddlers.

Most everyone was afraid of being laid off. I was concerned about my job, but at the level I was, it really wasn't a problem. The people they kept were the most highly qualified. The fact is, we were loaded with dead wood.

Grady Hall

I was laid off from Lockheed in 1973. It was devastating. I didn't think it could happen to me; after all, I was in management. I had been with them since 1951 and although there was some severance, it was very little. When the regular paychecks stopped, that was really something, especially since I had not saved anything to speak of, and I had already lost my house though a divorce. The house was in the Saratoga hills with a beautiful view of the valley lights and was built by George Day, the premier builder in the area.

The next thing I knew, I was selling used Pontiacs at a dealership on Stevens Creek. That wasn't quite paying the bills, so I was also selling soap through an Amway-like company that has long since gone bust.

Looking back on it, perhaps it was the best thing that ever happened to me. I had to face life as it was, and I realized I could live without Lockheed. I had become so dependent on the company that I was lacking in a wide range of skills.

But I sure was happy to be rehired in 1980! Later, after I retired from Lockheed, I started up a machine shop in my garage making one-of-a-kind small parts or short runs. In a few years, I moved the shop to a small industrial park in Santa Clara. The ability to manage that shop and business came in good measure from those laid-off years when I was forced to think on my feet more and didn't have everything done for me. [6]

***

The next three stories are about some difficulties the semiconductor industry experienced during this time period.

Norm Tarowsky

In early 1969 a number of Hewlett Packard scientists left HP and joined Fairchild Semiconductor to start up their Microwave and Optoelectronics Division (MOD). This group was led by M.M. (John) Attala, John Moll, and Gerry Pighini. Moll was an eminent physicist who was teaching at Stanford University and consulting for our HPA Division. He is known for his work on the "Ebers-Moll effect" in semiconductor physics. Gerry Pighini was the manufacturing manager who transferred the technology to our division. I was asked to join them at Fairchild in 1969.

Over the next four years, I transferred to manufacturing, started up assembly plants in Hong Kong and on a Navajo reservation in Shiprock, New Mexico, and was going to school evenings at Santa Clara University to get my MBA. If that wasn't enough, I joined with two other engineers to start up a small company (garage-type operation) building precision temperature-controlled equipment for the industry. (The units were sold under the Hughes aircraft label.) But after a few years with each of us working full time, we decided to close the business.

I kept the original [1969 MOD] division phonebook at Fairchild that had about 250 to 300 names in it. When I left four years later, I went through the book and found that only four people were still there from the original group. I was one of them.

This continual churning and loss of personnel was becoming a problem for Fairchild, and to retain people they created a retirement program in which you became vested after five years. After promoting this program heavily, corporate found that less than 5 percent of the employees had signed up for the retirement plan. They asked the divisions why the sign-up was so low, so we surveyed our employees and found that the reason nobody signed up for the retirement plan was because almost no one expected they would still be there in five years. [7]

***

By the early 1970s, the semiconductor industry had gotten way ahead of itself and was rushing defective products—products that had not been thought out well—out the door. In many cases, the "bugs" in these products caused huge problems, not merely for those who bought them but also for the countless people affected by the use of those products. We had entered a brave new world in which a few people in this industry could unwittingly inflict significant discomfort on vast numbers of people. The following story is told by a former Intel employee, but it mirrors the problems that were common throughout the industry. Needless to say, Intel learned from its mistakes. By the time personal computers came out, it had a stellar reputation.

Albert Yu

I think it was a big economic downturn in '73, '74 timeframe, and a lot of our product ran into trouble in reliability, moisture, and stuff like that. So they asked me to go into reliability engineering. And I was not very happy about doing that. I thought, you know, manufacturing our products is where I wanted to be. Reliability seemed to be something that didn't require that much technical knowledge. It turns out I was totally wrong. The technical content of reliability engineering was very high, plus I think that was the first time I began to interface with customers. Before, I was the inside person. I dealt with R&D; I dealt with manufacturing. But in reliability, you got to talk to the customers because there were problems. You got to go understand the problems, work with them to solve it. So that turned out to be one of the jobs I learned the most, both on the technical side as well as the interfacing, talking to customers, and understanding what their concerns were and how to make things better for them. [8]   ***

Here are a few comments about how things were economically in the Valley in the mid-1970s from the perspective of the Indiana farm-boy-turned-venture-capitalist who later kept Applied Materials from dissolution.

Jim Morgan
It was a tough period. I think probably in October of '75 you could have purchased all of the high-tech stocks except Hewlett Packard and Varian for maybe a few hundred million dollars. Maybe three or four hundred million dollars. So it gives you a sense as to just how tough things were. [9]

***

Although unbridled development of the Valley had ceased by 1970, there was still a lot of construction going on. That is, until 1973.

T.S.
Construction in the Valley, which had experienced only brief pauses since 1950, came to an abrupt halt in September of 1973 due to rising interest rates. It would remain halted for a few years. Of the building projects that were already under way, many went into receivership as banks pulled their construction loans. I was working for a midsized custom home builder at the time as a carpenter, building the Sobey Meadows tract in Saratoga. The owners laid off everyone except for one nonunion laborer. One owner picked up a hammer himself to try to finish some of the houses.

Anonymous
When I graduated from high school in 1968, it was easy to get a good-paying job working construction. I became a carpenter and joined the carpenters' union because you wouldn't get hired without your union card. There were construction projects everywhere. You just walked on the jobsite, found the superintendent or foreman, and got put to work. If you were not needed at one place, you were at the next, so it was no problem. With the change that came over the Valley, though, and with a long downturn in building that began in 1973, I realized I was going to need to do something else to support my wife and two children. I decided to go back to school and study computer science, which was pretty new at the time but looked promising. It was tough going back to school. I was in shape physically but out of shape mentally. I did make it through my course work, although it was considerably more difficult for me than it was for most of my classmates. Nearly all of them were several years younger than I, and very few were married, let alone had children. [10]

***

The International Environmental Dynamics building on Castro Street in Mountain View, the floors of which were constructed on the ground and then jacked up into place, sat unfinished for many years after its financiers pulled the plug. It is now called the Mountain Bay Plaza Building.

Photo courtesy of Mountain View Historical Association and Library

Water Challenges

The increasing population of the Valley gradually strained water resources. The effects were many and widespread. By the early 1970s, many Palo Alto residents noticed that their drinking water had become increasingly salty. Here is one small part of that story.

Anonymous

In the late 1970s, I was on a research project on the Palo Alto bayfront, where we drilled several wells for the purpose of trying to offset saltwater intrusion from the bay. It was a joint project, mostly paid for by the federal government through the EPA. As I recall, NASA paid for some of it, and the water district, for which I worked, picked up a small portion of the tab. It was a USGS [U.S. Geological Survey] project, and I worked with their staff to drill the wells and to test the water's conductivity and pH.

In the older parts of Palo Alto many landowners had their own water wells, and they were complaining that their water had become too salty. The project was designed to try to stop that. It was obvious where the salt was coming from (the bay), and was equally obvious that if something was not done right away, that aquifer could be completely lost. The plan was to drill injection wells and recharge the aquifer using reclaimed water from the wastewater plant that we operated. That plant was right across the street from the well field. The water used was of very high quality. As far as the tests go, it was better than the tap water Palo Alto was getting at the time.

Many new methods were used there. The first ozonator on the West Coast was used on that project. We also had the first carbon recycling system there. (Carbon is used as a filtering medium.) The ozonator was about four feet in diameter and contained glass tubes that had what looked like bottle brushes inside. They would glow purple as the ozone was being produced. The ozone was used to disinfect the water.

We had two 12-inch PVC supply pipes that ran from the treatment plant to the well field. In all, nine wells were drilled and three or four were very effective for recharging. The others wouldn't take much—too tight of strata or some kind of blockage or something kept them from being used.

At the time, we reclaimed more water than we could use, so we had plenty of available water. The golf course also wanted it and got a lot of the water at the time. They were happy to have it. Regardless of the quality, we could not call it potable water. That was also before the color-designated purple pipe came out.

It was a research project to see if we could prevent losing the aquifer to saltwater intrusion. How well we did in that regard, I don't know. [11]

***

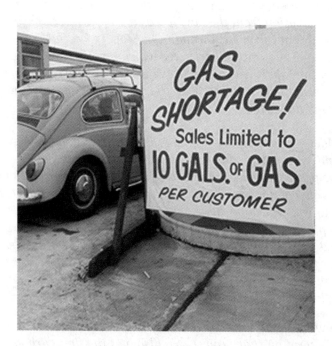

1973 Gas Crisis
Photo Copyright © Owen Franken

In the fall of 1973, in response to American involvement in the Yom Kippur War, the Organization of Arab Petroleum Exporting Countries (OAPEC) flexed its muscles for the first time and announced an oil embargo against the United States, Canada, Japan, the United Kingdom, and the Netherlands. The resulting shortage was felt at the pump immediately. At first ten-gallon limits were imposed, then limitations on the days you could purchase gasoline (odd or even, according to the last digit on your license plate). Long lines at gas stations became common, as were "Out of Gas" signs. This precipitated construction of the Alaskan Pipeline, the stated goal of which was to make the United States energy independent.

Chapter 14

The Fourth Wave: Minicomputers, Late-1970s-1980s

It could be said that the era of the minicomputer began on December 9, 1968, at the Fall Joint Computer Conference in San Francisco. On that day, what became known as "the mother of all demos" was given by a fellow named Douglas Engelbart, who headed up a team of computer engineers at Stanford Research Institute. In that ninety-minute live demonstration, Engelbart and his team showed a stunned audience almost all the features of a modern computer: windows, graphics, video conferencing, a mouse, word processing, a real-time editor, revision control, and, perhaps most shocking of all the individual parts: the efficient navigation throughout the computer system. Some of these features had been demonstrated before but never as a single system. During his presentation, Engelbart highlighted text, moved windows around the screen, and performed remote, real-time, collaborative editing with team members stationed at Stanford, who showed up in a window on the screen.

After this demonstration, Xerox established its Palo Alto Research Center, locally known as PARC, which several members of Engelbart's team eventually joined. In 1973, a team at PARC privately introduced the Xerox Alto, the precursor to desktop computers. Senior management chose not to market the product but to use it only in-house, much to the chagrin of the team that had developed it. The same pattern evident in the development of semiconductors would repeat itself again and again in the development of the mini and personal computers. Key people who actually wanted to market a product, instead of conduct science experiments, left the older, slower companies, joined up with others of like mind, and either started their own companies or went to work with others who already had and were pursuing the same goals.

After the success of the Apple II, which was released in June 1977, Xerox management was convinced they could not succeed in marketing a personal computer and invited Apple's senior management to Xerox PARC to show them parts of the Alto in order to see if they could collaborate. When Steve Jobs saw the graphical user interface, the mouse, and several other features of the Alto, he became very excited and could not understand the apathy of most of the others. But that is getting a little ahead of the story.

Xerox Alto

At the time Apple executives were visiting Xerox PARC, Atari led the computer game craze with its machine that hooked up to a television set. So games and "home" or "personal" computers were linked from the beginning.

Most of the initial home computers never got off the ground, but many contributed to the knowledge bank of the industry. Video Brain, another local product, is a good example.

Albert Yu
I was born in Shanghai in China and moved with my parents to Taiwan. It was kind of interesting as my father was opening a sales office in Taiwan, and we were supposed to go back to Shanghai after a couple years. But we couldn't go back because the communists took over mainland China. So I went to high school in Taiwan. And then my father's job moved again to Hong Kong. So I moved with the family to Hong Kong. Then I came to the United States for undergraduate studies at Cal Tech in Pasadena and then graduate school at Stanford. . . .

When I got out of school, at that time with a PhD, most of the jobs were on the East Coast—the classical places, Bell Labs, IBM, RCA, and so forth. And I didn't really want to move from California. There was only one company that interviewed me. It turned out to be Fairchild. . . .

I think soon after I joined Fairchild, Andy Grove, Gordon Moore, and Bob Noyce left to found Intel. That was in 1968. So I was still at Fairchild. As time [went] on, I got increasingly frustrated because the Fairchild R&D lab was in Palo Alto, and the manufacturing [was] in Mountain View, and the two never seemed to talk to each other. And I felt I [had] developed a whole bunch of interesting devices, but nobody ever wanted to pick [them] up. What is interesting was that Fairchild had a diode plant in San Rafael, and the fellow there, Ed Browder, was interested in what I was doing. I actually transferred the process from Palo Alto to San Rafael all by myself. I went there every week to get the product into production. That was the most exciting thing for me—to get products into production.

I was pretty frustrated after about four and a half years at Fairchild. Andy Grove called me and said, "Do you want to join Intel? They're looking for somebody in the manufacturing area." I had no experience in the manufacturing area. I was then more of a device researcher. But I thought, "That's great because I could work on something that actually would go to the customers and go to the marketplace." So I said I'd be happy to come and work on manufacturing.

That was 1972. So I joined Intel in 1972. Intel was in Mountain View, in one small building, and everybody was there. It was just a small place and construction was going on to improve the [fabrication] capabilities all the time. I was responsible for taking two-inch wafers to three-inch wafers in Fab. That was my very first project.

What struck me was how open and helpful everybody was at Intel versus Fairchild, where there was a big gap between R&D and manufacturing. I didn't really know much about manufacturing, but the people there were very knowledgeable and taught me. [They told] me what the right thing to do [was] and some of the secrets of some of these processes. Our team also came up with new processes. It was a phenomenal time for me. I learned and contributed so much about manufacturing. So that was the beginning of my Intel days. . . .

Then something kind of clicked in my head in 1976: we already knew about Moore's law—that transistor density would double every eighteen months or something of that sort. So if you did a simple extrapolation, you said, "Oh, my God, we're going to make millions of these microprocessors!" We were making lots of memory chips, and the application was obvious. You put them in computers [because] the memory usage in the computer was limitless. But for [the] microprocessor, it is a different picture. Where would you use it? At that time, they were used for traffic controllers and some industrial controls—pretty mundane applications, [and] not particularly of high volume at that time. In 1976, I sort of came to the realization that there's going to be millions of microprocessors produced as time went on. So where was it going to go? Well, I thought it was obvious. It's going to go into the home.

So home computers were going to come and be in the millions. But, remember, that's 1976. That's before Apple was founded. I actually got so excited about that [that I] left Intel, got together with a couple of friends, and started a company doing home computer. That was [the] really early days, if you will. There's no floppy disk drive. There's no operating system. And in fact [the] only thing that's available is BASIC from Microsoft. And so we worked with Bill Gates about having a BASIC running on our machine and developed a whole bunch of software. But we were way ahead of [our] time. . . . So I was a little crazy and way ahead of time and did a home computer called Video Brain. It was kind of interesting for me because I had to sell the computer through retail channels—Sears Roebuck, Macy's, all these people, and I went on the retail counters to sell to the consumers directly. It became very clear to me after a little while that people didn't know what that was. At that time [1977], Apple introduced the Apple II computer. That was aimed for a totally different audience. It was for computer enthusiasts and so forth. And the Apple obviously took off from that point on.

My home computer never really took off. But I learned so much about it. Would I do that over again, given what I know [now]? I think I probably would have done it over again, because I learned so much during that period of time [about] everything—not manufacturing, not R&D, but marketing, sales, cash flow, products, getting software put together on the computer—that helped me a lot later on. So it was a phenomenal experience but not financially very successful.[1]

***

Gene Carter, a South Dakota kid who played piano in a dance band to get through school and then went to work for the Atomic Energy Commission, developed a keen interest in semiconductors. Frustrated with his work, he came out to Fairchild Semiconductor in 1966, then moved on to National Semiconductor in 1969 where he eventually became marketing manager for the microprocessor group. After a short time of designing and producing calculators, and pushing for better and better product, his relationship with the executive staff became strained. It was time for his career at National to end. I will let him pick up the story from there.

Gene Carter

Well, what brought it to an end was when I made the presentation to Charlie [Sporck] and the executive staff of making small computers, and he suggested that there was no market for small computers, that I could go to work in the marketing group and research it more if I wanted to. I said, "No, I'm gonna take my ball and go home."

So I took that business plan. I went home and did nothing. I thought, "Well, I can live without working for a while." I was forty-three. "I don't have to work." And within three months I was stark raving mad. I don't sit well. I'm not an easy sitter. I've got to be moving all the time.

I left [National] in the fall of 1976. So I took the business plan, and, knowing Don Valentine as I had from Fairchild and from National (and he was at Sequoia Capital), I took my business plan and I went over to Sequoia and told him what I wanted to do. He says, "Well, what do you want to do?"

I said, "I want to sell computers. I'm not an engineer. I'm tired of marketing, and I want to sell computers. And I think there's a market out there for small computers. I've got this business plan here designed by Steve Leininger, who's now at Radio Shack [and] did the TRS 80. All I need is some funding, and tell me how I go about getting it funded." And he says, "Well, do you know what your friends Markkula and Scott are doing?" I said no.

Mike Scott and Mike Markkula and I [had] shared an eight-by-twelve cubicle at Fairchild for three years. And then Mike Scott worked for me for four years at National. . . . And those two had—well, Don said, "I had these two scruffy-looking kids show up in my office last November and they wanted money for their computer." And he says, "I called Markkula," who had left Intel because he'd been passed over for the director of marketing job, or VP of marketing, so he left. And he says, "I sent Markkula over there to check them out, and he never came back. . . You might want to go see what they're doing before you decide you want to start another company." So I went over to see what they were doing on Bandley Drive in Cupertino.

They had a twenty by sixty-foot cubicle, you know, an office space in an office complex there, right behind Target now on Stevens Creek. And, I mean, he gave me the tour of the place. And this [was an] order of magnitude better than what I was going to do. So I said, "I'd really like to join." And I said, "I'm interested in selling computers." He says, "Well, we don't need any marketing guys. We've got two marketing guys already. We don't need more."

I said, "No, I don't want to market. I want to sell. I'm tired of building marketing plans that the field ignores. So I will be in the field. You tell me what you want done, and I'll do it your way. If it doesn't work, it's your fault, not mine."

And so I went home and I wrote up a little plan, and I took it back to him and said, "OK, here's what I want. I want a percentage of the company. And I want to be vice president of sales." And he says, "I didn't give the president that much. I'm not giving it to the sales guy.". . .

I asked for 10 percent and he offered me two. And I said, "No way." And he says, "OK." He wadded it up and threw it in the trash can. So I went home and I was sitting there having lunch with my wife, and I said, "I really want to do this. I really want to do this. If it doesn't work, I'll go find another job, but this is really something I want to do."

So I got back in the car, drove over there, reached in the trash bag, straightened it all out, and laid it on his desk. [Same day, within an hour.] Got a deal. So he says, "Well, I can't hire you because I don't have any money." So I said, "OK, but I want the job." "You have the job."

So I show up every day. I work every day, sometimes weekends, until the fifth of August. And we shipped fifty systems on the fifth of August. Apple IIs. . . . So I worked from April to August [1977] for nothing.

In those days we had Byte Shops [that had sold the Apple I]. *And there was a group of stores called Team Electronics that went across the northern part of the country, which were like Radio Shack. They were all kinds of electronics—they sold components, hardware, phones, all those things. And when I started, that was my outlet. We had zero software, had no program capability. Mike Markkula had written a checkbook program in BASIC. That was our program.*

And so all of those engineers who had always wanted a computer of their own were buying the Apple. They were programming it in programing language or in Basic, and they were programming their

own applications. And that was the first year; that's what we had to sell.
. . .

But in the meantime, more people started to open up stores. And as time went on we had ComputerLand and BusinessLand. [i] And we had a lot of good dealers that sold audio equipment, so they had at least access to techies. . . . But that was in '77. When I left in 1984, I had twenty-seven hundred dealers. [2]   ***

Barry Yarkoni came out to California from the University of Rochester to work at Intel in 1975. Later he went on to Apple.

Barry Yarkoni
I started at Apple in November of 1979 as employee number 102 and was part of a wave of a few Intel people. Mike Markkula was ex-Intel and knew the Intel folks to be 1) very hard working, and 2) very capable. Interestingly, Apple did not place as much weight on technical cred[entials]. At that time, the entire Intel sales force had engineering degrees.

A few notes about those early days at Apple:
1. We worked very hard. Everybody. 100-hour weeks were not uncommon.
2. It was not always fun, but it was always exciting. We KNEW we were changing the world, hopefully for the better.
3. We were doing a lot of things that had never been done before, so there was no established wrong or right way to do things. As a result, a lot of mistakes got made. Most, but not all, were forgiven.
4. The company grew so fast that things were often totally out of control.
5. There were some very dark days too. The worst experience was "black Friday" in early 1981 where forty people got fired. For most, there were good reasons, but not all. I thought I was a goner, too, and waited all day for the axe to drop. It didn't.
6. Steve [Jobs] could be the world's most charming person, and the greatest ogre, all within ten seconds. He could turn it on and off at will, and often did. With Steve, everything was personal. [3]   ***

---

[i] ComputerLand opened its first store in 1976 and had eight hundred stores by 1985. The standardization of the personal computer, that is when it became a simple commodity, was the downfall of the business. Most stores were closed by 1990. (*InfoWorld*, August 13, 1990, Vol. 12 no.33. p.34) BusinessLand, the fast-rising company that became the largest computer retailer in the nation, was on the brink of bankruptcy in June 1991. (*NY Times*, June 5, 1991.)

Apple II

In the Valley, hopping from one electronics company to another was standard fare. For the most part, people simply jumped to where they thought the action was or where they thought they could make more money. Some took this further than others did.

Jeff Ronne
I worked in Silicon Valley at twenty-two companies in thirty-one years, about half that time as an employee, the other half as a contractor.

In 1980, fresh out of Cal Tech, I went to work for a small company in Pasadena called APH Technological Consulting. They developed video games and a console for Mattel. The company was essentially an informal partnership of pretty close friends, and they only hired Cal Tech people. When I joined them, there were about twenty of us. Although my background was chemistry, they knew I could learn programming and they trained me.

Among other products, APH had an LED football game in the late 1970s that sold for about $20 and was very successful. They kept leveraging greater contracts with Mattel and kept increasing their slice of the business by outperforming Mattel engineering. Initial underbidding helped, along with a vision of putting in a BIOS in the Intellivision console, which was specified by APH.

The big payoff was an approximately $10 million multi-game deal with Mattel, which included games for the Atari 2600 console (which I did one of). The only problem was, when the ship came in with the cash, senior staff was not satisfied with how it was distributed and quit en masse, all fifteen or so, leaving about that number of junior staff. I was offered double my salary to stay on, but I sensed that there was a better offer, and shortly after that, Activision and Imagic started bidding for the remaining junior APH staff, who were still valuable and were skilled video game programmers. Both of these companies had goals of passing Atari, which was losing engineers to these start-ups, as they were not paying as well. So, in late 1982, I took a job in Silicon Valley with Imagic.

At the time, there were very few people who could program video games, so I was in a fortunate position.

Imagic made games for all consoles, and it was a plus that I knew Intellivision, and the Atari 2600 to a lesser extent.

Imagic was located in Los Gatos, so that was my move to Silicon Valley, where I stayed for the rest of my career. The company was funded by Kleiner Perkins, one of the top venture capital companies.

Imagic was in a building in an office complex in Los Gatos on University Avenue, which was shared with Eagle Computer, another company seeking an IPO. Unfortunately, the CEO of Eagle was killed in a high-speed crash in his Ferrari on the day of the IPO. I saw the parked fire trucks handling the traffic death from my office window facing south. He wrecked right on the last bend in the road, fifty yards from his office. The popping of champagne corks turned surreal when the happiest day of their lives was stopped just after noon by their CEO's death.

Eagle had to pull the IPO but filed again a couple of months later. Not long afterward, IBM filed suit against Eagle for copyright infringement right when Eagle stock was at its height. They never recovered.

But it was the Atari crash that killed us. It didn't help that a couple of Atari executives were charged with insider trading. So Atari ruined it for everybody in the industry. The stock market dumped video game stocks. We still hoped for an IPO, but then the Eagle IPO demonstrated what we had likely missed out on.

Imagic imploded. The real surprise was that we were not going to go public.

As for me, I was going to try to make it rich and figured out that I should pay attention to who was doing what, and to the venture capitalists. I always had two contracts or two jobs. Either you have two, or you have none for a moment. It is less risky to be busy and have backup. I would often book the next contract before the current contract ended. Clients would wait. Sometimes they would just have to take me working evenings as I already had a full-time commitment.

I had a lot of connections and stayed connected from the beginning. This was before the Internet. It was mostly phone calls.

But I stayed one tier removed from being a principal in a start-up. I was never inclined that way. I was hustling contracting, mostly at pre-IPO companies. Confident of my skill set, I actively chose jobs by experience as opposed to pay.

Being close to the bleeding edge means you are always in demand because your one or two years of experience trumps all others. You do have to pick winning horses, but I could see the use cases and need. You also have to put up with some instability, but that keeps matters interesting. [4]

***

In the world of minicomputers in the late 1970s and early 1980s, there were three main categories: toys, personal computers, and business workstations. Workstations are super minicomputers that are linked to other computers through a network and a multiuser operating system. I will say a little about workstations next.

First, there were a lot of players in the game. There was also a lot of excess technology in the industry that had been discovered and was not being used, and many companies were founded to capitalize on it. At the beginning of this period, standardization was nonexistent.

I will mention two local firms, long forgotten, that had different approaches to workstations, or super minicomputers:

- Convergent Technologies was founded in 1979 by a group of people who left Intel and Xerox PARC. They produced integrated workstations based on the Intel 8086 processor and used their own in-house operating system.

- Elxsi, also founded in 1979, was the brainchild of Joe Rizzi, a former manager at Intersil, and a couple of Stanford professors. It also used an in-house operating system. The machines filled a niche as a super minicomputer that took the place of a mainframe, but the market segment for Elxsi disappeared after microprocessors were improved.

Silicon Graphics and Sun Microsystems, two other local companies, both started in 1982. They were far more successful, and the two of them, and a few others, took the computer workstation into almost every industry.

Sun, founded by three Stanford graduate students, used the popular UNIX operating system. The company quickly jumped to the forefront and was profitable in its first quarter.

Silicon Graphics, started by a Stanford associate professor and seven of his graduate students and research staff, was at the forefront of the 3-D graphics industry.

The term *personal computer* was perhaps first attributed to the Altair 8800, which was introduced in 1975. It was a kit sold to hobbyists who assembled their own computer and it was a great success in that market niche. In June 1977, a couple of Cupertino kids in their twenties took personal computing a giant step further with the introduction of the Apple II, which was already assembled. You just needed to plug it into a television set. It also came with two game paddles.

IBM's release of its personal computer, or PC, in August 1981 was the game changer. The IBM name on the machine essentially declared, "Here is a small computer that is a business tool and not a toy." And with WordPerfect, the premiere word-processing program of the time, it was indeed a serious tool. However, it was the release of the spreadsheet Lotus 1-2-3, in January 1983, that revolutionized businesses everywhere over the next several years.

T.S.
There was a lot of hype about the Apple computer when it came out. I knew people who bought them, were really excited about them, and told me about the great things the computer could do. But when I questioned them, I found that what they were actually doing was

playing with them, not producing real work. Then, probably in mid-1981, a client of mine, a CPA, told me I needed to look into this seriously. He gave me a short demo of how he used his Apple computer to keep track of his household finances. He was working with numbers, which I needed to know in my construction business, so I was impressed. However, the whole concept was so new that I could not relate to it, especially when he told me I would have to program it myself—whatever that meant.

A little later, the IBM PC came out. OK, I thought, this computer thing is for real. So over the next couple of years, I went to trade shows and saw demos of programs that were designed for use in the construction industry and also for business in general. Most were behemoths with little or no flexibility. These programs could produce all kinds of reports I did not want but could not produce the kind of reports I did want. Furthermore, using them would require me to fill in a lot of data that I did not care about. The question quickly became, "How can I get a machine to work for me instead of me working for it?"

Somewhere along the line, someone told me about spreadsheets—how they were just like a large sheet of graph paper with individual cells that could be connected in any way you wanted with mathematical formulas. I was also told that outside of calculating ability, the computer had no brains, only an excellent memory.

OK, I thought, if that is all these programs are, I'll design my own and get what I want. So I got out my yellow writing tablet and on a few pages sketched out exactly what I wanted. It was really pretty simple. All I wanted to do was estimate a construction project by breaking it down into its parts and then take that estimate and use it to track costs as a job progressed. And I would need flexibility for change orders.

So I took my yellow tablet to a couple of high-priced computer consultants to see if they could give me what I wanted. They studied it, frowned, shook their heads, and said no.

OK, I'm back at square one. But about this time a computer store opened in our neighborhood, so I went down there to see what they had. All these beautiful machines were displayed on desks. Very impressive. The IBM machine was there too. Even more impressive. The salesman came over. I showed him my yellow tablet and told him what I wanted to do. He turned me over to another salesperson, a very young woman. I told her, "I'll buy a machine if you can give me this," and handed her my yellow tablet. She looked at it for a few minutes and said confidently, "I can't give it all to you, but I can give you 90 percent of it." "What can't you give me?" She showed me. "No problem, I don't need that."

She said she would need ten hours to set it up and she would teach me how to do it. Her fee was $30 an hour, $300 total.

So I bought the machine, an IBM PC, with Lotus 1-2-3, Release 1A, and that twenty-one-year-old brought me into the computer age. It was an absolutely astounding experience that I still marvel at.

Up until that time, Deborah, my wife, had been working in the business about twenty hours a week. Some of that time she was typing proposals and keeping the books. She also tried her best to produce reports that tracked job costs. No matter how hard we worked on those reports, they were never really what I needed, could not give me "what-if" examples, and were always too late to be much good.

With the computer, I would spend about two hours a week doing input and analyzing the results. I had exactly what I needed to make crucial decisions. Furthermore, as I did more projects with computerized job cost reports, I had easily accessible data with which to hone my estimating skills. The net result was that from that time I accepted only the profitable jobs and let the unprofitable ones go. In effect, from a numbers standpoint, I could see the end from the beginning.

Not only so, with the word processing program (Word Perfect at the time), I was producing highly professional proposals, which my clients greatly appreciated. In short, I was catapulted into a whole new realm of professionalism and profitability, and for about seven years I enjoyed a great advantage over my competitors. However, I did not yet understand two crucial things: how to manage a business, and the need to subcontract virtually all my work instead of spending so much time on employees. I mention this last part to underscore the statement that a computer has no brains. I needed to supply that, and in some areas I was deficient.

With the arrival of the computer, all the work Deborah had been doing in the business was no longer necessary. I could do it all much faster and with greater accuracy—and I could quickly make all the changes I wanted (and that my customers demanded).

Being replaced by a machine was a real blow to Deborah. She didn't like the machine. I fixed that one pretty quickly, though. One Saturday morning I encouraged her to write her mother a letter using the word processor. After about twenty minutes she was hooked. The gray box, a former enemy, had become a friend. Whew!

***

That story of mine is typical of many thousands of others. Of course, there are also plenty of other stories, maybe more, of business owners who were not as fortunate. They did not understand the basic concepts of computer use, leased ill-fitting programs, or did not get the help they needed and consequently suffered—a lot of them greatly.

Notice I said *leased*. It was, and remains, a common misconception that software is purchased. Not so. And that can be a painful awakening when it comes time to upgrade either hardware or software.

After IBM entered the personal computer market, standardization was the name of the game. As it was, IBM owned nothing but its name. Intel owned the processor, Microsoft owned the operating system, and various other companies owned the software that ran on that processor and used that operating system. Several companies cloned the IBM machine and sold it cheaper, which destroyed IBM's market dominance within two or three years. Intel won the PC processor wars by marketing directly to the consumers and convincing them that Intel alone could be trusted to be reliable. And Microsoft eventually subjugated most of the early major software companies because they owned the operating system on which their programs ran.

By the end of the 1980s, nearly every office had some kind of computer system. Getting people accustomed to working with a computer, however, was quite another matter as the next stories illustrate.

Anonymous
Word processing was the precursor to the [mini, or workplace,] computer. At Lockheed, they introduced it at the top levels first. My boss called me in one day and said, "I want you to see something." He showed me this machine.

I didn't like it at first; it was usurping my position. I was my own worst enemy in that regard. Eventually they established a secretarial pool where people would drop stuff off and then pick it up. To me, it was getting to be too mechanical. Whenever I had to do anything with the computer, my assistant would do it for me. It drove me crazy. One day my boss told me, "You're going to become obsolete." I told him, "No, I'm going to quit." [5]

Anonymous

My dad was with IBM after he was discharged from the Air Force. During the Korean War, he was stationed in a small northern radar base that was part of the early detection system. At the time, the threat was not missiles but long-range bombers coming over the pole from Russia.

IBM was interested in him because of his training in electronics. At IBM, he was trained to maintain and repair large mainframe computers. He actually had to climb into them to repair them. The computers had vacuum tubes and also some solid-state electronics. He became a specialist on the computer that was nicknamed "Stretch." [The 7030.]

Later, he was sent to a government facility to work on IBM computers there, although he was on call and flew all over the States fixing those computers. Those trips were always urgent.

In 1971, he was transferred to San Jose. By that time, the handwriting was on the wall that the big mainframes were done. He was retrained as a programmer and later became a manager of programmers, and eventually became a manager of their managers.

The strange thing is this: in 1987, he was the only one of his colleagues at IBM who was using a PC to do his work. He would finish his work in eight hours and go home, while the others put in long hours to get their work done. A new boss came in and marked him down in a performance review because he did not put in the hours his coworkers did. He refused to sign the review. When he questioned his boss about it, he was told flat out that he "was not committed." My dad asked him, "What did I not get done? What could I do better?" He got the highest score.

IBM was very loyal to their people. They paid well, had medical insurance and a good retirement, so most people didn't leave. In the early 1980s, Intel and others approached my dad and tried to hire him, telling him, "We'll pay you much more than what you're making now." His reply was always, "In ten years IBM will still be here; I don't know if you will be."

Anonymous

In 1988, I was an assistant manager of a major chain grocery store in San Jose. The only thing we used a computer for was payroll calculation. It used to take four hours to do that work, but with a computer, it was fifteen minutes. But they didn't trust the computer and required us to do the same report by hand also. Another manager and I trained the assistant managers in all the chain's stores. Sometimes we did troubleshooting over the phone, but you would be amazed how hard it was to get across some very basic concepts. For example, many people just could not understand that the "0" (zero) and the "o" keys were not the same. Another example: at certain intervals, when they were finished with a task, their computer would prompt, "Strike any key when ready." There would be a long pause. "You got it?" "Give me a minute." Another long pause. "You got it?" "No. I'm sorry, I can't find the 'any' key."

Dick Karp

There were a lot of microcomputer and personal computer start-ups [in the 1980s], now pretty much all gone because of the commoditization of computers. In the middle of the decade, their father having sold the family supermarket chain, the Fry brothers started the first electronics superstore in Sunnyvale. Today, going to Fry's Electronics is something you have to do, but back then, it was something you wanted to do. 6

Chapter 15

Stories from New Immigrants

Here are some representative stories of immigrants during the time period of this book. I think you will enjoy reading them.

Dione Chen

My father, Reno (Jia-ling) Chen, grew up in Shanghai, the happy-go-lucky oldest son of a middle-class, educated family. He was twenty-two when, in May 1949, the communist forces were on the verge of taking Shanghai in China's civil war. There was incredible uncertainty and anxiety about what would happen when the city fell. No one knew. My father's family was not political but they worried. Unless you were rich or had connections, there was no way to escape.

Unexpectedly, one of my father's good friends asked if he wanted to leave Shanghai on a United Nations fishing boat for Taiwan the next day. There was no time to think about it or to prepare. His family decided he should go, just to be safe, and so, with less than twenty-four hours' notice, my dad packed a few things. His parents gave him the equivalent of US $100 (a lot of money in those days) and a gold ring. He left early the next morning on one of the last boats out of Shanghai before the city fell. Gunshots could be heard as they motored away. He didn't really want to leave and thought it wouldn't be for long. He had no idea that it would be thirty years before he would see his family again.

Taiwan was poor and not industrialized at the time, and two million mainland Chinese refugees had fled there. There was little support for refugees and it was hard to find work. My father was lucky to get a job fishing with a United Nations program aimed at developing the fishing industry in Taiwan. He had studied accounting in China, and in contrast, fishing was brutally hard and dangerous. It was a very rough life.

Five years passed and during this time, he said he didn't have any goals or hopes. He lived just one day at a time. There was little freedom living under martial law in Taiwan, and he couldn't get another job. He desperately wanted to go to America, but that seemed like an impossible dream.

He became close friends with some of the other single men from China who were in the same predicament. One day, my father's friend and fellow fisherman Paul Chow showed him a news article about a trans-Atlantic yacht race from Rhode Island to Sweden. Paul got the crazy idea to enter a traditional Chinese junk in the race, even though they didn't own a junk and didn't know the first thing about sailing. They also didn't have a visa or money or sponsors. Nevertheless, Paul applied. To their surprise, his application was accepted. My father was the first person Paul asked to join the crew. My father didn't hesitate for one minute before signing on, even though he didn't know how to swim. Now all they needed to do was make it happen.

Eventually, three other young men joined my father and Paul. Between the five of them, not one knew the first thing about sailing, but they were determined. They finally found a junk but had no money to purchase it, let alone to perform the repairs needed to make it seaworthy. Despite their protests, a reporter published an article about them that caught the attention of the Taiwanese government. The mayor of Keelung offered to buy the junk for them. The governor of Taiwan trumped the mayor's offer and bought the junk for them with the stipulation that they name it Free China.

My father decided it was time to choose a Western name. He was very social and loved to play cards. He had read that Reno was a fun city whose residents were down-to-earth, good people, and that's how he chose Reno as his American name.

Next, they went to get their visas. The young U.S. vice consul there, named Calvin Mehlert, a Cal grad, asked the men if he could join them on their voyage. They couldn't help but say yes. Calvin became the sixth and final crew member of the Free China.

It is amazing, but things fell in place for them. The Rotary Club donated food provisions. The U.S. government donated life preservers and film for Calvin, who had been appointed the ship's photographer. People from Taiwan and the U.S. were supportive; they wanted the crew to succeed.

Finally, after overcoming many challenges, they set sail for San Francisco. They encountered serious problems—including heavy storms, losing their compass, breaking their wooden tillers, and being stranded at sea early in the trip—but eventually arrived in San

Francisco in August 1955. They arrived far too late to be able to join the trans-Atlantic race but received a hero's welcome by San Franciscans when they docked at Pier 43.

The members of the crew had different reasons for making the trip. Some did it for adventure, others to prove a Chinese junk could compete with Western yachts. My father was pragmatic. He joined the crew of the Free China *junk because it was his only way out of Taiwan, his only chance to start a new life in America. He dismissed any claims of heroism. "When you're desperate and have no choices, you take chances," he said.*

After spending a short time in San Francisco, the Chinese crew members went their separate ways, one returning to Taiwan, another going to Washington State. The American vice-consul had to return to his post in Taiwan—flying back, of course! My father and his friend Paul were determined to stay in America. But how?

Many people wanted to help these young men get established in America. Members of the Chinatown community, Rotary Club, and a cross section of San Franciscans welcomed them. A UC Berkeley professor suggested that they apply to Cal, but the admissions officer there told them they would need to provide transcripts of the two years of accounting study they had completed in China. Impossible! Communications between the U.S. and China were cut off, and it would have endangered their families to ask for records.

Eventually, they went to the admissions office at San Francisco City College but were told they needed to prove they were high school graduates. Again, an impossibility. They were about to give up when Dr. Jacobson, the foreign student adviser there, walked by and asked if he could help. Thanks to him, they took a high school equivalency test, easily passing the math and science sections. Dr. Jacobson advised them to study engineering.

They now had student visas, but their first year in America was very difficult. In addition to taking seventeen units of math and science classes, my father had to find work. In exchange for room and board, he and Paul washed dishes until 9:30 every evening. By the time they were done, they were too tired to study. And they still needed to earn money for tuition and living expenses. On weekends, my father tried to get odd jobs pulling weeds, washing windows, or anything else to earn money.

He was exhausted. He was 5'-10" and kept losing weight. At 135 pounds, he had tightened his belt to the last notch, but his pants still hung loosely around his waist.

He was fortunate to get a job as a houseboy for a well-to-do family, the Bakers, in San Francisco. Upon hearing about his circumstances, in exchange for household help, he got free room and board and a little spending money—about $25 per month. This was much easier than living at the boardinghouse, and he was able to finally settle down and study.

My father was always grateful to the Bakers. Every year when we were growing up, we would go to "Grandma" and "Grandpa" Baker's home to deliver a box of yellow roses on Grandma Baker's birthday.

Still, my father found continuing his studies was difficult. There was always the question of money, and he decided to get an AA degree in electronics instead of continuing to get a BS degree in electrical engineering. He got a job working on the assembly line at Ampex, a successful electronics company in Redwood City.

He told his friend Paul, "I am going to work for both of us. You go on to school." With my father's help, Paul went on to graduate with a BS in physics from UC Berkeley. He then earned a PhD at Northwestern and become a physics professor at Cal State Northridge.

My father was very lonely once he moved to Redwood City. Not long afterward, he met my mother, Iris Louie, at a small party in Palo Alto. Within a year, in 1960, they were married at the courthouse. They didn't have a wedding. My mother's parents were dead set against my dad because he was a poor northern Chinese refugee who didn't speak their dialect of Chinese. They themselves were poor and uneducated, but, still, they thought my mother could do better.

My parents decided to move to Palo Alto because they had heard the schools were good. They never earned much money, but they were very frugal and Palo Alto was more affordable then.

It was a good thing that my father left China when he did because the following years were very hard on his family. They were an upper-middle-class, educated family and not at all political but still suffered. It was dangerous for my father to communicate with them. His family *destroyed their family records and any trace of him, including letters, documents, and photographs.*

In 1979, when the relationship between the U.S. and China finally opened up, my father's parents wrote my father at an old address. Luckily, their Palo Alto mailman found their letter in a pile of unclaimed mail and gave it to my father. That year, my parents and youngest brother traveled to Shanghai to see my father's parents. Thirty years had passed.

My father spent his whole career at Ampex. After starting on the assembly line, he was promoted to assistant engineer and later a full engineer in the research division. He was very proud of his work at Ampex. He worked alongside PhDs and gained a reputation for solving technical challenges and maintaining high quality standards.

My father never got a bachelor's degree; he studied on his own. He set high standards for himself and said he figured things out based on intuition. As a manager, he made it a point to give other immigrants a chance, taking them under his wing, just as he had been given opportunities.

Although my parents never had a lot of money, my father was very generous, "loaning" money to friends, knowing he would never be repaid. He was very loyal and honest—blunt even—and sentimental. He believed it was important to treat people with respect, to give them a chance, and to always do the right thing.

He was proud that my brothers and I all graduated from college, something neither he nor my mother had been able to afford to do. I earned BA and MBA degrees from Stanford, my brother Eric graduated with a BS in engineering from San Jose State, and my brother Mark graduated with a BS in biology from Pomona College.

My father always considered himself a lucky man.

The story of my family is the American dream. [1]

Anonymous

I grew up in Taiwan. It was the goal of many parents there to get a good education for their children so they could go to university in the

United States. So, after high school, I was sent to a university in the Midwest in 1969 to study mechanical engineering. It was very difficult for me. I knew hardly any English, and there were very few Chinese-speaking students there. I was lonely. Terribly lonely. I cried a lot when by myself in my room. But I made it through. It took me five years, but I made it through. Many years later, after I was established and married with children of my own, I sent for my parents. [2]

Armando D.

I left Cuba when I was seventeen years old. These guys drove into our village and told us to get into the truck. They said, "We need you to cut sugarcane." They had guns. What are you going to do? They told us we were going to work "for the people." Yeah, what people!

A while after [Castro] took over, we went to the market. There was nothing on the shelves. Nothing. We had money, but we could buy nothing. Later, there would be long lines for bread. People standing in line for hours for a loaf of bread. Maybe there would be some for you when you got to the front, maybe not. The same thing on the days they were supposed to have flour. Some days, nothing.

On the day they came to take us to cut sugar cane, I had a short-sleeve shirt on. You don't cut cane with short sleeves. I got all cut up. Everywhere. All up and down my arms, bleeding. Look at these marks on my arms! The leaves are very sharp. I said, "That's all; no more." [A little later] I swam out into the ocean. I didn't care. I would try to make it to the American base. If not—[shrugs].

A boat picked me up. It was American military. They asked me questions. I told them I was not going back. They told me if I wanted to go to America, I would have to join the military and fight. [This was during the Vietnam War era.] *I told them, "No problem." So I joined the Navy. After I got out, I moved to California. I couldn't see my mother for thirty-five years. I couldn't go visit her because I would be in big trouble. [And] they would never let me out. Thirty-five years!*

For a lot of years my work was on and off. I worked construction, odd jobs, anything. Sometimes I made good money; sometimes nothing. I have a good job now. I'm a janitor at the college. It took me four years to get on full time but I finally did. [3]

Anonymous

I came here from Mexico when I was seventeen. We hired a coyote. [i] *He got us across—no problem. I learned to do drywall. The contractors like my work. They keep me busy and they pay good. Jorge and Alberto work with me. We are a team. We have an apartment together. I miss my family in Guadalajara, but what are you going to do? Are you going to eat dust? I send money home and visit sometimes. Not for long. This is my home now. I got my citizenship two years ago.* [Big smile.]

T.S.

I taught English to immigrants for a while when work was slow after 9-11-2001. Most of the class was Spanish speakers, but there were also some Chinese speakers and a woman who spoke Farsi.

One day one of my students, a woman about forty years old, came in very shaken and upset. The day before, the immigration service had raided the beauty parlor where she worked and arrested some of the people in the shop who were undocumented. I did not understand enough Spanish to get the full story, but apparently one of the women at the shop had told her that every day, when she and her family members left home, they knew one of them could be picked up and deported. They had a specific plan in place if that should happen. My student must have had a green card herself, but the whole matter was obviously too familiar to her, and she was quite shaken.

Anonymous

I grew up in the hills above Sarajevo. It was beautiful there. The Winter Olympics were there in 1984, you know. People talk bad of Tito, but when he was in power, there was peace. You didn't cross the government, that's for sure, or you were in real trouble, but there was peace. After he died, there was all this celebrating, "We are free! We are free!" Yeah—free to kill each other. A few years later, after the Olympics, the war broke out. Kids I grew up with—you wouldn't believe. . . . We were in each other's houses. . . . But they told them, "You kill that guy, or we'll kill you." After the first one, it was easy for them.

I was lucky to get out. My brother got out first and he helped us.

---

[i] A person who smuggles people across the border.

Anonymous

My parents are from the state of Tamil Nadu in southern India. My father was a lecturer at the Indian Institute of Technology in Bombay in 1969-71. He studied geotechnical engineering and was interested in teaching. Later, he won a contest, the prize of which allowed him to come to the United States on a grant to further his studies. He already had his master's degree, and he enrolled in a PhD program at UC Berkeley. That was in 1971. The next year my mother and I joined him. I was four years old.

There were four or five other Indian families living in the campus housing off San Pablo Avenue in Albany at the time. They were all young—either recently married or soon to be married.

To come to America from India back then was a very big thing. It was an awe-inspiring "wow!" Life is easier here but especially at that time. In terms of traffic and dealing with other people, day-to-day life was just so much easier. This was before India opened up for commerce, which, based upon what I have heard from other Indians, was about 1995. Everything is available in India now, but it was not so then.

My father was able to stay in the United States because he got an offer from the University of Wisconsin, which also sponsored him, allowing him and his family to get green cards. So we moved to Wisconsin in 1978, a year after my sister was born. We stayed there until the fall of 1980, when my dad got an offer at Lawrence Berkeley Labs doing research.

Being from southern India, Wisconsin was hard on my mother. But as a kid, I enjoyed it very much. We got to take road trips a lot—my dad always looking at rock formations. Milwaukee was quite central so we went to the East Coast, to Florida, everywhere.

In the 1970s or 1980s, when we saw another Indian person in a store or wherever, it was, "Wow! Hi!" At least we smiled at them. Now there are so many Indians in the Bay Area, it is not like that at all.

The differences between people as to region, class, or caste and all that were forgotten here. My parents were Tamilian, but they had friends who were Bengali or whatever. There are different caste dialects, and my father would speak to some others in their (lower) caste dialect to make them feel comfortable. [That was not done much in India.] *The barriers seemed to go away in terms of friendships.*

As far as assimilating is concerned, I have to say that I never felt any racism here. I was a little different because I was vegetarian and that was not common at the time, so people would ask questions. You know, "What do you eat?," and things like that. I had a harder time assimilating in high school because my parents did not allow me to date or go to any of the dances.

I was interested in art and painted a lot. Eventually I got my undergraduate degree in architecture at UC Berkeley. I was not allowed to live in a dorm. Commuting was a little difficult because the BART did not go all the way to Hercules, where we lived.

I met my husband at Berkeley in a Tamil class. That was in 1988. He was taking engineering/computer science and was a senior. I was a junior. We got married in 1992. At the time, I was working on my master's degree in city and regional planning. [Later] we lived in Fremont, so in the morning I went one way, to Berkeley, and he went the other way to 3-Com in Santa Clara.

The elementary school our children went to had almost all Indian students. Indian or Asian, that is. The joke was, "Can you count the Caucasians?" I think there was one in the school.

We moved to Palo Alto primarily for the schools. The junior high in Fremont was not so good. We also disliked the suburbs and preferred the semi urban setting of Palo Alto, where you can go down the street to the coffee shop or bakery. For us, it was either pay a higher mortgage and send our kids to public school or stay and put our kids in private school.

There was also the matter that at the school in Fremont, they were not happy with families taking their kids out of school for an extra week at winter break. To take a trip to India in two weeks is tough; three weeks is OK. By this time, my husband and I felt it would be good to give our children some of their Indian heritage, so we began taking trips to India. The school had a waiting list and eventually said they would drop you if you took that time off. Whether they ever implemented it or not, I don't know. But there were a bunch of kids gone out of school at that time of year.

For me, as a second-generation Indian, I did not have that many friends in Fremont. But that changed when we came to Palo Alto in 2004. It was mostly Caucasian in Palo Alto but more Indians are here now. We have a lot of good friends here.

Poornima Kumar

I am from Kerala, India, which is one of the southern states. My husband and I both grew up there and attended university in India. Shortly after we were married, my husband was accepted at the Sloan School of Management at MIT, in Boston. He had an F-1 student visa, which is for full-time students, and as his wife, I received an F-2.

After two years at MIT, my husband was offered an opportunity in Sunnyvale with a computer start-up, so we moved to California. That was in 1980. Getting permanent residency took two and a half years. We became citizens in 1994.

My husband had wanted to go back to India after MIT, as he had an excellent career awaiting him there with the Tata Group. That is what we planned to do. When the opportunity in Silicon Valley came up, we thought we would try it out for a year or two and then return to India. Over the next few years, we often thought of returning to India, but work became increasingly interesting in Silicon Valley. In 1982, we had the first of our two sons. Once he was born, it was not so easy to move back unless we moved right away. Soon after that, my husband and a friend started a company of their own. One thing led to another, we got settled into California, and it was too late to go back. So we stayed.

As for me, I went back to school at San Jose State University. An American degree would help me in the job market, so I redid my master's in molecular biology and also got a certificate in biotechnology, which was a relatively new field at the time. I realized the biotech boom was about to happen and went to work at a company called Genelabs Technologies. The company worked on discovery and development of infectious disease therapies.

For me, job opportunities in India in the 1980s were not attractive. In the biotech industry there was nothing there. That was another reason why we did not go back.

I started as a scientist, eventually moved into marketing and business development, and built a successful career in the biotech industry for twenty-five years.

When I was in business development, I was required to travel a lot. Meanwhile, I had two children—boys. My husband was supportive in bringing them up; in fact, at one time I was posted in Geneva for some six months while he took care of the children in our home in Palo Alto.

What do I miss most about India? Family. They all wanted us to come back. My father had gone to Harvard and went back to India. None of them want to come to the U.S. now.

Also, in my early years here, I missed not having any help with the housework, which was readily available in India. Help is very difficult to get and was unaffordable in California when we were just starting our careers here. So I had to do all the housework, shopping, and myriad chores as my husband's job entailed long hours and frequent travel.

Outside of the career opportunities, what do I appreciate most about living in California? You can be much more independent here. In India, there are a lot of demands from the family, and one's time is not quite one's own.

I don't know if that is good or not. But it is hard that our boys did not grow up with their grandparents. We would send them annually to India, though, and we did the best to build their bonds.

We travel back and forth to India from time to time, mostly for special events, and we have done our best to help the family financially and emotionally. [4]

Ashutosh Mehndiratta

In 1995, when I was preparing to leave my hometown, New Delhi, for the United States of America, there were several beliefs prevalent about the U.S. There was no Internet in those days, and I hardly knew anyone who had firsthand knowledge of the U.S. There were American movies and TV shows that helped you make your own mental image of the U.S. I used to go to the library at the American Center, but most of the books were of the serious kind. There was a limited counseling session offered at the USEFI (U.S. Educational Foundation in India) to assist aspiring students. But there was no way I could have asked the questions that I had in mind, so I restricted my questions to admissions, scholarships, etc.

Interestingly, most of the following beliefs and stereotypes hold to date in India.

For one, America means skyscrapers, downtowns—New York City, Los Angeles. It is extremely hard for people outside the U.S. to visualize how spread out and vast America is. Most Indians cannot think of small town America, where millions live a "low rise," nonurban life.

Another stereotype: American parents lose connection with their kids as soon as they turn sixteen. Indians believe that American kids are abruptly on their own as soon as they are a certain age, and they all go work at fast-food restaurants. I recall discussions with my family and friends back in 1995 [about] why that would be so. Americans build big houses with multiple bedrooms, but why do they kick their children out? What's the point of building a big house? Likewise, when kids do well in their careers and build a big house of their own, why do they not have room for their parents? And if parents are successful and wealthy, why would a kid need to work? People knew that Americans adore their kids when they are young, but what happens all of a sudden on the sixteenth birthday? There was also a belief that children don't respect their parents. (In contrast, Indian children did respect their parents and hence the argument about [the] moral superiority of our culture to counter the progress and wealth of America.) In the Indian scenario, all these were illogical as most Indians live with their parents and vice versa well into their forties, fifties, sixties, and seventies! Fact is that kids in America do leave home for college and often never return. The individualism in the culture is such that they get to have more independence in terms of choosing their career or partner, etc. However, it is misinterpreted by Indians as a disconnect, which may not be true. There is plenty of love and respect between American parents and children, just that it may not be as explicit as in India.

Another thing [Indians] believed is that Americans are always in a hurry. Thanks to TV shows and movies, where the actors are often running in a hurry—they walk into the office, grab a coffee mug, and pour from a pot while running around and talking. One of my cousins had visualized that I would be driving with one hand while having a hamburger in my other hand! I used to wonder why I would always be late, though, and why I would be eating a hamburger early in the morning. Heck, I didn't even know what a hamburger was.

One last one: American or Western culture involves smoking, drinking, promiscuity, partying. . . . I was surprised to know that several of my American friends did not drink at all. . . . It was rather a shock to see that Americans were early risers, had lunch by noon, dinner early evening, and Monday through Thursday they led a disciplined life.

Again, thanks to movies and TV shows like Sex in the City, *they promote an image of a highly promiscuous society.* [5]

***

One of my relatives had a neighbor who is from Singapore. Around 2005, as stricter H-1B Visa laws were being argued by our lawmakers, he told me this: *"They're crazy for limiting the visas in that way! How do they think Silicon Valley happened!"*

Good point.

Another point I should make in this chapter is something of the social differences between the Chinese and Indian immigrants. Indian kids are taught to speak up and to debate with their peers; Chinese kids learn to be quiet.

Joseph Wang
I don't think the fact that Chinese are more careful about what they say is due to the educational system so much as the political system. Someone in China who says exactly what he or she thinks without thinking about who might be listening is going to get themselves in a lot of trouble very quickly. If you want someone in China to talk freely, you need to convince them that you aren't working for the Ministry of State Security. [6]

***

I will close the chapter with this next story.

Monica Huang
I don't know if you are familiar with China's one child policy. It started in the 1970s with encouragement. Later it became mandatory, and eventually it became a law. [That law was in effect until January of 2016.]

In China, when a couple gets married, before they have a child, they have to go to the local Community Committee to get a permit that allows them to have a child.

After you get pregnant, when you go to the hospital to see the doctor, you must take the permit. This is how they control it. If they find out that you violate the policy and you are pregnant, most of the time they will try to terminate it.

At one point it was very strictly enforced, especially in the countryside. In the city, because of the economic development, people have more ways. If they are rich, they may be willing to pay the fine. So it was more relaxed in the city.

Another way they enforce the law is through the company you work for. If you work for a state-owned company, which was the case of my husband, they have annual checkups for the female. If one couple is found violating the law, not only he or she will lose their job but also the whole company will get fined. Maybe everyone in the whole company will lose their bonuses or will get deducted in some way. So there was big peer pressure.

In my case, I worked at a U.S. company. When I was there, it did not have power over personnel management. All the employees had to go through a government agency. So technically, we were government agency employees, but they "lent" us to work for this U.S. company. So the one child policy was strictly enforced on us too.

I had my first baby, a daughter, in 1999. After you have your first baby, you must have an IUD put in the womb, and it would be checked every year. I had a huge reaction to it. Heavy bleeding. Very bad. It is very hard to take it out, and the hospital will not allow that. The consequences are too big. My mother had the same problem for more than ten years before I did. Even with the IUD she got pregnant, so she had to have an abortion. Finally, when she was forty-five, they took it out. She suffered a lot.

I had an IUD for about a year. My health got worse and worse. They would do nothing.

In 2000, I had to go on a business trip to the U.S., but my health was so poor due to the IUD, I figured I had to get it out before I went on the trip. My mother went to the hospital with me. She pleaded and pleaded with the doctor for me. Eventually, the doctor found the IUD was not in the right position; that's why it was causing the heavy bleeding. Finally she removed it.

In 2001, I had to go on another business trip to Los Angeles, San Francisco, Seattle, and then to Oregon, where the U.S. company is. I was very sick before that business trip. I had a cold and fever. When I went to see the doctor for some medicine, I heard an inner voice, the Holy Spirit, telling me, "You have to get a pregnancy test." The voice was so strong. I had the test, and I was pregnant. Then I started to pray. I talked to my husband. What should we do?

The next day I had to get on the plane. At that time, my thought was abortion—not that God wanted that, but I was living in a country that has this "one child policy" law. Should I obey the government? I had a struggle. I was not clear. And I am not that brave to fight it, so I really struggled.

I prayed. There were two things I needed to know. First, what is the difference between when somebody is born and an aborted child? And, if You want me to keep this baby, what should I do? Should I go to the U.S. or stay in China?

So those are the two things I was praying. I didn't know what to do. I would trust the Lord to lead me step by step. With these questions I went on to take the trip. During the trip, God answered my first question. While visiting a friend in San Francisco, I saw he had a book on Madame Guyon. This was the original translation, not the abridged version. In the first two chapters, she tells the story of her birth and early life. She was born with very weak health. Her parents prayed and prayed for her. Eventually, God saved her life. Later, she realized God saved her life for a purpose. She can be a vessel of God's grace in this world. To honor God. That answered my first question.

I was very encouraged. I knew God wanted me to keep the baby. So I made up my mind—I would just pray and see how God would lead.

I went back to China and talked to my boss about the situation, and he talked to his boss. I would have to quit; they could not do anything for me. But they agreed not to tell anyone.

So I started to look to see how I could have the baby in China. Either you have to hide during the whole time or go to some illegal private clinic for delivery. For me, since I quit my job there was no problem; but for my husband it would be a very big problem. I can't go to a hospital. I would have to go somewhere that has no license. If I was found out, no matter in what stage of my pregnancy, I would be forced to do an abortion.

I went to talk to an old Christian brother who was in the house church fellowship. He told me if there was any way to leave the country to have the baby, do it. In that church, there was a sister who two months [before] was going to have a second child. In her eighth month, [the authorities] took her out and killed the baby inside her. Her husband turned to God because of this. He saw how cruel and how unreasonable the government was, and he saw the love the people in the church showed to his family.

This pushed my decision to come to the United States. But where would I go?

I have an aunt and uncle who owned a Chinese restaurant in California. I know my aunt would be willing to care for me, but my uncle—he had not yet believed in the Lord. He was very focused on his business. I had visited them before and knew how busy their lives were. If I would go there and I couldn't help them, or if my aunt needed to take care of me, it would cause conflict in their marriage. This is something I did not want to do.

My thought was that I would have the baby safe, in the U.S., then go back to China, and there would be no consequence. That is what I thought. So I thought I needed someone to care for me for a few months, then a month after the baby I could go back.

One week before I quit my job, in my daily communications, one of my U.S. colleagues, who lives in Maine, called me about something. We had met a few times and he had come to China to visit. We talked about some business, then at the end he said in a cheerful way, "See you later, Monica," because we had another conference coming soon. Out of my sadness I told him, "I probably won't be able to see you again." He asked me, "Monica, what's happening? What's wrong?" "Oh, oh, nothing. I'm just joking, you know—" But he kept asking; he wouldn't let it go. I told him it was not a good time to talk—if he really wanted to know, call me at night at home. He called that night. I was surprised because I was not very familiar with him. But since he called, I told him what happened and that I would be quitting soon and that I might be going to the U.S. to protect my baby. He was Catholic. All of a sudden he said, "Come to my house. If you have nowhere to go, come here." I thought he was joking, but he was very serious. I did not feel so good to go there though, he being a man, I being a woman.

It worked out that I would stay with a friend of a friend of his. She was willing to have me. This was risky, of course—they did not know what they were going to end up with. How difficult were things going to be? The hospital bill? There were many questions.

I brought all my savings and came, September 1, 2001, ten days before 9/11. So I flew to Maine and I stayed with his friend—a very nice American family.

After I came to the U.S. I had a big relief. My baby was safe. So I called my husband to prepare for my coming back—what kind of documents they require, what we needed to do, and how to register my baby with the local Community Committee. I was due in January and thought I would come back in February.

My husband found out that even though the baby would be born in the U.S., we were still going to face the same consequences unless I had a green card. He would get fired from his job. Maybe his whole company would face the consequence. Also, as soon as I got back, I would be forced to have a hysterectomy. We were also facing a big fine. It was years of our income—enormous. We could never pay it.

I was shocked to find that out. I knew some would ask, "Why didn't you find all this out before?" But the thing is, we were so nervous. There was no one to go to. The Internet was not much at the time. And if you called, it is quite a sensitive topic. I didn't know what to do. The only thing I was thinking was, "I want to keep the baby safe."

My friends in Maine and I started to look to see how I could get a green card. They helped me talk to the lawyers. We figured the only way I could get a green card was through asylum. The problem was that there were no immigration lawyers in Maine who knew how to do it.

So I came to California, to my aunt's, in November, to try to get a green card in order for me to go back to China. When you come to the U.S., you have an I-94, which allows you to stay here legally for six months. So I had to finish everything before that time.

After I got to California, I realized the dirty part about applying for asylum is that people just lie. They make up stories. Just claim whatever they are not. I told the lawyers I am qualified because of my situation, but they wanted me to make up something. It would be faster. I told them no.

At the time, they were only granting asylum to a thousand a year for China's one child policy category. I would need to wait eight years to be granted asylum—and be separated from my family during that time. Then I could start to apply for them to come here.

So for me, if these were the only ways to get asylum, I would go back and accept my consequences. If my case can fit into the asylum category, fine, but I was not going to lie.

The attorneys had me write my whole story out in detail. So they knew I was a Christian and that I was meeting with a home church. I told them I had never really been persecuted. The church I met with was not registered with the government. The older brother there, the leader, had been put in a labor camp for twenty years. Because of him, the police had an eye on us, and some were called to the police office for inquiry. But personally, I was never arrested or beaten—anything like that. I told them my case could fit in the asylum category because I did have a fear what would happen to us. But I was not going to make up any story. I would tell the truth.

I went to the first asylum interview a month after my son was born. Normally it takes two weeks for them to give you the results of the interview. It took me eight months. That was a hard time. But God used that time to work in me.

The result came back. They rejected me because I had never been persecuted. That is why so many people make up stories, because it's hard to prove the "future fear." But if you had past persecution experience, it automatically proves that you have a fear to go back. That's why [some] just go the easy route.

My husband told me strongly I could not come back. So I went to court to appeal. In the meantime, he and our daughter applied for a visa to be able to join me. After 9/11 it was so hard to get a visa.

About that time, I attended a Christian conference at a retreat center in the mountains. The speaker spoke on the Lord's words: "Ask, and it shall be given to you, knock and it shall be opened to you, seek and you shall find." During that retreat, I lost my tiny phonebook that was on my key chain. It had all my numbers on it. This was before you had all your numbers on cell phones. It was so small and the grounds were so large. We couldn't find it. Those words came to me: "Ask!" I did. I also asked the brother who served in the camp, but we did not find it. He asked me to leave my contact information with him, saying if it was found, he would contact me. Of course, I think that was only out of courtesy; there is no way to find such a little thing in this big camp on top of the mountain.

About one week later I received it in the mail with a card. This brother's grandson had found it. He looked inside and saw all the Chinese characters. He showed it to the brother's wife, who threw it away. At dinner he mentioned that this Chinese girl was looking for her little address book. His wife cried out. . . and they retrieved it out of the trash.

As I'm holding that little book, amazed, God said to me, "That little thing. I took care of it. What about your family? I will take care of them!" My heart was full of joy. Such peace. I knew our prayer was heard. Sometimes you pray with good intentions but you are not sure. But from that moment I knew they would be coming. They got their visa and came in July 2003.

It took six years to get legal status. But through those six years God was doing an awesome work in me.

The first three years were terrible. I had to prepare so many documents. I went to court two times a year. Every time they told me, "This or that document is not ready." And then they started a new procedure, requiring background checks. So I would do what they asked and go back. Sometimes [the court] would just say, "Sorry, I don't have time to look at your case." It would be the same thing again and again. This was a hammer on my faith. But I just kept asking God.

My parents were still not believers. They kept asking me, "Why are you having such a hard time? Why is your God not listening to your prayers?" Every time I come back and cry before the Lord.

But after three years, I was reading in the Bible—Romans, chapter 4, that talks about Abraham's faith. Even though in the environment there was no hope, he still had this faith in him to sustain him, to carry him through the circumstance. I realized that the faith in me was not the same as the faith that was in Abraham. My faith depended on the environment.

I said, "How can Abraham have such faith?" You know what? After three years I realized that there was faith in me that was growing. After that time, every time I got delayed, I had a bubble of joy in me. It was for real. Not like something you talk to yourself and try to make sense of. It's just something that comes up. It's like, "I have less hope in this, but I have more hope in You. I know that You are taking care of it. I know my time is getting closer."

The last time I went to court was September 2009. Finally, the judge said, "I will listen to your case." My lawyer asked me some questions to bring out my case. Then the immigration attorney representing the government was called to question me. He stood up and said, "I have nothing to ask. I request she and her family be granted asylum." [7]

Chapter 16

More Convulsions: Mid-1980s

By the mid-1980s, it was apparent that employment in the technology sector in the Valley would continue to be a revolving door. Overseas competition and the short life span of tech products combined to make the workforce increasingly transient.

The openness between companies and the sharing of ideas that had characterized the early days of electronics in the Valley had long ceased to exist. Business in the Valley was no longer a science project, with people working in different companies openly sharing their knowledge to advance ideas. It was big business—world-shaking big business—and a large number of attorneys moved in to protect the interests of those who could pay for their services. Bigger companies bought up the smaller ones. In most cases, there was no choice.

Due to the increased ability to collect, sort, and manipulate data, the entire fabric of American business had changed. Aided by database technology, it was during this time that the conglomerates perfected the shell game of buying and spinning off companies to avoid paying taxes, and this affected nearly all businesses.

Home Depot and others became powerhouses largely due to their advanced use of data. Oracle, in Redwood City, became the king of databases, and major companies paid dearly to use its wares. Smaller companies could not pay the freight, and by the mid-1980s the replacement of independent businesses with chain stores and services, which had begun in earnest in the 1960s, was nearly complete. Management was centralized at faraway locations. Employees found their responsibilities narrowed and spoke more and more in prescribed sound bites. And as a result, a significant part of human interaction was lost.

Perhaps the most notable change in the Valley was the increase in leasing of both facilities and workers. Because the cycles of innovation and obsolescence were so fast, there were commonly plenty of facility vacancies. Temporary employment agencies also did a thriving business. In times of increased workload, instead of hiring more full-time employees, temporary workers increasingly made up the slack—even at Hewlett Packard and IBM, companies long noted for employee loyalty.

The Valley's technology had been touted as making life better, but you would have had a hard time selling that notion to the average local worker. Of course, if you're at the top, you're at the top. But most people weren't.

A *San Jose Mercury News* survey, taken in 1984 at a peak in the Valley's prosperity, found that while Silicon Valley production workers were working overtime and valuing work at rates well above national averages, more than a quarter of them expected to be laid off soon. [1]

The time of the itinerant computer professional had arrived, and many engineer specialists found their knowledge base obsolete and retraining a tough nut to crack. People who had been on the top because of a new technology found themselves at the bottom when that technology became obsolete. Some people had a very hard time with this, many were greatly humbled, and thousands left the Valley. I saw this several times, and so has nearly everyone else who has lived here.

From the early days, the labor unions made several attempts to gain a foothold in the local electronics industry, especially with production workers. They did not win an employee vote at any major employer until 1993, at Versatronex, an assembly facility in Sunnyvale. The company shut down shortly after the vote. The company had been there for twenty years and assembled circuit boards for IBM and others. [2]

Some local companies did well during this period; some did not. Apple Computer entered a difficult time after the IBM PC came out and before the Macintosh hit its stride. At a time when many local chip manufacturers were closing up shop, Xilinx was formed with the idea of producing a new kind of chip that users could program themselves. The advantage of these chips was that the same chip could be customized for individual market segments. As was almost always the case, key people from a local chip maker (in this case, Zilog) left to form a new business based on a technology they had developed but their employer would not fund. The Xilinx founders secured venture capital and found a growing market niche with their product. Gold was struck once again in the Valley. The company would later take over the golf course at Branham Lane and Union Avenue and turn the site into a design and manufacturing facility. [3]

Abandoned plant, Santa Clara

T.S.

While I was doing research for this book, I struck up a conversation with a man in his seventies outside a local library. He had moved to the Valley to open a local office for an East Coast tech firm. When I told him about the book and this chapter, he shook his head and rolled his eyes. He then began telling me about his career in the Valley and what happened to the company he moved here for. A few months after he arrived, the company was sold. A short time later it was absorbed in a merger, and then a little later that company split up. He told me he jumped ship somewhere along the line and went to another company, which lost a large contract and went into receivership. He then went on to talk about many companies by name—ones that during the 1980s and early 1990s had similar histories. As he was telling the story he was reliving it. He had hit the Play *button and a full-color motion picture was running in his mind.*

I wrote him a few months later, reminded him of our conversation, and asked if he would like to share something of his story for the book. He replied that, after careful consideration, he had decided to decline. Too many of the principals were still alive, and he thought some of them would not appreciate his view.

His comments bring out the hard fact that company breakups are always messy at the upper levels. Reputations and big money are always on the line. Loan payments are missed, lawsuits follow lawsuits, wounds are inflicted and received, and too often friendships are poisoned.

***

Unfortunately, not only friendships were poisoned, as the next story attests.

Anonymous

I worked on the maintenance crew for the city for many years before I retired. Part of our responsibilities included the routine maintenance of the city sewer lines. The city was smart to have a regular schedule of jetting the lines, rather than waiting for a problem to develop. In the late 1970s, we began to notice something we had never seen before. In several places in the city, we would lift the manhole cover and down below it would just be gravel. The concrete had just been eaten away. It didn't take long to realize that these locations were always directly across from an electronics plant. It was obvious they were dumping something down the drain that shouldn't go down the drain. We reported this to our supervisor, who at first listened. At a certain point, though, we were all told in no uncertain terms to keep our mouths shut.[4]

Anonymous

The polluted groundwater from the electronics industry in the early 1980s was the big story, of course. The solvents used to clean the wafers were highly toxic, and eventually they began showing up in well water. I was put on that project, probably from the beginning. At the start, I was one of two technicians.

We were monitoring all the municipal wells in the county. Some of them were on the grounds of electronics plants. I was on this investigation full time for four to six months, then sporadically afterward. I drove samples to a firm in Dublin to get them tested. The water district did not have the ability to make the further tests that were needed, but our lab had picked up indicators that were alarming. A flag had been raised, and it became evident that there was a much larger problem. We looked to the regional water board, whose response was, "You guys are going to have to handle this!" No one knew what to do.

One time, early on, I drove into one of the plants late in the day and went by a maintenance shop. The roll-up door was open and inside was a large dumpster, but it was shaped differently than a typical dumpster and had a pipe going into it. There was also a fresh patch in the asphalt there. Something didn't feel right, and I said to the fellow who was there, "What is this?" He told me that the water in the dumpster was so polluted it had to be hauled off to Kettleman City.

During this time I got a threatening phone call. The caller just said, "Mr. ____, you watch your step!" and hung up. To say that this was stressful is an understatement. The whole situation was charged. It was the most stressful time of my life, by far. Sometimes my wife would pick me up at work. The kids would be with her. I can't tell you what that meant. Somebody cared about me!

We found some real problems. There was a well that was out by Kaiser [hospital in south San Jose], that we shut down within a couple of hours of testing. Eventually, we had to shut down a lot of wells.

There was a plant down in that area on Bernal Road, and another was nearby too, but who knows where the stuff was coming from. Exactly where those electronics plants were located is now (2015) difficult to tell. They quietly abandoned those sites, and now there is no trace of many of them.

There were five electronics plants that I went to on my rounds. They had very high security and sure didn't like me coming onto the property. The water district was doing its duty, but who knows what was going on. The corporate lawyers for these companies were really putting pressure on the water district too. We all knew we were in the middle of a very messy situation.

We had some authority but not much. It was not like it is today. The pendulum has swung way over to the other side. Today the environmental concerns have most of the authority. It was not so then. [5]

***

Ted Smith was born in 1945 and grew up mostly in New York. His father was a GE man who worked at GE's atomic facilities in Schenectady and at the Hanford Atomic plant in Richmond, Washington, and then was transferred to headquarters in New York City.

A couple of years after Ted graduated from Wesleyan University and had become involved in politics, he came out to California. That was in 1969, and by that time, he said, "I got so frustrated I decided to go to law school." He did, and later started a small law practice in Palo Alto with a couple of partners. They specialized in health and safety issues but had to take drunk driving and divorce cases to help pay the bills. He also married an attorney. I'll let him pick up the story from there.

Ted Smith
My wife began realizing that this new industry that we saw growing up around us, the high-tech industry, the electronics industry, was actually a chemical-handling industry. The way that she learned about that was she started getting some clients, in her own legal practice, who were getting sick on the job and were pretty sure it was connected to the chemical exposure.

I wasn't that interested in it because I didn't see how that related to making social change. There was a few people getting sick, and that was too bad, but how was that going to change the world? She kept talking to me about how this was horrible, what was happening to people, and that nobody understood what was happening. She and some friends formed an organization that originally was called PHASE, the Project on Health and Safety in Electronics. They actually got a little money from the federal government during the Jimmy Carter years, through an OSHA grant program called New Directions. They were able to hire some industrial hygienists and some other technical people and were able to document the chemical-handling patterns of the industry . . . . [They were also being] contacted by workers who were getting sick on the job, and [they] increasingly began to get a little notice about what was happening.

It was around that time that Lois Gibbs started speaking out on Love Canal, and I began paying attention to that. It was around that same time that people started talking about this concept of the public's "right to know" and "workers' right to know." The workers' right to know had begun as part of OSHA in the 1970s. For the first time, OSHA established the principle that people who were exposed to toxic substances had a right to know about what was happening to them. And then people started thinking about that from the standpoint of augmenting [workers' right to know] with a community's right to know.

So all this stuff is going on around me. I'm continuing to practice in a small law office and not feeling terribly fulfilled or satisfied. What we were finding is that, increasingly, as we got into bigger and bigger fights, the law firms got bigger and bigger and better financed with lots and lots of lawyers. They were beginning to use what was becoming known as "computer technology," and we were using our little [IBM] Selectric [typewriters]. We would spend all night typing briefs, and they would push a button and spit out a hundred pages of interrogatories. The technological warfare involved in the practice of law became pretty unbalanced.

So I was trying to figure out something new to do, and my wife, Mandy, kept talking about the occupational health stuff. I kept thinking that was not going to create a center of gravity that's going to help change the direction of things. I think [that was] what I was trying to find, because people found it too easy to write off worker health issues as somebody else's problem, and it didn't affect people personally.

It was at that point there was a little story in the newspaper that groundwater contamination had been discovered in south San Jose. That was the Fairchild leak. And a lightbulb started going off in my head, that whereas I still thought that people didn't care that much about toxic exposure to somebody else, if people could see that there was drinking water pollution, all of sudden it could become, "Oh, my God, this could be me."

And that was the connection, the lightbulb, I saw. The same concerns that Mandy had been talking about could now become concerns that could have a mass base behind them. They could then provide enough momentum to change things.

There was a woman in the south San Jose neighborhood called Los Paseos named Lorraine Ross, who had just given birth to a daughter with a heart defect. She began to speak out about this and go door to door talking to her neighbors. She got in touch [with us] and said she wanted some help in trying to figure out what to do.

We started having some meetings and began to realize two different things. One is that there was a potential to get some local legislation together that would have a major impact. It was [also] around that set of issues that I saw the need to develop a community-based organization, and that's what ended up turning into the Silicon Valley Toxics Coalition. [i]

At the same time, Mandy began to work with Lorraine and some of the other neighbors to develop legal strategies for how to deal with the terrible health problems people were running into. Pretty soon there were several hundred people who came out of the woodwork, all in that same neighborhood, that had a range of problems but mostly people with reproductive health problems and people with cancers. [6]

***

The Santa Clara Valley eventually became the home of twenty-three EPA Superfund sites. Most were semiconductor fabrication sites, and the Valley gained the distinction of having the highest concentration of Superfund sites in the country. Most of these facilities were bulldozed, and, after some remediation work, the sites were redeveloped. It is difficult to find any trace of them now. I will mention just one because it is an example of the extreme volatility of the times. A Fairchild plant in south San Jose was in operation only about seven years before it was shut down in 1984, partly, if not entirely, due to the contamination at that site.

What happened in the semiconductor industry in the Valley was just the most recent in a long line of local poisonings. Before this, for more than a hundred years, mercury had been leaching out of cinnabar mine tailings in the Almaden area and had gotten into some of the local creeks; airborne lead from the tailpipes of cars using leaded gasoline not only poisoned the air, it had also been washing down in the rain on the valley since the 1920s. And DDT, which was widely used to control crop pests after World War II, had also left a residue in some places.

It is easy to look back and criticize these things. But mercury was convenient for extracting gold, lead was convenient for eliminating engine "ping," and DDT was convenient for killing crop pests. The

---

[i] Formed in 1982.

silicon chip may be the most convenient of all. Unlike the others, it was soon used in virtually every industry and the mad rush to produce these chips in an environment of global competition is understandable. Today, texting is convenient too. But at what cost? Granted, the texting problem is inward rather than outward, but my point is that many people believed all these things made the world better. But trust placed in technology is misplaced trust. We have more than ample evidence to say the world does not become better through technology without the right actions of individuals. In contrast with technology, the virtues of gratitude, honesty, self-control, kindness, goodness, faithfulness, and the like have no downside.

As the Valley filled in, housing became increasingly expensive. Younger families that wanted to buy a house in the Valley could not afford to. As a result, the sleepy little towns of Tracy and Los Banos, on the eastern side of the Diablo Range, saw a huge surge in housing development. The next story is a typical tale of commuting.

Anonymous
After growing up in San Jose and living there for more than thirty years, I bought a new house in Los Banos in 1990. At first, I tried to drive the commute every day but soon found that to be impossible. It was making me old. I would stay over in San Jose some nights, and that helped a lot, but. . . . I joined a vanpool and that was extremely helpful, but, still, getting up every morning at 4:30 and getting home around 7 p.m. was a killer. It just sucks the life out of you. You can sleep on the van, but the sleep was not the same, not of the same quality. It was not as restful and I never felt refreshed by it. Relieved, yes; refreshed, no. There were frequent accidents on Pacheco Pass too. Lots of bad accidents. People just fell asleep at the wheel. I did it myself. That's why I joined the vanpool. A lot of people were killed or maimed. You couldn't help but think about that. You knew the risk. It was always right there before you.
***

While I was gathering stories for this book, someone wrote me: "As the years passed, the boys grew up and left the area." Countless others would say the same thing. The exodus from the Valley of those who grew up here was enormous. I think it is safe to say that by the mid-1980s the majority of the kids who had grown up in the Valley in the fifties and sixties had left. It was probably a large majority. The situation was not that different from when the GIs were returning following World War II. In a large percentage of those cases, other than Mom and Dad, there was not much for them back home. And so it has been for their children and grandchildren after the Santa Clara Valley became Silicon Valley. If they were not engineers of a certain stripe, or if they wanted to raise a family, it was, and is, considerably less attractive to stay than to find somewhere else to live that is more accommodating.

Young people who had grown up here were not the only ones deserting the Valley. So were many of the World War II veterans and others who had moved here in the first two waves of migration after the war. They were retiring and moving out in large numbers. One of their favorite destinations was the Sierra foothills. New communities such as Oakhurst and Paradise sprang up in places where there had hardly been a wide spot in the road, and old gold-mining communities like Nevada City, Placerville, Auburn, and Grass Valley were deluged with retirees from the Bay Area.

The Valley had changed radically on these people, and it had also become an expensive place to live. Few places have inflated as fast. The cost of housing, which was low in the 1970s, began to get ridiculous by the mid-1980s. For those who left, rarely has the saying "You can't go back" proved more true.

Chapter 17

Growing Up in the Valley, 1980s to Early 2000s

In many ways, coming of age today is much the same as it was in the 1950s and 1960s. Young people in the Valley grapple with most of the same issues we older folks did. But kids of previous generations were not subjected to many of the issues they are now, and the environment in which they grow up is quite different. The bicycle as a mode of transportation for kids has largely been replaced by Mom carting them everywhere. Free time to play outdoors has been replaced by organized everything. Working to earn what you need or want has been replaced by allowances from parents and fundraisers. And as always, there is pressure to conform to whatever the current social norms are.

I'll let the young people take it from there.

Jenny Du
I thought it would be nice to give you a child's view of Silicon Valley. Now that I've left the place, I realize that the culture in Silicon Valley is often fantasized, but you also get a sort of artificial feeling from people. It's the general mind-set of the place.

Silicon Valley is very fast paced and it's a place for people to work hard to achieve their dreams. This means that people are extremely, extremely competitive. When I was little my mom always told me about workplace drama. . . . She told me about how project managers took credit for other people's work. . . .

The overly competitive adults pushed their kids to be overly competitive. When I lived there, I was enrolled in ice skating, piano, violin, and drawing lessons—all by the age of seven. This was the bare minimum, though; most families had their kids preparing for the SATs before high school or going to extra tutoring outside of classes that they didn't need. Everyone wanted their kid to be the best, and they put a lot of pressure on their kids. There is a high school in Silicon Valley where we often heard of students committing suicide on the train tracks. The drive to push them toward Ivy League schools was really strong, and the other Asian parents were constantly comparing their kids to each other. It made children turn on each other; it made some of them jealous and conniving.

Although the parents care about their kids and believe in their ability, there isn't a lot of time to spend with them. Most Chinese people sent their kids to Chinese school after school, and I assume that with the level of diversity there, there were similar schools for other highly represented cultures. Both my parents worked, so I didn't really talk to them much or get to know them as people until we moved away and had more time to do things.

In the Bay Area, everything moves faster: the curriculum at school is more advanced than in other regions, companies rise and fall very quickly, and you age faster. There is a lot of stress and the traffic can be kind of stressful too. People usually aren't friendly to each other unless they get something out of it because there simply isn't enough time to be friendly. [1]   ***

A 2014 graduate of Lynbrook High had this to say of his high school.

Tony Jiang

If you are academically minded, or even academically obsessed, this is the perfect place for you. The highest people in the social hierarchy seem to be the ones who are the most academically successful. It's very easy to focus completely on academics without risk of missing out socially. In other words, being smart is cool. [2]

Matt Williams

As a young person who recently grew up in Palo Alto and attended Gunn High School (the pressure-cooker school where many people, including two of my friends, committed suicide), I feel obligated to share my experience.

Though people here are very nonmaterialistic (compared to L.A. and NYC, yet this has changed after the recent influx of tech/VC money), there is an extremely high value placed on education and intellect. Many exceptionally brilliant people live in the area, but most of them have achieved success in life solely through their academic endeavors, and they struggle to empathize with those whose talents extend beyond the classroom.

Children who cannot keep up with the academic rigor of the top 10 percent of their class become invisible to the school until they begin to dramatically fail. And the top 10 percent isn't doing just the usual accelerated math/science classes; they have parents who are ushering them through to the upper levels of academia at a very young age. I had a friend who was taking math classes at Stanford in the ninth grade. Children this successful are obviously very exciting for schools because they greatly improve their overall test scores. But many schools fail to realize the potential in the vast majority of children, many of whom have tremendous talents, yet they cannot compete at a ridiculous academic pace. Because of the intense competition, there is a huge amount of pressure placed on students by both parents and the children's social group—to "keep up" with the top students in their class. And when they can't keep up, their otherwise noteworthy achievements become invisible, and the kids feel worthless, which is what led to the suicides at my high school, kids doing lots of hard drugs, and many reckless decisions. Many great people were lost because of the intense competition by both kids and parents to prove who was "ahead of the pack." I can't stress this enough, but Silicon Valley is not a good place whatsoever for a child who struggles academically.

I will ask the all-important question: Would I raise my children here, after growing up in the area myself? The answer is yes. The amount of opportunity for children here is vast, and despite the ridiculous cost of living, I would much rather have my children surrounded by brilliant minds and resources. [3]

D.M.

Kids don't worry much about being popular. While almost every teenager makes an effort to fit in, Palo Alto doesn't really have popular kids. Maybe it's that the high schools in general aren't at all like what they're reflected to be like on television, or maybe it can be credited to Palo Alto's uniqueness, but the high schools in the area don't really have many cliques. The kids do, however, worry about not being smart enough. (Being a nerd is cool here!)

Most people surrounding you are very smart and educated. Kids that grow up here have very high educational standards. They strive to be the very best, and while many times that leads to unbearable stress, it also leads to incredibly innovative and intelligent teenagers.

Growing up in Palo Alto can make you pretty spoiled (even if unintentionally). However, it also makes you dedicated, hard-working, and tough. The people surrounding us worked extremely hard to get to where they are. It's not like we are surrounded by people who inherited all of their money and never had to work for anything they've earned. We are surrounded by people who busted their asses in school, and in the workplace, to get to where they are. No matter how spoiled you can get when being surrounded with rich people, we most definitely do not live up to the public's view of rich teenagers who go to private schools. We work hard and we want to make a difference (and not just one in our parents' bank accounts.)

On the downside, going to high school here is extremely difficult academically and, as I said, causes the teenagers here an immense amount of stress. The standard at Palo Alto schools is very high. People who would be top of their class in any other school are completely lost in the middle. They sometimes barely even make the top 20 percent of their class. It makes you feel pretty worthless. You work your butt off, and yet there will always be a bunch of people who are much better than you are. I'm talking about people that are taking multivariable calculus as freshmen. People who got 2350s (or higher) on the SAT in sixth grade. People who went to your middle school and yet somehow now attend a world-class university such as Berkeley or Stanford (at the age of fourteen). People who have founded their own companies (with parental help) at the age of fifteen. There are so many of these people that it's almost become normal.

High school is a living hell for many of us (but I guess that is true for many people anyway). Don't get me wrong: it's awesome that as kids we are pushed to work hard and that we are surrounded by very intelligent people. However, many times it gets to be way too much.

Also, growing up here gives you a relatively naive view of the world. We live in a very rich and privileged area. We have no idea what the real world is like. I wasn't even going to mention it because it seemed so normal to me, but the reality is, most people do not have the newest iPhones and iPads. Most people don't own MacBook Pros or have their own Google Glass. It's not normal for your high school's parking lot to be filled with cars that cost over $30,000.

There is a huge divide between the wealthy and the working class, and the area is extremely expensive. Our teachers can't even afford to live in the area. Some of them drive over two hours every morning just to get to school. There are also a lot of kids that live in East Palo Alto who attend Palo Alto High School. Their lives are drastically different from ours. There is a huge divide between the kids living in East Palo Alto and the kids living in Palo Alto. Although people are generally accepting, there is definitely this idea of them not being "as good" as us. If your parent isn't an engineer, a doctor, or a lawyer, then people generally look down on you. It may not be evident in our actions, but it's definitely what the people around here think.

Another downside is that we barely value anything other than STEM (science, technology, engineering, and math) classes. Most people that I go to school with think that English and history are a joke. Math and science are ALWAYS the classes that people place emphasis on. A large number of my friends' parents let them (and tell them) to skip these classes in order to study for their math and science classes. This is even worse for the arts. The kids and parents here barely care about the arts.

We have been raised to value careers in STEM, and so we barely hold any value for other career options.

As a parent, I would most definitely want my child to grow up in an environment like this! But as a student, I'm not so sure. [4]

Anonymous

It is well known in the high schools here in Silicon Valley that behind the college prep stuff is a system of deceit. Phony clubs exist on campus for the sole purpose of stuffing college resumes. The only reason many clubs exist is so you can write down that you were president of the Whatever Club. That's what they want to see on the resume, so you put it down. Then there is the phony volunteering. They want that too. So you write that down. Do they really think we have the time to take all those AP courses, go to club meetings, and volunteer at the old folks' home? Supposedly, they want us to become good, socially responsible citizens, but they're making us into something else. [5]

***

While writing this book I had the privilege of talking to some young community college students. Here is a little of what they had to say.

Anonymous

What was it like growing up here? Growing up in a Latino family there was a lot of gender bias. My brothers can stay out late; I can't. They can do a lot of things I'm not allowed to do.

My mom is pretty strict with me because she doesn't want me to make some of the mistakes she made. My dad's not around, which is good. He is an alcoholic and into drugs.

I know my mom wants the best for me, but it's hard sometimes. Not so much now, but it was when I was in high school. I wasn't allowed to have my own phone until I was sixteen. Even then, use was restricted and she took it away at night.

When I was in junior high and high school she kept me very busy with activities. I think my mom kept me busy so I wouldn't think about my dad not being there. I guess it worked.

Ain Phan

I'm a Vietnamese-American, so growing up was go to school, come home, do homework—that's it. Same thing for summer vacation—if you don't have homework, we'll give you some. That's the whole summer. Some Vietnamese families are like this and some aren't.

I went to Andrew Hill High School. My sister goes to another high school and her experience is completely different. Different teachers have different ways of presenting the lessons. For her it was a completely different approach for all subjects, so I wasn't able to help much.

What do I want to do? I'm not sure. I thought about having a coffee shop. Then I started taking business classes. Now I'm thinking linguistics. I really enjoyed French in high school and recently took Japanese. So maybe something along those lines.

My major wasn't what my parents wanted it to be. They would have preferred I go to UC.

During high school there was a lot of parental pressure; now not so much. I came to San Jose City College so it would be less pressure on my dad. He works in a small tofu shop. My mom is a stay-at-home mom and works hard to help my sister, who is still in high school.

My biggest challenge? Trying to meet the basic minimum expectations of my parents—what I can do for them. They want my sister and I to get a better future faster.

Immigrant families don't learn as fast as others. My parents came here several years before I was born but they really don't know that many people.

First-generation Vietnamese immigrants think that if they push their children through university we will have a better future—better than they had. When I was younger, I wanted to go to work with my dad but he didn't want me to go. He said it's just hard work.

Vietnamese parents want their kids to stay at home. I have some friends whose parents want them to move out and be independent. My parents? They want us to depend on them until we can achieve that better future that they wanted. For first-generation Vietnamese it's this way.

I have worked some. I worked at a couple of the farmers' markets for a while to sell the produce. [6]

Angelina M.
Academic-wise, De Anza College definitely has everything you need. There is a nursing program, health technology programs, and a ton more to choose from. The counselors are extremely helpful in choosing a course of action to put your educational plans in motion.

On the other hand, you will have an extremely hard time finding parking the first couple weeks of school, so [you need to] show up thirty minutes early for classes, and prepare mentally for a high chance of getting your car dinged/hit/smashed. Unfortunately, I had this happen to me a couple of times, both with no note.

Also, if this is your first quarter attending, don't be surprised if all the classes are full when you try to register. They have the system set up so that returning students have priority and new students get the last pick of classes. So De Anza has its positives and negatives. [7]

***

Here are a few random, but classic, comments I heard from young people while working on this book:

A computer science major: *If I had my way, I'd play computer games all day. But I probably shouldn't do that.*

A first-year student: *I get financial aid, so my classes and everything are paid for. I hope to transfer to San Jose State University in three years—if I can get the classes.*

Another young man of Vietnamese ancestry: *It's study, study, study; work, work, work; and then you die.*

A high school student: *Lynbrook High School is about 86 percent Asian; Saratoga High is about 50 percent.*

During a recent dinnertime conversation with some friends, we were talking about how so many younger employees do not realize they need to produce something and the problems that causes in the workplace. The youngest among us, a college student, commented: *What do you expect the millennials to do? You [parents and teachers] told them they were great; they could do anything they wanted to do. You gave them ribbons and awards when they had done nothing. What did you expect?*

Obviously, parents of Asian and Indian ancestry didn't buy into that approach.

I saw a sign in front of a community college that underscores my young friend's comment. The sign said: "Your success is our commitment." Huh?

Anonymous

My great-grandfather came to San Jose from Mexico in the 1940s. He was a farm worker. All but two of his children were born here. They all worked the crops—the whole family. When the children grew up, they all stayed in San Jose.

Then my grandparents had six children, and when they grew up they all stayed. The same with my parents and uncles and aunts—they had children and most of their kids stayed too. San Jose, east side. A few of us moved away for a while. All but one came back. My brother? He'll come back. There are sixty-eight of us now. We are very close. Family is what is important. That's the way we were taught.

My grandparents bought a house on the east side and are still there. Most of us live close—some of us within walking distance. Except for my older brother, the farthest away that any of us lives is in Hollister. We get together all the time. All the time.

Nobody in my family went into computers or anything like that. One of my uncles is a mechanic and some of my cousins work with him. Two of my uncles are truck drivers and some of my cousins are too. Two of my aunts work in elder care, one of my cousins is a teacher for special needs kids, another is a hair dresser. Things like that. I work as a social worker for the county.

A few [family members] got into drugs, but not many. That's because we are family. We take care of each other. Hispanic culture is different. We stick together. That's it.

Chapter 18

The Fifth Wave: The Software and Web Developers

Software developers, that is, people who design and write the commands for computers to follow, began arriving in Silicon Valley in large numbers with the development of minicomputers. It was the construction of the Internet and the World Wide Web, however, that opened the floodgates to these newcomers.

In the 1850s, wagon trains headed to California, the land of promise, causing horrific traffic jams on all the trails and leaving huge clouds of choking dust in their wake. In the 1990s, a deluge of software engineers, programmers, and related folks hit the Valley, causing horrific traffic jams and leaving huge clouds of choking dust behind them too. The first group settled in California and transformed it into a mining and agricultural powerhouse; the second group is in large part responsible for giving us access to the web.

By 1990, the great majority of the semiconductor plants in Silicon Valley had closed down. This probably had as much to do with the fallout from the poisoning of the groundwater as it did inexpensive labor overseas. From the early 1990s on, for all practical purposes the Valley has been Post-Silicon Valley. Design work on the integrated circuits remained, and experimental and specialty fabrication remained, but the big manufacturing plants were either gone or were on their way out.

The Internet, the global system of local area computer networks, carries the traffic of the web, which is a system of interlinked documents created in what is called hypertext. The two together are similar to a system of roads and the traffic on them, including the postal carriers, who handle electronic mail. A server is like a traffic light that allows travelers to get onto a local area network and access the web.

Like the construction of the Interstate Highway System, the Internet was built mostly by large companies. The web, or the vehicles on the information superhighway, were for the most part developed by thousands of smaller companies and by millions of individuals.

Software programs, that is, computer instructions, are built using what is called binary code, which as its name implies, uses two digits, 0 and 1. These 1's and 0's correspond to the commands "on" and "off"; and when fed into a computer, they turn transistors on or off and enable that "data" to (hopefully) communicate something.

Of course, to write everything out in 1's and 0's would be time prohibitive, so clusters of 1's and 0's are bundled together. Link enough large clusters of this kind of data together in a particular format so they interact, and you have what is called a programming language. The programming language, then, will translate what is written into the 1's and 0's that a computer can deal with.

I hope all you tech people will forgive the simplicity of the above. It is meant to communicate ideas, not to be precise in every detail.

The nature of coding, or writing computer code, is unforgiving. That is because computers are in fact as dumb as a load of asphalt. A single programming error will cause a wrong gate (transistor) to open (or close) and that causes problems. Sometimes very big problems. As one programmer so eloquently put it: "If you write bad code, you are going to cause a lot of people a lot of pain."

I used the term *programmer* above as it is often used, in a broad sense. There are software designers or architects, software engineers, and there are programmers. I think the terms are somewhat self-explanatory, it's just that the term *programmer* is frequently used not only to refer to someone who writes code, but also to a software engineer or even to someone who designs software. Software is a very big field with enormous variations in complexity, but to the outsider all these folks are commonly lumped into the term *programmers*, or sometimes into the less flattering "you know, those guys."

OK, a couple more terms and general histories and we can go on to our oral history.

A web browser is a computer program that allows you to see websites, not as a bunch of lines of code, which is the way they are written, but as an intelligible page, as you see it. A search engine is a website that allows you to (hopefully) find other websites based upon information you supply. Without these two, the web would still be confined to the Department of Defense (where it got started) and to academia (where it was further developed) because nearly no one would be able to readily access the information they wanted.

As with most products that Silicon Valley is known for, the first good web browser was not a local creation. The Valley has been, and remains, more of a development center than it is a research center. That is not to put down the research that has been done here. It is just to say that the Valley's ability to develop products that are put into widespread use far outshines its greatness as a research center.

Mosaic was the first really good web browser. It was developed at the federally funded National Center for Supercomputing Applications at the University of Illinois, Urbana-Champaign, beginning in 1992. Mosaic opened up the web and clearly established that it was destined to be used by millions of people.

The obvious next step was commercialization. Marc Lowell Andreessen, coauthor of Mosaic, and several others on the Mosaic team joined up with James H. Clark, the founder of fabulously successful Silicon Graphics. The result was Netscape and the Netscape Navigator, the browser that put the web into the hands of anyone who wanted to access it. Wisely, Netscape management intentionally did not use any code in Navigator that was used by Mosaic.

That brings us to the story of search, or search engines, which is in large part a local story, emanating from Stanford University.

In the early days, way back in the early 1990s, if you were working at the Department of Defense or on campus and wanted to access a particular document on the web, you had to know its precise address, or uniform resource identifier, better known as a URL. That limited access to the web because you frequently could not find what you wanted because you lost the slip of paper with the URL on it, or you could not read the handwriting of the librarian who wrote it down for you, or you wrote it down incorrectly, or someone electronically moved the document you were looking for. So people started writing and publishing directories and putting them on a compact disc (CD). The problem with these directories was that as soon as they were published and distributed they were obsolete. The web was developing and growing too fast. Commonly you would look up a URL and it would be gone. At the same time, more pertinent websites were being added.

In early 1995, a couple of Stanford graduate students decided to take their directory, "Jerry and David's Guide to the World Wide Web," and make a serious business out of it. They renamed it Yahoo and built it into a multimedia company. By 1998, Yahoo was probably the most popular starting point for web users. You could search for websites or content on Yahoo, but to the user it was obvious Yahoo was programmed to lead you where Yahoo wanted you to go, not necessarily where you wanted to go.

Yahoo had a tremendous head start, but so far as search is concerned, it behaved like a new, old company. They were making money—a rare thing for computer-related companies at that time—and could not see the need to develop search for its own sake.

Search, or programs designed for searching the web, started out with the simple ability to identify key words. That method worked (although somewhat poorly) while the web was in its infancy. As the web grew, that method became useless because no one wanted to scan 2,391 search results for "codling moth" or whatever it was that they wanted information about.

The first really good search engine was probably Alta Vista, the brainchild of a Stanford PhD named Paul Flaherty and a Frenchman named Louis Monier, both of whom worked as research engineers at Digital Equipment Corporation's Western Research Lab in Palo Alto. They proposed building a search engine that could load all Internet content onto DEC's new Alpha computer. At the time, such a thing was unheard of. That was the birth of Alta Vista. It was launched in December 1995 and was quickly recognized as the most efficient way to search the web. But DEC management did not see the value in search. They thought that what Flaherty and Monier had done was simply a nice way to showcase its Alpha computer, and they starved the project out of existence. In the meantime, many people got a taste of being able to research something using the web.

As the web grew, Alta Vista didn't and it fell by the wayside. Increasingly it could no longer get pertinent results. Into the void jumped Lycos, Excite, and many others of lesser notoriety.

Excite was started by a bunch of Stanford students who got a little venture capital from a Stanford alumnus and formally launched their product in December 1995. The difference between Excite and Alta Vista was that Excite had financial backers who believed in what they were creating. To get ahead of the pack, the company purchased two popular search engines of the day—Magellan and WebCrawler, in 1997.

A couple of other Stanford undergraduates also wanted to sell their search engine to Excite because maintaining their school research project was taking too much time away from their studies. They asked $1 million for it and were shown the door.

But the two believed in their search engine project and decided to stick with it. They developed the best search engine yet and released it as Google in early 1998. Their approach was quite different from all the others. First, their homepage was uncluttered. On a white background, it said "Google" and gave you a box to enter your search, and that was about it. Second, there were no obnoxious advertisements cluttering successive pages. Simple text-only ads were off to the right and were well marked as advertisements. Third, their methodology of search was advanced.

All search engines of the day used algorithms and "crawlers." An algorithm is a step-by-step process, or set of rules, followed in calculations, data processing, or automated reasoning. An example is the Sort command on an Excel spreadsheet, where, for example, you can sort data first according to column D, second according column C, and third according to column A. In this way a search engine takes data and classifies it (hopefully) to render better search results. A crawler is an automated program that methodically searches web content and sorts it into indexes. These were the means that search engines used before Google.

Google took the art of search further by using an algorithm that counts the number and (perceived) quality of links to a web page to determine roughly how important that website is. The thought behind this method is that a website's importance is related to how many other websites link to it, how many websites link to those websites, and so on. Although similar to a high school popularity contest, and with the same inherent flaws, initially this method led to superior search results, and in very little time, probably by early 2000, Google was well ahead of all other search engines.

The ability to search the web changed just about everything other than human nature. One inherent flaw in the use of search engines, however, is that they are programmed to believe the world began in the mid-1990s. If you need something older than that, and do not have a specific title of a work you want, it is common to have a tough time getting relevant search results. For the most part, general searches will only yield contemporary commentary. Add into the equation that it is easy to change web content and you have a pretty good understanding why there is often an enormous disparity between what is popularly accepted and historical fact. Due to this, and the decreased use of books, there is a lot of history revision going on.

Nevertheless, with the web being developed and much, much more going on here, the Valley became the place to be if you were a software developer.

Anonymous
If you want a job in software engineering, you can work just about anywhere. If you want to have a lot of options, though, or if you want to be immersed in the software culture, you need to be with other people who have the same interests. You need to come to the Valley. The opportunities you are exposed to here are unlike anywhere else. I came from Redmond [Washington] and worked in Austin for a couple of years, too, and they are software hubs, no doubt. But they pale compared to Silicon Valley. [1]

***

With tens of thousands of young engineers pouring into the Valley, stories like the next one were (and are) common.

S.P.
I'm from the Midwest and took computer programming in college. When I got a job offer from a company in Sunnyvale for $80,000, I thought I had hit the jackpot. Then I looked on the web to find out where to live, and all there seemed to be was negativity about how much things cost and how expensive it was in the Valley. I couldn't believe it. I was single at the time, and I knew how to be frugal, and after all I wasn't asking for much—just a nice apartment in a safe neighborhood somewhere in the suburbs with a maximum thirty minute commute.

Live and learn. I was barely making it on the $80k. Everything is expensive here.

***

Yahoo building

Top: Apple offices on Infinite Loop, Cupertino

Bottom: Google headquarters

Here is the story of a young engineer who came to the U.S. from Spain in 1997. She describes the process by which she was able to work here and the makeup of a typical software development team in the Valley.

María García Herrero

I wanted a change from my engineering life, so I enrolled in a summer session at UCLA. I chose two classes: literature and economics. After that, I decided to move in with a family until Christmas in order to perfect my English. Then I took the TOEFL. . . . [i]

I met somebody and decided to look for a job and stay in Los Angeles. The problem was that without a green card, nobody wanted to hire me. Companies sponsor visas for high-tech immigrant workers only if they have expertise in some area, but I was fresh out of college. I successfully passed a number of interviews to finally hear, "Oh, you don't have a green card? Then we can't hire you."

My friend encouraged me to apply for jobs here, thinking that the greater demand of the Silicon Valley offered better chances for new grads to be sponsored. I didn't follow his advice because I wanted to stay by his side, but somehow my resume got in the hands of a Bay Area company, Divicom. They called me for an interview and made me a good offer. After more than four months looking for a job, I couldn't say no. I worked for them for two years before joining Monterey Design Systems. . . .

Monterey was a Silicon Valley EDA company with approximately a hundred employees. EDA stands for electronic design automation, a set of processes defined by algorithms that automate integrated circuit design. Its customers are semiconductor companies that design chips and need software tools to do it efficiently. . . .

I was really excited to have been assigned to one of the two native speakers of the group. I liked each member genuinely, but I had a hard time understanding some of the accents of my other colleagues. So, as lame as my rationale was, I was pleased not to have language as an extra barrier. I would meet enough challenge in the routing arena. . . .

Five p.m. on Friday was time to socialize. Monterey provided food and beverages to its employees for their weekly happy hour. We gathered in the lounge, a central space that separated the front of the building,

---

[i] Test of English as a Foreign Language

where the upper management offices were, from the remaining cubicle-populated work space. The lounge had a few tables for those who wanted to socialize at lunchtime. Moreover, it had two important assets for our group: a pool table and a Ping-Pong table. At happy hour Archie, Tong, and Sam played pool, while Shankar and Nanto played Ping-Pong.

Over time, Friday evenings proved to be a great occasion to meet people from other groups, but in the early days, I focused on getting to know those in my group. Everyone was young, twenties or early thirties. I learned that Brendan spoke Spanish and that he had been in Salamanca (Spain) taking language classes. His father was of Cuban descent. Only he and Archie could properly say my name. Hua was Chinese and married. Nanto was Indonesian and single. Shankar was Indian and still single, but his family was working hard on arranging his marriage. Sam was Korean and in the process of celebrating his wedding for a second and third time, to please the many relatives both his and his wife's family had in different parts of the world. Archie's parents were both Chinese, but his maternal great-grandfather was Austrian and his paternal great-great-grandmother was Dutch. [2]

***

The development of the Internet and the web was not carried out only by the young. Many people who had been in industry for years caught the bug and joined the effort, bringing with them technical expertise in a wide variety of fields. Through their efforts, the huge infrastructure on which web content is carried was put into place. Dial-up connections on telephone lines, which were sufficient when few people were using the Internet, increasingly got bogged down. They were replaced with far more sophisticated systems using coaxial and fiber optic cabling, complete with all the switching, relay stations, and satellites.

Doug McNeil

Up until 1990 I was working for the DOD. Then, all of a sudden, the Soviet Union fell and all of our (Lockheed's) contracts came to a close. My boss told me, "We're sort of shifting gears, but there's something exciting going on at Motorola," and told me about the Iridium system of satellites. He said, "Doug, the world is all about communication." I could see the company making a quantum shift—getting into commercial applications.

From 1990 to 1999, we were focused on building next-generation commercial wireless communications, optical remote sensing, and direct broadcast satellites for a variety of customers.

In 1999, after twenty years in aerospace, and with the dot-com bloom at its peak, I was curious how I could reinvent myself and retool my skills for launching high-volume commercial products. All this commercial experience opened my eyes to expanded opportunities to leverage my skills in developing cutting-edge technologies in wireless computing, optical communication systems, material discovery, smart sensors, homeland security, and home automation design products.

My first experience working in the greater Silicon Valley (outside of Lockheed) was working for Cisco Systems in the Wireless LAN (local area networks) products division. It was a great transition for me. In five years, this division would grow from a $15 million per year revenue run rate to $1 billion. After taking part in helping to successfully launch the 802.11 enterprise wireless system at Cisco, I joined a team of former Lockheed engineers to help package and product-ize smart sensor technology. This would be my experience on a road less traveled for a former aerospace engineer and my first true start-up. We founded a small company of seven people and were given a budget for one year to prove that our technology was ready for commercialization. We were successful in proving our technology was ready for the marketplace but lacked the funding to get the product certified for the OEM market, which would take two to three years for market adoption. [i] With lack of funding, we dissolved the company, sold the patents, and repaid debts. This product later won the innovation of the year award via John Deer Tractor Company.

Next, I joined a company that was developing optical wireless communications and advanced biometrics. [ii] Over the next five years, we developed, tested, and started commercializing products for both homeland security, military, and commercial applications. When [U.S. government budget] sequestration started, we were forced to cancel

---

[i] OEM refers to original equipment manufacturer, a company that makes parts or subsystems for another company's end product.
[ii] Biometrics is the application of statistical analysis to biological data. Different forms are used to verify identification. Older methods include finger and palm printing; newer methods include iris recognition, voice recognition, face recognition, DNA, and even typing rhythm.

these critical projects. It was a classic example of great technology with market timing and funding out of sync.

With no promise of job security, financial security, or fame, technologists simply engage in the creative process of developing the next new technology. Hope and faith are part of this process, which, at the core for some of us, is the underlying desire to make the world a better place than we found it.

I have had several discussions with fellow engineers regarding "how did we get here?" Most of us seek the challenge to do new things, create, and explore ways of doing things. Product development cycles are becoming increasingly shorter and faster, and none of us are comfortable being spectators in the process. Later in one's career, the opportunity to imagine and create better futures for others becomes a chance to help the next generation of engineers navigate new pathways to the future. [3]

***

The mingling of experienced professionals with young, inexperienced people, who have received their formal education in a new technology and are eager to put it into practice, inevitably brings about conflict, as the next story describes so vividly.

Stan Hanks

I was in grad school and working on the side for a company that had a mature software product that they decided needed to be ported to UNIX, to 4BSD in particular. They needed some people who knew the ins and outs of getting commercial and OEM UNIX licenses, buying and setting up VAX computers, writing device drivers, figuring out how to setup "binary distribution builds" and teaching programmers how to code in a different paradigm. I'd done all of that. It was just my kind of gig.

I worked for them for almost a year and really liked the VP who brought me in. However, he had a counterpart in the California office who was a real ___. Anyway, this guy was a first-class idiot when it came to technology. I wasn't terribly shy about pointing out everything that was wrong with pretty much everything he said, with the support and encouragement of most of the rest of the tech team.

One day, I show up, and my key doesn't open my office door. I head to the front, get security to let me in. Two guys come back with me, one opens the door, the other walks around the corner, comes back with a box. "Put all your stuff in here. You don't work here anymore."

What? Um. . . OK. I do so, and go to leave the building, figuring I'd better get out before I start breaking [stuff]. On my way out, the guy from California stops me. He says, "Oh, there was a management change. I'm the new CEO, but I guess you found out about that already."

I was dumbfounded. I went and hung out at a library for the rest of the day, then went home at the usual time, just before my wife went to work. She asked how my day was. I mumbled something nondescript and said I was going to school. She left, and I collapsed.

I was mortified. I was the hotshot, the bright and burning star, the "I can fix that in N-1 lines of code" guy. I'd excelled at everything I'd ever done since grade school. Me? Fired? Noooooo!

I didn't tell anyone. I went to classes, symposia, study groups, and worked on various projects in the lab. I hung out with the other grad students, taught my classes, all that jazz. But the time I was supposed to be "at work"? I lied. I hid. I did things to distract myself from how horrible and worthless I felt. Some of those weren't very helpful to an already struggling marriage. Most I couldn't really afford—my graduate stipend covered all the base living expenses, my wife's salary covered a lot of the extras, but my outside income covered all the really expensive stuff, and with that gone, everything ate into savings, fast.

Eventually, like about eight months later, I ran out of money. From that, my wife figured out I'd been lying—about a lot of things—and we separated for a while. I took a year off from school, got a great job with a boss who proved to be my first real mentor.

And I eventually realized that I'd done it to myself. If I hadn't treated that guy with such contempt, none of this would have happened. He clearly had something going for him, something that I didn't see or didn't value, or he wouldn't have become CEO.

It was a huge lesson for me. About not saying the thing that's first to come to mind. About getting to know someone instead of rejecting them out of hand. About how no matter how good you are or how critical the work you are doing, you are not indispensable.

Getting fired changed my trajectory completely. The year off from grad school made me reevaluate what I was doing and why. The separation made me think hard about what I wanted from a relationship and realize that I didn't have it. And the whole thing crushed my sense of invulnerability.

It made me who I am today. Painful and ugly as it was, I wouldn't take it away. [4]

***

The software industry is dominated by young single men who know they are vulnerable.

Anonymous
You have to be constantly updating your skillset in your spare time, and you have very little of that. The problem is you don't really know what [programming] language you should learn next. Should you learn C++ or Java? What about Python? Regardless of what you are working on now, you know that within a short time your skills could be obsolete. Everyone knows that and carries it around with them. That is at least part of the reason why, as a group, we tend to be defensive, opinionated, and sharp in speech.

***

That may have something to do with why, in 2012, fewer than one in five computer science undergraduates were women.[5] That's not because they aren't smart—over half of newly minted medical doctors and attorneys are women.

Businesses are also aware of an imbalance in a lot of their software and are trying to do something about it. *Wikipedia* recently admitted that 80 percent of its users are male. That is better than the ratio of men to women in the software business, but. . .

Dennis Hayes tells of another common characteristic among software developers.
The computer professional's relationship to work approaches a compulsive masochism of the athlete in training—pain and the lonely allure of an endorphin high. [6]

***

Many programmers speak of that endorphin high but also add that when things go wrong they can be in a foul mood for days. I suppose that's true of any job, but there is a feeling of total absorption and an addictive sense of control that are somewhat endemic among programmers.

Anonymous

The Valley is a mecca for workaholics. People come here from everywhere for the same reason I came—to get rich. Of course that's just a dream, but we believe it, and, besides, most of us are young and single and we're willing to work around the clock, at least for a while.

We know the odds are against us but we do it anyway. We're chasing the big bucks and you can't do that passively. There are plenty of companies that are glad to hire people like us, and when we burn out there is an endless stream of new blood to offer all the same perks to.

The perks are there for a reason. The free meals and snacks, the workout room with showers, the sleeping pods, the laundry service— are there so you can keep working. (By the way, daycare is usually not one of the perks. Children aren't so conducive to what's going on in a start-up.)

The work-life balance is just not much of a priority. People talk about a work-life balance, but I haven't seen much of it in my seven years in the Valley. People do not come here to take it easy.

There have been plenty of cases here where people have been in the right place at the right time and have gotten fabulously wealthy, but that is not the typical case. So you decide how long you want to play the game.

Anonymous

The perks and benefits that the companies offer are an illusion. They exist for one purpose: to keep you at work. The culture here is that you work long days and weekends too. That's the way it is. If you want to work here, that's what you do.

On the positive side, the work is interesting and super challenging, and you work with some very smart people. You also hope that what you are doing will have a positive impact on the society, although I believe that less now than I used to. When I first got here, I was all charged up, thinking I was part of changing the world and all that. We are changing the world, but not all the change has been for the good. Some of it has been, though, and I try to choose my assignments accordingly.

The weather is great here, not humid like the East Coast, where I'm from. It's sunshine most days and seldom hot or cold. People from California don't know what cold is.

***

One cannot tell even a little part of the story of software development without saying something about the independent contractor. Before the tech explosion, we rarely heard the term *independent contractor*.

As a former employer, I can tell you straight up that no one wants to hire an employee unless he or she absolutely has to. Talk about a ball and chain! And I have had some of the best employees anyone could want.

What growing businesses need is help, and hiring an employee is usually the most expensive way to get it. When you hire someone, you marry them, and maybe you're not ready for that kind of commitment. Enter the independent contractor. If you can get them through an employment agency, you do that. That is a layer of insulation between you and an expensive divorce settlement or long years of paying alimony.

Employers have to deal with a set of employment laws, proposed and passed by lawmakers who like their jobs and want to keep them, and a way out of those laws so businesses can survive. This is a dance that has been going on for decades.

Silicon Valley has been somewhat a capital for the temporary worker since the days of the semiconductor plants. Actually, it has been no different from when the local farmers hired seasonal workers to get their crops in. Both kinds of businesses need a much larger number of workers at certain times than they can possibly maintain all the time. When you have two hundred tons of ripe apricots in your orchard, you had better get them in. When you are developing a hot tech product, you had better get it out. This is hard to swallow for those who think in terms of "jobs" and not "work."

Maybe it would be nice if we could go back to the days of paternal organizations, like HP and IBM were several decades ago, but that is not how the Valley came to be the economic powerhouse it is. For better and for worse, the gears spin fast here—too fast for that kind of thinking. As one so eloquently put it, "You can't come out here expecting to make a killing and have job security too."

Anonymous

I was a contract worker for Google for years. Like many of the other companies, Google does not hire all their people directly. They hire a lot of contractors. Some are individuals; others are companies that supply many workers. Contractors do the same work, but the employment status is different. Many people go to work as contractors hoping to be noticed by Google and then be hired directly. From what I saw, that almost never happens.

For me, the breaking point came when I found out they had other teams working on the same project my team was working on. We had no knowledge of each other. There was a redundancy built in. At a certain point, my group had no tools and no direction. We were still there, but it's like we got unplugged. In essence, we had nothing and could get nothing done. Although the pay was good, after a short time that alone could not override the feeling of uselessness, so I quit. I wasn't moving back to Indiana, so I got over it and got another job here in the Valley, which isn't hard to do.

***

Many have asked, "Why don't more software developers work remotely?" The thinking is, if they're mostly writing code, why do they have to drive in to work every day—especially since the Valley is so crowded and the traffic is so bad? I'll let a veteran answer that.

Greg Kemnitz

Engineers in a nontrivial software development group are discussing coding and engineering approaches, finding and fixing each other's bugs, meeting with product managers and customers to figure out requirements, working with test groups, operations groups, and other groups who are affected by the software. Oh, and they're also sometimes socializing and having a good time.

Trying to do all this stuff remotely has several effects, most of which engineers find unpleasant. For one, everything is done through e-mail, docs, or formal meetings. Impromptu hallway conversations, which is where a whole lot of engineering gets done, don't happen.

Specs have to be written to excruciating levels of detail. Some people of a more bureaucratic mind-set regard this as a good thing, but most engineers hate it; after all, they want to code, not get into tedious arguments about the exact phrasing of something in a spec over e-mail [late] at night.

[Then] everything takes longer. Find a bug that the guy next to you just checked in, and you just show it to him and he fixes it in five minutes. Find the same bug in the code that someone in Malaysia checked in, and you get several back-and-forth e-mails over the course of a couple of days to accomplish the same thing. And both you and the guy in Malaysia spent several hours composing the e-mails. And you don't know these people. All your interactions focus on tedious e-mails, irritating spec lawyering, and strange accents on conference calls at odd hours of the day. You don't get to have lunch with them, learn about their families, know what ball teams they root for, hear about their difficulties with their kids/boyfriends/in-laws, or all the other little things that make people human. So ultimately you end up with a much less cohesive engineering team, which will have a much harder time getting stuff accomplished, particularly if things become difficult. [7]

Unknown
Software development is very complex. You're never finished with it, and if you don't get it out in time, it can be useless, so you're under a time crunch. Sometimes the team you're working with is very tight, sometimes it's not. That's when you have a real problem. If it's bad enough, it's time to bail. Anyway, you're under pressure all the time. The approach is: "Build it, hype it, release it, and fix it when the bugs come out." [8]

***

The fact is, software projects are never really done. There are always loose ends. That is why you need support. A case in point is computer-aided design, or computer-assisted drafting, better known as CAD.

T.S.
CAD came into widespread use during the 1980s with AutoCAD. By the early 1990s, several small software companies had come out with house design software, and, being a builder, I looked at several of these products at trade shows. AutoCAD did not come to the shows, even though there were about ten thousand attendees, mostly builders, in attendance. I suppose the makers of AutoCAD understood that their product was ill-suited for one-of-a-kind home design. It was also very expensive, and the learning curve was such that people who used it tended to be those who used it all day, every day.

In about 1992, after I had seen a couple of demos of a particular program, I decided to take the plunge and purchased a license agreement to use a Canadian company's product. Since I was pretty good at understanding my clients' needs and visualizing what would please them, I had been hiring draftsmen to work from my sketches. They did a good job, but by the time revisions were made, too much time had elapsed. The fact is, my clients lived in the fast lane, and when they wanted something they wanted it now or they would lose interest. Consequently, I lost a lot of projects because I could not move fast enough.

Since I usually had the designs in my mind, I figured, "I've learned how to build spreadsheets and do word processing; I understand drafting and design—how tough could this be?" Well, I put a lot of time into learning how to use that program and after about two years gave up on it.

By that time a new kind of program had come out that dealt with objects that contain data and attributes instead of just lines and shapes. Instead of drawing lines to represent a house foundation, for example, you draw that foundation and in that foundation are the components you select for it. The technology is called object orientation, and I thought it looked very promising.

So I decided to try an object-oriented program. The software I invested in was developed by a Stanford graduate who started his company in Morgan Hill, and of course I thought it was the best of the lot.

After spending a few hundred hours on it, it became apparent that the program was not going to do the job. Ah, but I only had Version 3, and the company was coming out with Version 4! By that time I had spent a lot of time on the phone with their leading support engineer (the only one on the support staff who was truly knowledgeable), and he assured me that the new version would address the problems I had encountered. He also asked if I would like to be part of the "beta team" for Version 4. In other words, I would participate in testing the new product before it was released. He would send me a copy of the program free of charge, and I would use it and report any problems I had with it. I agreed.

The next release was indeed much improved over the previous version, but it still fell considerably short of being able to produce a professional set of plans. Eventually, the lead support engineer told me the truth of the matter: I could take my plans only so far and then would need to finish them by hand.

Later I purchased Version 7, which was a big improvement but still left a lot to be desired. The impressive (and deceiving) thing was that you could get 90 percent of your drawings done very quickly. That's where the fun stopped. The next 5 percent you had to accomplish with work-arounds, many of which were hard fought and painfully slow. The last 5 percent you just were not going to get, or it would take so long that I opted to draw those things in by hand, which required taking the electronic file to the blueprinter, then adding the necessary information, then taking the corrected drawings back to the blueprinter. For most projects, this process had to be repeated at least twice because my client typically made some changes and the city plan checkers also wanted additional detail or revisions.

I took my study of the program so far that I wrote a 96-page quick reference guide for it, put it in booklet format, and sold it on the web. Actually, it was something I needed to refer to when drawing my plans and I shared it with others. (Don't ever believe the line: "It's intuitive.") The guide was valuable to some users because it showed the necessary sequences (which if you did not follow, you would go in endless circles), provided work-arounds, and discussed the limitations of the program, none of which were in the manual and most of which tech support was unable to address. That was in 1996. So, yes, I suppose one could say I started a dot-com. [i] *And, yes, I lost money on it. Nevertheless, I was helped and so were some other people.*

After Version 7, it was apparent that the software developer was going in the direction of renderings and exterior landscaping and such, and was not going to improve the program to meet the needs of someone who needed to get working drawings through a building department. I suppose the money was in the glitz.

My experience with the program was not entirely a fun process, and few things in life have frustrated me as much. I was embarrassed of the way some of my plans looked. While parts were very good, overall they were not up to my standard. Granted, I am a stickler for quality, but that is what my clients demanded, my name was on those plans, and I hate making excuses.

At the trade shows where the software was demonstrated, you could always tell the newbies. They were so excited and bubbly, "Oh, I've got

---

[i] This is a joke. But you would be amazed what some people in the Valley call a start-up.

my plans almost done. I'll have the rest of it in no time!" Those of us with more experience just smiled, looked at each other, and shook our heads.

I tell the story for several reasons. First, because mine was, and is, a common experience with work-related software. Second, to balance the spreadsheet story I told you in chapter 14. Third, to show that some programs are far more complex than others. Fourth, to make the point that if you actually need to produce something with a software program, you are not going to learn it adequately by yourself. There are always too many nuances. You must be around or associated with other people using the same product. Fifth, to say that there are a lot of people working for nothing who are trying to get their work done and are greatly frustrated by having to work around somebody's shoddy software. And, last, to make the point that there is no money made fixing software, which is why so many bugs and seemingly stupid features remain in successive releases.

All things being the same, would I do it again? Well. . . probably so. (Grumble, grumble.)

***

Multiply the last story by several thousand and you see why Silicon Valley works. To develop software, it is highly advantageous to be in a software environment where networking occurs spontaneously and immediately.

However advantageous that may be, there is something even more important.

Unknown
I've been in software development in the Valley for over thirty years and have worked for several companies. Regardless of the company's prestige, it is the manager you work for who will make your work life pleasant or miserable. One more thing: everyone around here is smart or at least thinks they are, but for all but the truly brilliant, that only goes so far. Engineers who have people skills have greater value. After all, software is about communication. You would be amazed how often that is forgotten during the development of a product.

***

The reach of software has already extended into almost every industry and has radically changed many. It seems the only things that are not governed by software now are toothpaste and toilet paper. (Oh, no! Now they'll go to work on them!)

The changes in society have been enormous and will continue to be. Although I am an advocate of work as opposed to jobs, I am only stating the obvious when I say that software is a job killer. While the software industry offers high wages for some people (at least for a while), at the same time it moves a much larger number of people out of the middle class and into the ranks of those earning a minimum wage. The formula is simple: software developers are paid high wages because software replaces countless workers at *every* skill level.

Here is a story from a technical writer who makes several points.

Cousette Copeland
Technical writing was once regarded as a unique profession, allowing those of us with humanities degrees to participate in Silicon Valley's high-tech market and make a living instead of working as a sales clerk. However, now I often joke that the technical writer is one of the lowest positions in the high tech company. I think that there may be a tie between the janitor and the tech writer, with the janitor being more necessary for day-to-day functions. I do say, "Without the technical writer, all the R&D and marketing hype is not enough to make thousands of products able to comply with government requirements or to satisfy user needs." I'm not sure if anyone believes that anymore. . . .

As a technical writer, I am not just a wordsmith. I must be a user advocate, understanding what the end-user needs to know, as well as function as a technology expert, assisting R&D in resolving "bugs." I interact and communicate with personnel from the highest levels to the lowest. I have to ignore the quirks of engineers who are borderline autistic (as they clip their toenails in their cubicles, forget to bathe, and steal salt and pepper shakers from the cafeteria). . . .

In 2004, I was working at hpshopping.com. The project that we contractors were working on was to develop a knowledge base and training materials for all functions, which were being outsourced to India. When one of the writers walked off the job on the third day, I told the recruiter what to look for in a writer. Based on our conversation, he asked if I would take over the interviews and select someone to work on our team. . . .

During those interviews, I found the perfect candidate. Her name was Rekha Raman. She was the most qualified, had the best writing samples, and spoke in such a manner that I knew she would be successful in gathering information from difficult engineers who knew that they would soon be losing their jobs. [9]

***

According to *Bloomberg Businessweek*, in 2015 there were eleven million professional software developers worldwide and another seven million hobbyists. They were programming everything from Microsoft Windows to how to change channels on your TV, from mobile applications to databases, from hearing aids to financial market programs, from controllers that turn on your sprinklers to those that turn the lights off after you leave a room, from medical devices to automotive controls. [10]

That last one is interesting because just about any command you give your car goes through software. You punch the accelerator, and your car says, "I beg your pardon, sir, but that is not in accordance with fuel efficiency standards, therefore, you are wrong and I am right, and we will accelerate gradually." You slam on the brakes and your car says, "You want to stop; that will be fine, but I will control how long the pedal pressure is maintained." You push the button to roll down your window, and software takes over and says, "You want your window down; so be it!" "But I only wanted it down a little," you protest. "No. You are wrong. You pushed the button; it is not my fault that you do not want your window down." You put a couple of heavy bags of groceries on the front passenger seat, then walk around the car, get in, and turn the key. "Oh, no, you don't, you lawbreaker! Fasten that seatbelt so your child is not hurt!" "But I don't have a child," you complain. "Don't argue with me! I'm here to protect you, you dunce!" And on and on it goes. No doubt we will be better off when we are taken out of the equation entirely and are only allowed to have cars that drive themselves. Ah, bliss! A perfect world!

The software revolution has invaded our homes as well. At the end of my contracting days, we were required to put motion sensor light switches in the bathrooms we remodeled. So my client is taking a shower late one night, and the light goes out on him, and it's pitch black in there. The electrician made a trip out to change the program setting because, of course, most people cannot do that. When our old washing machine conked out, we bought a new one—the simplest we could find. After washing a couple of loads, we realized that when we selected "hot," there was no hot water. Turns out the energy police had gotten into that too. We not only cannot be trusted to turn the bathroom light out, we also need to be told that we don't need hot water to wash our clothes. When I took the washer back, I found out that (at least at the time) you couldn't buy a home washing machine that gives hot water, because that is governed by software that someone decreed should have only the options of cold and lukewarm. The electrical company also installed a "smart" meter on our house (we had no choice). Since then they have been sending us notices that we can sign up for an *optional* special savings program that allows the company to shut off our air-conditioner when there is a "flex" energy alert. That is psycho-babble for "when you'll need it the most." Water heaters now cost $700 instead of $300. Software. Is there any reason to believe that this kind of intrusion into the way we live is going to stop?

A professional class has emerged whose work is increasingly shaping our daily lives. Many of these folks have strong opinions about how our society (we) should function, and the heavyweights among them have the money to lobby our lawmakers. Therefore, whether it is your car, your home, your medical care, your use of utilities, or anything at your kid's school, more and more when someone enters a command into a computer program somewhere, an edict is set in stone.

While we appreciate the convenience of some software, we must also wade through mountains of personalized, computer-generated mail, e-mail, and automated voice recognition phone calls, which are all now a way of life. We deal with forced "upgrades" to Windows and with the upgrades of other software systems used by the businesses and government agencies we must interact with. Put all this together, and we find that a large portion of our time is eaten up in the process of conforming our lives to someone's software. In this environment it is easy to wonder if there is not an army of people out there working to make our lives impersonal, if not take them over entirely.

It is telling that even some leading experts in the software business have warned us about the use (and misuse) of artificial intelligence.

Elon Musk, Bill Gates, and others came out in mid-2015 warning about the dangers inherent in the development of artificial intelligence. Musk says that AI is inevitable, which is likely true, and why he himself is developing it. The only question is, Who can you possibly trust to control it? We have already seen the beginning of it, as in the examples given here. Can the end be better?

This is the "cloud of dust" I referred to at the beginning of the chapter. I suppose it is in the realm of possibility that we don't really have "a better world through technology," as is so often claimed by those who make their living selling it.

Chapter 19

Blowing Bubbles and Funny Money: 1995-2001

The history of California is one of booms and busts, and the dot-com era in the Valley is as good an example as any of the phenomenon. The boom gathered enormous momentum with the Netscape IPO in 1995. What was unique about this IPO was that it was for a company that had not yet made any money. Typically, businesses are supposed to do that; but suddenly with Netscape that became irrelevant. And since Netscape's stock price maintained an upward trajectory, its business strategy became an accepted business model. You didn't need to make money; you just had to look like you would make lots of money sometime in the future.

The gold rush was on again and in a big way. It was spurred on by this mantra, coined by one of the top local venture capitalists: "The Internet is the largest legal creation of wealth in the history of the planet."

Young engineers and other tech professionals of every stripe flooded the Valley. A common saying at many of the start-ups was, "Everyone here is from somewhere else." They came from every corner of the world, and it was not just money that brought them here, although that was by far the dominant motivator. A religious zeal also motivated many of these newcomers, especially among the recent American and European college graduates. It was a secular religion, but a religion nonetheless. Many people genuinely believed that the Internet was going to solve our social problems and make the world a better place. With unflagging confidence they were amped up to change the world.

Unknown

I never liked being somebody's employee so I have worked as a consultant for several software companies. During the bubble years, a lot of start-ups burned a million dollars or more a month. [i] Everything was outrageously expensive, but nobody cared. Computer science graduates with no experience were offered $100K salaries, and often signing bonuses on top of that. Then the companies spent more to train them. That's why so many consultants like myself were hired. We

---

[i] He is referring to "burn rate," the monthly net loss a company is incurring.

already knew how to code professionally, they didn't, and we could contribute immediately. Also, the new graduates made the transition from what they learned in school to how it applied to the real world by seeing how we approached problems. [1]

J.S.
I had a roommate in college who was a computer science major and was a lot of fun to be with. After he graduated in 1997, he moved to Silicon Valley to work for a start-up in Mountain View. When I checked up on him several months later, he was working virtually all the time. He hardly ever left the office. He was even sleeping under his desk at work. He was hoping his company would have an IPO and he'd get rich along with everybody else. [2]

Unknown
I came from China in 1999 and went to work for Nvidia. It was easy to get a job here then. I had a few choices. The whole area was so starved for engineers. There were just not enough to meet the demand. I had a friend from China who did not understand hardly any English, and even she got a job right away. They didn't care that she didn't know English. She knew engineering and that was enough; they took her.

T.S.
When it became evident that the web was for real, everything changed. I was a residential remodeling contractor and suddenly began getting calls that were totally different. In the late 1980s and early 1990s, people wanted to add fancy master suites to their homes. Others were giving their homes a facelift or having a luxury kitchen put in or doing all those things at the same time. But nothing could prepare me for many of the calls that started coming in during the mid-1990s. A new kind of client emerged. They wanted expanded home-office space and additional workstations, and they wanted them now. They added living space, not for a growing family but for growing in-home businesses.

The homes of these people were war zones. There were no kids, no dogs, nothing extraneous. Computers and cabling were all over the living room, dining room, and everywhere else. And these folks, themselves, were at a fever pitch. How soon can you put on a fourteen-by-twenty foot room and upgrade the electrical panel and air-conditioning? How soon can we get built-ins?

These people hired me because I had an established reputation for keeping a schedule. On these jobs, we were in and out in a month or two, and by the time I went to pick up my final check, the place was buzzing. It was open season. Some of these people were working full time to claim and register domain names. Many, if not most, companies were caught sleeping and not a few paid a king's ransom for their domain names to people like my clients, who had registered them first. Other clients of mine were building web pages. At the time, few people knew how to do this, and there were very few tools.

***

Multiply this story by thousands, and you get a feel for the kind of gold rush that was going on. It was frantic—even more so than a tax accountant's office in early April. The difference was, the tax accountant could file for an extension; these people were in a race where coming in second meant losing money.

Anonymous

I know a fellow who had recently graduated from a prestigious law school when he took a job at a major law firm in Palo Alto. The firm was growing rapidly and had become largely an IPO farm during the bubble. He worked under the tutelage of senior associates and was responsible for certain aspects of some of the deals. He had hardly started work there when he became alarmed. It was apparent to him that the dot-com companies he was working with had all based their company's value on projected advertising revenue, and a good amount of that revenue was coming from other dot-coms. Granted, these companies had a lot of capital, but they were not making money or, if they were, they were not making much. They had investors— knowledgeable investors—behind them, but to his Midwestern mind the whole thing didn't make sense. How did they know the advertising money would come in? He talked to others in the firm privately, but it seemed that no one wanted to admit how shaky the whole business was.

But he was drawing a good salary, had student loans to pay off, and was not the final say on the deal, so he tried to put the concerns out of mind. Then he visited one of the businesses that he was working to position for an IPO. What he saw was extravagance everywhere. In itself that was bad enough, but added to it was an attitude of pretentiousness among the founders that shook him.

He didn't have to worry about it long. Shortly thereafter (that would have been in the spring of 2000, I believe) he was laid off along with several other people in his office. The firm called it a "performance-

based firing," but everyone knew they were really being laid off because the capital markets had dried up and their work had dried up with them. He was consoled by that but was shocked by the suddenness of the events. The whole dot-com thing crashed not long afterward. Within a year or so, we read that more than half of the attorneys at his former firm had been laid off. [3]

***

I should say a little about how all this built up. In the financial world, you have investment bankers, who are trying to make the deals, and you have business analysts, who are supposed to be guarding the reputations of the brokerage houses and of the markets. In the bubble, the two blended together into one big frat party where the golden beer of other peoples' money was flowing. The analysts—if they wanted to stay employed—rubber-stamped whatever they were told to rubber-stamp. That is the essence of what happened; the rest is details.

This kind of manipulation was not new to financial markets. Consider the Dow Jones Industrial Average. In a hypothetical case, if you ask an average sixth-grade class how to make a stock index chart go up from left to right, they will eventually come up with, "You take out the losers and put winners in their place." Have you ever seen a list of the companies that have been taken out of the Dow because they were "no longer representative of our economy"? That is why we keep hearing newscasters say, "The Dow is reaching new heights."

In 2001, the venture capitalist's quote was revised this way: "The Internet is the largest legal creation *and evaporation* of wealth in the history of the planet."

I remember reading someone's inside account of what it was like working at Excite when the bubble burst. The company employed about three thousand people and was seemingly one of the most stable of the new Internet companies. Their search engine was popular, and the company was bringing in revenue from advertising, but it was a house of cards, and it fell suddenly and dramatically like almost all the others. Everyone was laid off, the whole place shut down, and the office furniture and equipment were auctioned off for a pittance because very few buyers had any cash.

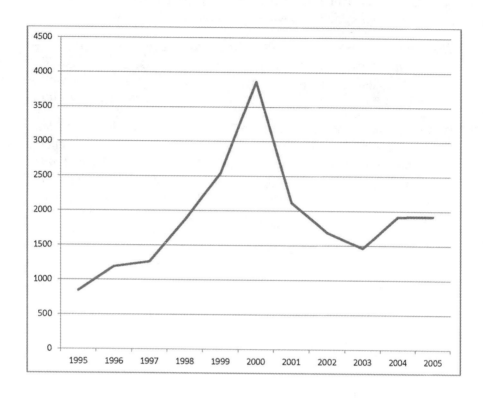

The NASDAQ Composite chart tells the story of the bubble.

Another graph, showing the rise of the number of tech IPOs during the bubble years, is similar to the left side of the above graph. The difference is the right side of the graph. Tech IPOs fell off a cliff in the year 2000—from a high of about 360 in 1999 to about 25 in 2001. [4]

Here are some more stories of the times.

Lawrence Coburn

Oh, man, it was brutal. As a youngish start-up guy, everyone I knew was affected. Most everyone I knew lost their jobs. Soon after, most everyone I knew moved away.

We were [at] the epicenter of the financial collapse. There weren't enough eyeballs on the web to support all of our e-commerce-related businesses, and when we all scrambled to go B2B, the phantom contracts we all signed with each other dissolved into dust. [i]

The contrast between the bubble years was epic. Gone were the open bar events and fabulous launch parties. Gone were the jobs and companies. And soon after, gone were most of the entrepreneurs without a safety net—many back to live with their families to regroup.

When a promised term sheet[ii] didn't arrive, my cofounders and I laid everyone in our start-up off, shut our office on Fourteenth and Valencia, and moved in together to try and keep the boat afloat. I worked for a year without seeing a dime. My monthly budget was $2,100, including rent. Not easy to do in San Francisco. My low point came when [I was] out in North Beach, [and] I thought I had $100 in my checking account but then was denied by the ATM increasingly smaller deductions all the way down to $20. I went home and the next day cashed in my 401k. Then I took a real job for eighteen horrible months and banked enough to go independent again.

Those years left a permanent impression on me. [I'm] not big on excess these days, because you never know what macro conditions are going to lay the hammer down. [5]

Michael Stricklen

On paper, I stood to make a small fortune. My job had stock options attached, and at the time the company's stock was trading at $175. My shares were struck at $125. Fast-forward two years, and the stock is trading at $0.17 (yes, that's 17 cents per share.) I survived five rounds of layoffs before it was my time with the axe man. It was a tough period. I was in my mid-twenties when it happened, and I remember thinking that I'd made a mistake in career choice. For a short period, I worked part time as a ski/snowboard instructor and stayed technically relevant by contributing to open source projects.[iii] Throughout the period of unemployment, I kept tapping my network for opportunities. After a few months, I landed a new job at a start-up. Fortunately, the start-up was a success and we were acquired. This led to a long-term job at a stable, large software company. [6]

---

[i] B2B: business to business. Transactions between businesses, such as between a manufacturer and a wholesaler, or between a software developer and an Internet service provider.

[ii] Term sheet: an investor's list of terms for putting money into a company.

[iii] Open Source software is software code that the copyright holder has made available for users to modify and distribute as they see fit.

Sean Corfield

I moved to America from England in 1999. I'd been doing consulting for a company in England that wanted me to create a software division in the Bay Area. I knew next to nothing about Silicon Valley but liked the idea of living in California (and knew a woman there I was very sweet on). We built software using BroadVision— insanely expensive stuff. They wanted us to take on the "small" projects (less than $1m licenses) because they couldn't really be bothered. It was what we'd been doing for them in England. It was crazy to visit these dot-com companies who'd happily pay half a million to a million dollars for a basic e-commerce website. But it was a fun kind of crazy.

I joined Macromedia in 2000. People were getting stupidly large signing bonuses everywhere (one company was giving new employees BMW 3 Series; I got $20,000 cash). Everyone seemed to have a lot of money to burn.

My stock options (yes, everyone got a ton of those when they joined any company) were granted at $80 and soared to $120 before the crash. They were valued at $5 when the company took them all back from us a few years later and then reissued them after six months at $12. Lots of layoffs. I remember the day that 25 percent of my colleagues in IT were let go. Brutal times.

On the plus side, I kept my job in a much slimmer, more sane company environment. . . . The roads suddenly became much more pleasant to commute on, and the Bay Area became a lot less crowded.

For those who lost their jobs, it was pretty rough, but. . . a lot of folks had moved here for the boom and simply moved back home when it collapsed and went back to their previous lives. For those who stuck it out, it got better in so many ways. Companies started taking hiring seriously and looking out for their bottom line so that they might actually make real profits they could share with employees.

Macromedia weathered the storm pretty well, considering it made web development tools and a lot of its customers disappeared. I stayed with them through the Adobe acquisition because it was a great place to work that steadily grew back up after the crash. I left Adobe in 2007 and have done the start-up thing, the consulting thing, and now the full-time employee thing.

I think the dot-com bubble was a huge anomaly, and life was really better before—and [for] some time after—once things had reset. It felt like a temporary insanity had gripped so many people in the Bay Area, like a mass drug experiment, and once the withdrawal symptoms faded, the Bay Area relaxed and became a really great place to live.

I love the Bay Area. I'm glad I was around to see the boom and bust (and very glad I wasn't really affected by it). It was an interesting life lesson in many ways. [7]

***

This next story is what a Los Gatos Realtor told my wife and me in 2005, just a few years after the bubble burst.

Anonymous
I've been selling real estate in Los Gatos and in the mountains for more than twenty years, so I lived through the bubble. No one who was in the business at the time can forget it, yet it seems more like a dream than something that really happened.

After a slower time in the early 1990s—now, remember, I'm talking about the local market here—there really are no slow times here compared to what the rest of the country experiences. Anyway, the market improved significantly by early 1995. Then it really started to pick up. There were more buyers than sellers and that led to inflated prices. It went on in this way for a while, and we all expected the market to cool off. It didn't. Prices continued to rise. Then the market went berserk. All of a sudden there were all these young people with money—lots of money—and they didn't care what they paid. The bidding wars were ridiculous. Some of the prime properties doubled in value—if you can call it that—I guess you have to; that's the way they were selling. Modest homes increased in value significantly also, although not nearly at the rate of the prime properties. It was funny money. Just funny money.

A lot of these people had no thought whatsoever about it, they just thought it was going to go on like this forever. Then there was the "correction," and you had all these houses in the middle of expensive renovations sitting. Just sitting. Some of the houses were mostly knocked down. No one could live in them. Many of the homes were bought for cash or with a lot of cash down, and the banks had been lending on them as if the prices had something—anything—to do with reality.

The banks ended up with some of these expensive homes and resold them, in some cases at a fraction of what had been paid for them. The modestly priced homes (if you can call anything here modestly priced) weathered the storm pretty well. They took a dip but nothing like the luxury home market did. There was, and still is, a backlog of buyers who are willing to pay dearly to live here.

T.S.

One of our neighbors was in the website design business. When things were booming, his company did very well. When it stopped, his company belly-upped, and he took a couple of years off to travel and afterward looked around for a job. Any job.

Another neighbor—he was a young guy, too—quit his job and became a day trader and worked out of his house. He thought, "With all this money waiting to be made, what am I going to work for?" That was a common sentiment at the time. His wife had "a real job" as an accountant, so that was their security blanket. When the bubble popped, they sold the house and went traveling the world, camping style. I don't know how bad of a hit either of these neighbors took, but it was evident that when the party was over, it was over.

As for me, I was in the middle of a major renovation on the luxury home of an IT fellow—another thirtysomething guy, for whom I had worked previously. Before the bubble began to pop, he was spending money as if he had an endless stream of it, and I am sure it looked to him as if he did. He kept increasing the scope of the project, and I kept writing extra work orders for him to sign that not only increased the cost of the project but also increased the time allotted for construction.

All that came to a dramatic halt one day when he walked on the job and started screaming at me that the bank was going to pull the loan and take the house if we did not have a certain inspection by a certain date. Although I was well within the time frame of the contract, that meant nothing. The deadline the bank set for the inspection was just a few weeks away and to meet it did not seem possible. So what do you do?

Well, the fellow had always been reasonable with me before, and I thought if I could get him out of this jam, I might be able to extract myself from it and still be in one piece. So I did something I had never done before and doubled up the amount of work in progress. There are good reasons never, ever, to do that—work becomes inefficient, accidents are more likely to happen, and quality goes down. But the alternative looked worse.

It was very fortunate that I had a group of subcontractors who had been with me, most of them, for many years. I explained to them what we needed to do and why, and underscored that if we wanted to get paid, we had better just pull it off.

Those guys were champs. They were almost working on top of one another, but they held their mud and got it done. I became a nearly full-time traffic cop and safety engineer on the job site. It all came out well in the end, but it sure could have ended differently.   ***

As the hype over the Internet increased and tech stocks soared, a ridiculous surplus of investment money became available to just about anyone who had anything to do with the Internet. Gold fever was probably never at a higher pitch. And, just as during the California gold rush, when a lot of people put their money into investments based on nothing more than hot air (e.g., Mineral King), so it was with the "Internet stocks" of the late 1990s.

Although there may be several examples of local companies that burned hundreds of millions of dollars very quickly, I'll name just one—a Foster City-based company called Webvan. Webvan delivered groceries to your door and was hatched by the fellow who, in 1971, founded Borders Bookstores. Some high-profile investors, including Goldman Sachs and Sequoia Capital, forked over a total of about $400 million to get things rolling, and the Webvan IPO raised another $375 million in November 1999. According to the Webvan IPO prospectus, the company was then valued at $4.8 billion—on revenue of $395,000 and losses of $50 million. (Huh?)

Not satisfied with those losses, and convinced that the way out was to get bigger fast, in June 2000 the company bought out the Bellevue, Washington-based HomeGrocer in a stock-only deal. HomeGrocer was another grocery home-delivery company backed by high-profile investors. They, too, had a successful IPO, which in their case had netted $288 million.

In less than a year all the money was gone. It seems that the investors did not understand that the profit margin for groceries, about 1 percent, is not like the profit margins commonly associated with tech products, which are often 200 to 300 percent.

The term *dumb money* is commonly used in the brokerage industry. I suppose the story of Webvan is as good an example as any. [8]

There were other factors that contributed to the bursting of the bubble—some closely related, some not. I will mention two. In 1996, with all the hype of quick money being made, California began to "modify" controls on its energy market. Translation: A company no longer needed to own any infrastructure, like transmission lines or power plants—those were things of the old economy. No, you could have a "technology company" that was more efficient and could sell electricity on the open market. In other words, you could have a (paperless) paper company and sell electricity that you did not produce, did not convey, and did not do anything with besides speculate on its future price. Not surprisingly, energy prices soared. The next thing we knew, we were having rolling blackouts in the Bay Area. This began in June 2000, and for the first time in memory, availability of electricity—which had always been taken for granted—was now questionable. As a result, hospitals and many other businesses invested in large diesel-burning generators.

The California electricity crisis of 2000 and 2001 was a wakeup call. Then 9/11 happened. By that time, most of the local Internet-based companies were already long gone. Few of those still standing were able to take that hit too. Even the large, established companies took a hit. Cisco, maker of routers, which had plans for a twenty-five thousand-person mega-campus in Coyote Canyon, scrapped those plans and hung on through some very tough years. Sun Microsystems, which in 1997 had built a large campus on the grounds of the old Agnews State Hospital in north San Jose, barely survived after selling prized assets. Even IBM had to take Hitachi on as a partner to continue operations in south San Jose. [9]

Unknown

You knew something big had happened just by the change in the traffic. By early 2001 my commute time was almost cut in half. It was eerie driving the 101 [freeway] during rush hour at nearly the posted speed limit in places. Obviously a lot of the workforce wasn't working. Thousands of cars just disappeared. Another big change on the freeway—empty billboards. During the bubble, all these companies with ridiculous names had rented billboards to tell everyone how smart and innovative they were. Then they were gone.

Chapter 20

After the Dust Settled. . . Or Has It?

The Athenians and the foreigners who were there spent their
time in nothing other than telling or hearing something new.

—Acts 17:21

Obsession with the next new thing is not new—the quote above is two thousand years old—but it has turned the economic gears of the Valley for more than a generation now. In that time the Valley has become an "economic zone" perhaps more than it is a home for a significant percentage of Valley dwellers. Those who feed that system can move in and stay as long as they continue to feed the system. Those who do not feed the system will eventually have to move out.

In one sense, the stability of the Valley is its instability. Perhaps the place can more accurately be called "Transient Valley" or "Adventurers' Alley." It has largely become a temporary stop for the most recent in a long line of Argonauts and adventurers. In the first three waves of migration to the Valley after World War II—the GIs, Lockheed, and the chip makers—most people stayed. Not so with the last two waves.

For newly graduated computer science majors, and many others, moving to the Valley today is like going to Broadway or Hollywood, and the lure of glitter and gold has the same pull as it did during the gold rush. So they keep pouring in. . . and out.

For the most part, by 2005 the Valley's economy had stabilized again. In the midst of all the craziness of the bubble years, enough sound technology not only survived but in fact flourished. However, the businesses themselves have rotated, including the most dominant among them. Silicon Graphics moved out, and Google took over; Sun Microsystems moved out of its expansive campus, and Facebook took over; Hewlett Packard moved out of its large Cupertino campus, and Apple took over. And on it goes.

For now, these three have come out on top. But if the history of the Valley is indicative of anything, they will not stay there. Prunes lasted longer at Cottle Road than IBM did.

One major difference in the Valley since the bubble years is that now small tech businesses typically cannot survive very long before they are swallowed up by one of the giants. Perhaps that is what drives the Valley technology culture as much as anything. Independence is usually not an option, as one of the giants will either buy them out or sue them. Either way, they're gone. This has become the accepted norm. Therefore, the primary goal of most startups now is to be acquired by a large company. While any particular technology project has only about a 10 percent chance that it will go anywhere, the hope of a bonanza is ever present, and that keeps companies that are flush with cash on a continual buying spree and keeps the Valley moving at a hyper pace.

Those who want a balanced life find that difficult to come by in the Valley. The culture is largely one of total commitment—to work. Official company policies may say they care about the life-work balance of their employees, but company culture is frequently something else altogether. Ask any software engineer who works at one of the prestigious firms. "There is no work-life balance—*none*," one told me, and many others concur.

Popular culture in the Valley has technology as its predominant value, which, when applied to life, can only lead to a shallow and warped view of things and a mocking emptiness that is deafening when the mind finally gets a breather.

Ultimately, the need is for wisdom, and that can be hard to come by in a place that worships innovation. You don't innovate wisdom, only what is currently fashionable, and these two are contrary to one another. Furthermore, in the fast lane, change and innovation are often the excuse given for not accepting personal responsibility. Wisdom insists otherwise.

Domination

There is money in dominating other people. Big money. The current trend is to come up with ways to occupy people's time and hence guide the way they think. In other words, control the thought processes of people who use your products. And we have to admit that some companies have become very good at doing just that.

In this kind of environment, the opportunity for evil is enormous. The Google founders understood this and adopted the motto "Don't be evil," and even put it in their company prospectus and employee code of conduct. They realized early on that users depended on search services to be objective and that they should not allow advertising dollars to direct search results. They also pledged that their company *culture* would avoid conflicts of interest, be objective, and avoid bias.

Users appreciated this, as well as their uncluttered screens, and the company thrived as few companies ever have. But now Google has lowered itself to occasionally, in a subtle way, promote its political views on its home page. Can we not assume that its search results are also tainted with the same biases? In the past few years it sure appears so. They are "doing the right thing" according to their viewpoint, but their stance is far from objective or unbiased. They have a political and social agenda, and choosing the name Alphabet for their new parent company is not an accidental statement about their desired place in the world.

Historically, monopolies have tended to enslave a society. Railroads were a great innovation. But when they became monopolies, they used their power to crush everyone else. In more recent years, Microsoft did the same thing. It was equally successful and used its influence to govern everything it could. Its stranglehold has now somewhat been broken, but others have moved in to take its place. So a great struggle is going on, and it isn't merely one of businesses competing. It is much deeper than that. The amount of influence a few Silicon Valley companies have on our society is enormous. They have the ability not only to put a spin on all communication, as newspapers and radio and television programming have done for decades, but the masters of the web also have the added power of making selected information disappear.

Web content is very different from book content. A printed book stands immovable. A book may contain inaccuracies, but there is an accountability with the printed page that does not exist with web content. Web content is continually and easily added, edited, and removed. So the history revisionists are having a field day. And, again, there is great opportunity for evil.

I met a fellow who works for Apple recently. We got to talking, and he told me about how he works with university leaders to help them tailor their curriculum in the direction Apple management thinks technology is going.

If it stopped there, that would be one thing. But it doesn't. Apple is now an all-encompassing culture. And that culture, with its many biases, is being pushed hard. It was one thing for some people to love their Macintosh computers. They numbered relatively few. But now, many, many more people have bought into a standardized, all-inclusive, and dumbed-down iPhone culture without realizing it. They are fine with someone else doing their thinking for them—telling them what is good, what is bad, and what is "trending." That's creepy. The days of Newspeak have fully arrived. [i]

The bottom line? When we use technology, that technology can use us. It seems to me we need the guarding attitude of: "All things are permissible for me, but not all things are helpful. All things are permissible for me, but I will not be enslaved by anything." [1]

Refreshing Reminders
In the midst of the standardized, short-sighted, and quick-buck culture around us, it is refreshing to visit some of the family-run businesses that have been in the Valley for generations: Gene's Fine Foods, Holder's Country Inn, Olson's Cherries, Garrod Farms, Spina Farms, Novakovich Orchards, Andy's Orchard, Rocca's Market, Peninsula Creamery, Hicklebee's Bookstore, Mountain View Lock, Yamagami's Nursery, Pine Cone Lumber, Sunnyvale Lumber, and Summit Store, to name a few. These folks, and many others like them—and how I wish I could name them all—are a real asset to the community not only because they provide a needed service but even more because they are a much needed reprieve from the standardization that deadens the soul of any community. These businesses are a gift to us all and stand in sharp contrast to the parroting of marketing folks who tell us their companies are "giving back to the community." A family-run business gives to the community just by being there. Thank you all!

Refreshing in a different way are the open space preserves, both in the hills and along the bay (where the birding is great except in the summer), that provide a much-needed reprieve from the hubbub of

---

[i] Newspeak: "A language designed to diminish the range of thought." From George Orwell's novel, *1984*. *Webster's* defines it as "propagandistic language marked by ambiguity and contradictions: double talk."

Valley life. The few remaining remnants of orchards scattered here and there around the Valley also provide visual relief.

Not everyone sees the value of these things. A few years ago, the Saratoga Heritage Orchard could have been lost to those who thought the land was being "underutilized" and wanted more soccer fields instead. The Los Altos Heritage Orchard is being eyed by those who want to develop the land. Thank you to all who have helped preserve these restful havens.

Wisdom and Technology

A while back, I met a woman on a hilltop overlooking the Valley. We got to talking and she told me she came from China about twenty years ago. She had done her undergraduate work in China, then came to the U.S. to do her graduate work.

As we looked out over the Valley and commented on some of the landmarks and businesses, she told me that she works for a company that is at the forefront of chip design.

As we marveled aloud about what was going on below us in the Valley she smiled and said, "My job is to find one bad transistor on a chip that contains a billion transistors."

I smiled, too, and we shook our heads, realizing something of the awesomeness of her comment.

She then told me that in China she had one set of clothes, but now if she wanted to she could buy all she wanted.

I asked her, "What's the downside?"

She paused for a while, then said: "What I do is so very narrow. You get very narrow in your field. I must do what I can to broaden my view of things. You have to work at it. Even the whole realm of technology put together is very narrow in the sense and scope of life."

Steve Jobs was known for boasting about how much Apple was changing the world. However, when he was forty years old and had a couple of children of his own, he finally realized that technology does not change the world and that constantly thinking in that way was fundamentally flawed. Having children and needing to raise them gave him some wisdom. But his devotees still chant his old mantra about how much they are changing the world and what a good thing that is.

Early in his life, Jobs understood something about the evils of television. He thought it was a conspiracy to dumb people down. Later he realized that was not the case; people were just getting what they wanted, and that depressed him. [2]

The ironic thing is that the man who felt so strongly about this is the one who, perhaps as much as any other single person, put an iPhone into the hands of millions of kids. He complained that "people are thinking less than they used to" because of television. Did he not know, by the end of his life, that he had done something even worse? Of course he did. He admitted that he kept the iPad away from his own children and that he limited their use of technology in their home. [3]

Good intentions are just that—good intentions. They have little, if anything, to do with results. Television was a good intention. Its result is largely something else. The iPhone was another good intention, and it can be a helpful tool when the user is not driving. But do we not know its net effect on most people?

Thank you, parents everywhere, who care for your children enough to keep them from being taken over by these devices, and who help them learn to read and write proficiently, be sociable, and to think outside of that little plastic box!

Alignment

Every car I have ever owned has the same alignment problem. They all have a strong pull toward the hills. Without exception, they tend to drive through Saratoga and just keep going up Big Basin Way. I don't live up that way anymore, and there is no practical reason for this, but all my cars have done the same thing.

Caught by the beauty of the scenery, I find myself driving slowly. If you've gotten in back of someone slow on that drive, I'm sorry, it might have been me. I use the turnouts, but. . . .

One day I was up in the hills for a short day-hike with my brother. We left our car in the Castle Rock parking lot and headed toward the coast. We walked through the Douglas fir forest, then along a small creek, and eventually into a mixed forest of redwoods, madrones, and bays. There was a little dampness under the forest canopy, and the fragrance of the forest was heavenly. After walking for about an hour, we suddenly popped out into a small clearing. The sky was clear and as blue as blue could be, and we looked out across the ranges of mountains covered with redwoods. It was early spring, and we saw nothing man-made except a small wisp of bluish smoke that rose in the distance, no doubt from the fireplace in someone's cabin. Monterey Bay was so clear it seemed like you could reach out and touch it. As we stood there in awe of what was before us, two eagles put on an aerial display I will never forget. Coming from the west, they shot down diagonally into the gulch below us, screaming as they passed at astounding speed. One followed the other by a couple of seconds. They disappeared down into the gulch and were gone. But not for long. They came back and did the same thing again and again. Neither of us spoke a word. There is nothing to say at such times.

The sanctity of the moment was interrupted by voices coming up the trail. Two young men walked past us at a good clip. We acknowledged them; they did not acknowledge us—too involved in their conversation with one another. They were talking about "doing" trails. One said something about "doing Berryvale," which I know to be a great hike in Big Basin Park. They were so much into their own exploits and planned exploits that they did not see the view of the bay. They did not see the gulch below. They did not see the uninterrupted forest. They did not see the eagles. They did not see the cluster of tiny wildflowers at the end of the clearing—even though they put on a dazzling display of variety in color and design. They saw nothing. Nothing but themselves. It was so sad. I did not say anything to my brother, and he did not say anything to me. We just looked at each other in amazement. As great as the miracle before us was, so great was the tragedy to miss it.

That scene, and countless others set in front of us daily, instruct those who will hear that it is not about us. It's about God. It is deep calling unto deep. It is the Spirit of God calling out to the spirit of man, "Here I am!"

The history of the Valley during the period covered by this book is an unusually good illustration of the transitory nature of life and of the value of what is called human progress. The GIs, the Lockheed folks, the chip makers, the minicomputer folks, the dot-commers and today's programmers were all looking for a better life and many seemed to have found it for a while. But even at the height of their successes they were often changing their environment in ways that were less than positive and would contribute to their own downfall. The wave of GIs gave us thick, choking smog by the mid-1950s. The missile work brought not only a high standard of living but also toxins we did not understand. The manufacture of microchips poisoned our ground water. Then the minicomputer revolution increased the demand for those chips. The dot-commers found out they were not as smart as they thought they were. And today's programmers are considerably less flowery than their predecessors were in their assessment of the good they are doing.

In the end, all our exploits added together amount to nothing. The center of everything, and that which has lasting value, is our Maker and Sustainer. May we honor Him and be thankful to Him.

God bless you all!

Tim Stanley

Saratoga Creek

Epilogue

The idea of this book came into being while I was writing my parents' story for the younger members of our family. The more I wrote, the more I realized there was a larger story that could be told.

As I mentioned in chapter 3, my parents were among the first wave of newcomers to the Santa Clara Valley after World War II. Their story, although unique, has many common threads with the stories of other GIs and GI families who came to the Valley after the war. And so it is with each successive wave of newcomers.

I decided to make *The Peopling of Silicon Valley, 1940 to the Present Day* an oral history because I wanted the people who lived the events to tell their stories. Although I lived a lot of the history of the Valley during the subject period, I realized the book would be better if I allowed a wide cross section of people to share their experiences as well. As I collected the stories, my own understanding of the Valley broadened, which confirmed my decision.

Looking forward, I hope Valley residents will preserve what is left of the natural beauty of the place. The value of that blanket of green that clothes the hills can hardly be exaggerated. Will we allow it to remain or will the hills gradually take on the appearance of the urban sprawl that characterizes so many of the world's cities?

On my father's tombstone are these words from Psalm 121: "I will lift up my eyes unto the hills. From whence comes my help? My help comes from the Lord who made heaven and earth." Dad drew a lot of strength from looking up at the hills. They reminded him of the one who sustained him. For him, looking up on the hills was like pushing a re-set button that brought everything into proper focus.

So if you are tired of slugging it out, look up to the hills and thank God for what you see. You may not be able to stop thanking Him for a long time.

Fog cascading over the Saratoga hills

Notes

Chapter 1

[1] Linda Lester, telephone interview by author, December 2016, and from materials provided by her. This and all other oral histories have been lightly edited for easier reading.

[2] Henry Petrino, e-mail to author, March 26, 2015.

[3] Figures for the fruit industry in this chapter are from the National Park Service and Santa Clara County websites.

[4] AFL connection is from Christensen et al., *Reflections of the Past, An Anthology of San Jose*, page 162; Unemployment Insurance is from "History of Unemployment Insurance in the United States," U.S. Department of Labor.

[5] Christensen et al., *Reflections of the Past*. One of these plants may have closed by 1940.

[6] Lois McPherson, undated letter to author, about 2012.

[7] John Giacomazzi, letter to author, June 10, 2015.

[8] Joan Huff Marschall, e-mails to author, July 16, 2014, June 25, 2016, and July 21, 2016.

[9] Rose Lesslie, Rosie the Riveter, World War II American Home Front Oral History Project. Interview conducted by Sam Redman in 2012. Regional Oral History Office, The Bancroft Library, University of California, Berkeley, California. Used by permission.

[10] Bob Norona, telephone interview by author, January 26, 2016.

[11] Edward Ginzton, interview by A. Michael McMahon, November 26, 1984, Institute of Electrical and Electronics Engineers, Inc. Used by permission.

Chapter 2

[1] Earl Warren, from The Earl Warren Oral History Project, Bancroft Library, University of California, Berkeley, California. Interviews conducted in 1971 and 1972 by Amelia R. Fry and others. Used by permission.

[2] From Donald J. Young, "West Coast War Zone," *World War II Magazine*, July 1998, pg. 26; display at the San Diego Maritime Museum.

[3] William M. Kays, interview, 2013, Stanford Historical Society Oral History Program Interviews (SC0932), Department of Special Collections and University Archives, Stanford University Libraries and Academic Information Resources, Stanford, California. Used by permission.

[4] Rixford K. Snyder, interviews March and April, 1979, Stanford Historical Society Oral History Program Interviews (SC0932). Department of Special Collections and University Archives, Stanford University Libraries and Academic Information Resources, Stanford, California. Used by permission.

[5] Dave Cochran, e-mail to author, July 16, 2015.

[6] Joan Huff Marschall, e-mails to author, July 16, 2014, June 25, 2016, and July 21, 2016.

7 George I. Rodriguez, telephone interviews by author, December 3, 2015 and January 26, 2016.

8 Lola Vaughn, interview July 17, 1979, "Joshua Hendy Iron Works WWII Women," by Sunnyvale Historical Society. Used by permission.

9 Most of the FMC story is from *Growing Orbit: The Story of FMC Corporation*, by Al Campbell and Mimi Real, 1992.

10 Rose Lesslie, from Rosie the Riveter, World War II American Home Front Oral History Project, interview conducted by Sam Redman in 2012, Regional Oral History Office, The Bancroft Library, University of California, Berkeley, California. Used by permission.

11 Gene Arnold, two telephone interviews by author, December 2015.

12 The Bracero Program brought about 4.5 million men from Mexico to the U.S. between 1942 and 1964 when this guest worker program was ended. Many stayed and eventually became citizens.

13 Interview by Craig Sherod, at the Mayfair Community Center in east San Jose, about 2006, posted on YouTube as *The Braceros at 80*. Permission to publish granted in September 22, 2016 e-mail to author.

14 Tower, Clarence Robert, *Seventy Years in the Silicon Valley: An Anecdotal History*, pages 36, 63, 115-119.

15 Richard Mesa, e-mail to author, December 18, 2015.

16 Henry Petrino, e-mail to author, March 26, 2015.

17 This story comes largely from the William and Flora Hewlett Foundation website.

Chapter 3

1 Earl Warren, from The Earl Warren Oral History Project, Bancroft Library, University of California, Berkeley, California. Interviews conducted in 1971 and 1972 by Amelia R. Fry and others. Used by permission.

2 See Preface concerning anonymous stories. And so throughout the book.

3 I learned of this story from the book, *Get Your Own Home the Cooperative Way*, by Elsie Danenberg, New York: Greenberg, 1949.

4 Robin Chapman, *California Apricots: The Lost Orchards of Silicon Valley*, pages 11-15.

5 Partly from *The Detroit News*, February 10, 1999.

6 Just as the GIs who had fought in the war did not talk about it, my parents never talked about the racial problem in Detroit. Only many decades later did my mother relate this story to my sister.

7 Geoff Goble, two telephone interviews by author, June 2016.

8 Excerpts from *From the Ground Up: Building Silicon Valley by Goodwin Steinberg F.A. I.A.* with Susan Wolfe, pages xii, xiv, 7-15, Copyright © 2002 by the Board of Trustees of the Leland Stanford Junior University. All rights reserved, Reprinted by permission of the publisher, Stanford University Press, sup.org.

9 Bill O'Dell, conversation, 1980s.

[10] Al Thompson, interview by author, January 26, 2016, and e-mail to author, February 1, 2016.

[11] Grady Hall, conversations, 1990s.

Chapter 4

[1] Henry Petrino, e-mail to author, March 26, 2015.

[2] Gene Arnold, interviews by author, December 2015, Irvine, CA.

[3] Rhonda Bump, e-mails to author, September 24, 2014, and March 26, 2015.

[4] N.M. letter to author, 2012.

[5] Eugene D. Sharp, e-mail to author, January 19, 2016, and unpublished stories he sent me the same day, copies in author's files.

[6] Evelyn Stevens-White, letter to author, 2015.

[7] Joan Fox, interviews by Allen Fox January 2016, voice recordings sent to author as e-mail attachments, February 7, 2016.

[8] Dave Pitman, interview by author, March 2010.

[9] See Preface concerning Unknown stories.

[10] Pier's Dairy info: from Harold Bacon interview, January 23, 1987, Stanford Oral History Project, page 7.

[11] Copyright © Rhonda Bump.

Chapter 5

[1] Rao and Scaruffi, *A History of Silicon Valley*, pgs. 32, 37; Lecuyer, *Making Silicon Valley*, pgs. 14, 15.

[2] Rao and Scaruffi, *A History of Silicon Valley*, pg. 37.

[3] Lecuyer, *Making Silicon Valley*, pg. 19.

[4] Harold Bacon, interview January 23, 1987, Stanford Oral History Project, Stanford Historical Society. Used by permission.

[5] Lecuyer, *Making Silicon Valley*, pg. 54.

[6] Lecuyer, *Making Silicon Valley*, pg. 56.

[7] Mostly from Lecuyer, pg. 40 and references there.

[8] Lecuyer, *Making Silicon Valley*, pg. 100.

[9] Edward Ginzton, interview conducted by A. Michael McMahon, November 26, 1984, The Institute of Electrical and Electronics Engineers, Inc. Used by permission.

[10] Rao and Scaruffi, *A History of Silicon Valley*, pg. 54.

[11] From *Stanford Magazine*, July/August, 1998. Reprinted by permission from STANFORD magazine, published by the Stanford Alumni Association, Stanford University. Used by permission.

[12] Gene Arnold, interviews by author, Irvine, CA, December 2015.

[13] Dave Cochran, e-mails to author, July 13 and 14, 2016.

[14] From IBM Archives, caption with photo of San Jose card plant.

[15] William D. Blankenship, from "Rey Johnson, a Full Life, a Fuller Future" from "*Think*" (an IBM employee publication), June 1971, pages 40-41.

[16] William D. Blankenship, "Rey Johnson, a Full Life, a Fuller Future" from "*Think*" (an IBM employee publication), June 1971, pages 40-41. Used by permission of IBM Archives, by e-mail February 2, 2016.

[17] William "Bill" Crooks, interview by Tom Gardner, November 13, 2008. Used by permission of the Computer History Museum, Mountain View, CA.

[18] James F. Gibbons, from Stanford Historical Society Oral History Program Interviews (SC0932), Department of Special Collections and University Archives, Stanford University Libraries and Academic Information Resources, Stanford, CA. Interview January 28, 2009. Used by permission.

[19] Tower, *Seventy Years in the Silicon Valley: An Anecdotal History*, pages 36, 63, 115-119.

Chapter 6

[1] Statistics in this paragraph are from a display at the Sunnyvale Historical Museum and from a booklet put out by the company titled *Lockheed, 40 Years of Leadership*.

[2] Glen Christoffersen, e-mails to author, January 22, and 23, and February 1, 2016.

[3] Dean Fisher, telephone interview by author, November 12, 2015.

[4] Telephone interview by author, January 21, 2016.

[5] Lane Pendleton, telephone interview by author, January 19, 2016, and e-mail to author, January 25, 2016.

[6] Jack Balletto, 2012 interview for Silicon Genesis, an Oral History of Semiconductor Technology, Stanford University. Used by permission.

[7] Gloria Beasley Lausten, *The Shirtsleeve Invention: The Story of a Man and an Idea*, pgs. 96-104.

[8] Telephone interview by author, March 2016.

[9] Al De Ridder, e-mails to author, January 26 and 27, and February 9, 2016.

[10] Al Thompson, telephone interview by author, January 26, 2016, and e-mail to author, February 1, 2016.

[11] Charles Chase, telephone interview by author, June 9, 2016, and materials sent to author by Charles Chase.

[12] Mark Twain, from *Life on the Mississippi*, chapter 27.

Chapter 7

[1] Department of Veterans Affairs, "Legislative History of the VA Home Loan Guaranty Program."

[2] Coleman, *PG&E of California, the Centennial Story of Pacific Gas and Electric Company, 1852-1952*, pgs. 5, 12, 300-308, 331-339, 343.

[3] Santa Clara Water District, "Timeline of the History of Water in Santa Clara County"; US Department of the Interior website.

[4] Coleman, *PG&E of California*, pgs. 300-308, 331-339.

[5] Ibid.

[6] This paragraph comes from a few sources: U.S. Census for population figures; Cal Trans, *Tract Housing in California, 1945-1973*, pg. 147, for area figures (the book quotes a non-local source, saying 157 sq. miles by 1980. Having some local knowledge, I have estimated the difference); annex quote from Henry Petrino's e-mail to author, March 26, 2015; and General Plan from Terri Christensen, et al., *Reflections of the Past*, pg. 183.

[7] Christensen, et al., *Reflections of the Past*, pg. 185.

[8] From Doug McNeil, "The Battle for Peaceful Mountain," a paper commemorating Monte Sereno's fiftieth anniversary, copy in author's files.

[9] Kushner, David, (2009), *Levittown: Two Families, One Tycoon, and the Fight for Civil Rights in America's Legendary Suburb*. New York, Walker & Company, pg.43.

[10] Annette Elissagaray, letter to author, May 16, 2016, and e-mails to author, May 2016.

[11] Joan Fox, from audio files made by Allen Fox, e-mailed to author February 7, 2016.

[12] Excerpts from *From the Ground Up: Building Silicon Valley by Goodwin Steinberg F.A. I.A.* with Susan Wolfe, pgs. xii, xiv, 7-15, Copyright © 2002 by the Board of Trustees of the Leland Stanford Junior University. All rights reserved, Reprinted by permission of the publisher, Stanford University Press, sup.org.

[13] Peter Gillies, e-mails to author, June 11, 2011, and November 18, 2015.

Chapter 8

[1] Skip Hazen, e-mail to author, May 26, 2015.

[2] Bill Sleight, e-mail to author, March 28, 2015.

[3] Thomas Hauber, e-mails to author, March 27 and 30, 2015, and September 22, 2016.

[4] Floyd Frederickson, e-mail sent to author, November 18, 2015.

[5] Debbie Hall, from her unpublished paper, September 2016.

[6] Doug McNeil, interview by author, February 28, 2016.

[7] See Preface concerning anonymous stories.

Chapter 9

[1] William Shockley, Lecuyer, *Making Silicon Valley*, pg. 134.

[2] Richard Hodgson, interview, September 19, 1995, for Silicon Genesis, an Oral History of Semiconductor Technology, Stanford University. Used by permission, and so with other Stanford interviews.

[3] Floyd Kvamme, interview, 2013, for Silicon Genesis, an Oral History of Semiconductor Technology, Stanford University.

[4] Charlie Sporck, interview, February 21, 2000, for Silicon Genesis, an Oral History of Semiconductor Technology, Stanford University.

[5] Tom Maher, *Silicon Valley Road*, pgs. 41-43, 49-51, 56, 63, 66-67.

[6] James Downey, interview, May 20, 1995, for Silicon Genesis, an Oral History of Semiconductor Technology, Stanford University.

[7] Jack Balletto, interview, 2012, Silicon Genesis, an Oral History of Semiconductor Technology, Stanford University.

[8] John East, interview, July 27, 2008, for Silicon Genesis, an Oral History of Semiconductor Technology, Stanford University.

[9] Jerry Sanders, interview, October 18, 2002, for Silicon Genesis, an Oral History of Semiconductor Technology, Stanford University.

[10] Jim Reynolds, telephone interview by author, May 17, 2016, and e-mail of June 24, 2016.

[11] H.P.S., telephone interviews by author, January 31 and February 16, 2016; corrections November 5, 2016.

[12] Todd Gilman, telephone interview by author and e-mails to author, August 16 and 22, 2016.

[13] Floyd Kvamme, interview, 2013, Silicon Genesis, an Oral History of Semiconductor Technology, Stanford University.

Chapter 10

[1] Vince S. Garrod , "Garrod Farms, 100 Years," Summer 1998, unpublished paper, copy in author's files, used by permission from Jan Garrod.

[2] Liz Iverson, e-mail to author, November 20, 2015.

[3] Tom Spink, e-mail to author, June 18, 2016.

[4] From Harold Voshage, *A Grateful Mennonite,* 2014; Harold A. Voshage, e-mails and letter to author March 25, 2016.

[5] John Giacomazzi, letter to author, April 27, 2015; "Giacomazzi Family Almaden Road Ranch History, May, 28, 2015," unpublished paper, copy in author's files.

[6] See Preface concerning anonymous stories.

[7] Paul McJones, originally posted on Quora, updated February 6, 2015. Permission to quote by e-mail to author, November 9, 2015.

Chapter 11

[1] Joan Fox, from audio files made by Allen Fox, January 2016, e-mailed to author February 7, 2016.

[2] Geoff Goble, interview by author, June 2016.

[3] Deborah Stanley, from unpublished paper; copy in author's files.

[4] See Preface concerning anonymous stories.

Chapter 12

[1] From the Bible, John 6:37. The treasure in the earthen vessel is II Cor. 4:7.

Chapter 13

[1] James F. Gibbons, interview January 28, 2009, Stanford Historical Society Oral History Program Interviews (SC0932), Department of Special Collections and University Archives, Stanford University Libraries and Academic Information Resources, Stanford, CA. Used by permission, and so with other Stanford interviews.

[2] John McGowan, e-mail to author (EarthLink), June 9, 2015.

[3] Robert D. Clark, President, San Jose State College, June 14, 1968, "Student Unrest at San Jose State College, 1967-1968." Used by permission.

[4] Mostly from *Saratoga News*, July 11, 2001.

[5] See Preface concerning anonymous stories.

[6] Grady Hall, conversations, early 2000s.

[7] Norm Tarowsky, e-mail to author, August 24, 2015.

[8] Albert Yu, interview September 15, 2005, for Silicon Genesis, an Oral History of Semiconductor Technology, Stanford University.

[9] Jim Morgan, interview July 20, 2004, for Silicon Genesis, an Oral History of Semiconductor Technology, Stanford University.

[10] Conversation, 1980s.

[11] About two million gallons of reclaimed water were injected per day. The project later also included extraction wells, "to avoid any possible degradation of the water-supply aquifers from this source, and to allow reuse of the reclaimed water." Water pumped from the extraction wells was to be sold for industrial and agricultural purposes. (From "Injection/Extraction Well System—A Unique Seawater Intrusion Barrier," by N. Thomas Sheahan.) The U.S. Geological Survey Water-Resources Investigation Report on this project (#82-4121, September 1983) states: "Overall, ground-water quality was greatly improved by injection of freshwater."

Chapter 14

[1] Albert Yu, interview September 15, 2005, interview for Silicon Genesis, an Oral History of Semiconductor Technology, Stanford University.

[2] Gene Carter, interview by Douglas Fairbairn, September 29, 2014, Computer History Museum, Mountain View, CA. Used by permission.

[3] Barry Yarkoni, from his post on Quora, 2015(?) and e-mail to author, both by permission granted November 5, 2015.

[4] Jeff Ronne, telephone interviews by author, November 2015, final edits approved in December 3, 2015 e-mail.

[5] See Preface concerning anonymous stories.

[6] Dick Karp, from his post on Quora, January 9, 2014. Permission to quote per e-mail to author, November 17, 2015.

Chapter 15

[1] Dione Chen, telephone interview by author, November 18, 2015; her edits in e-mail November 11, 2016.

[2] See Preface concerning anonymous stories.

[3] Armando D., conversations, 1990s.

[4] Poornima Kumar, interview by author, March 28, 2016; her revisions approved in April 22, 2016 e-mail.

[5] Ashutosh Mehndiratta, from his post on Quora, 2015, permission granted in January 18, 2016 e-mail (Cox).

[6] Joseph Wang, from his post on Quora, 2015(?). Permission granted in e-mail to author November 15, 2015.

[7] Monica Huang, interview by author, October 7, 2016. Final edits approved in e-mail of November 4, 2016.

Chapter 16

[1] Dennis Hayes, *Behind the Silicon Curtain: The Seductions of Work in a Lonely Era*, pg. 30.

[2] Various sources, including David Bacon's *Truthout*, a pro-union publication.

[3] Thomas Hauber e-mail to author, March 27, 2015; FundingUniverse.com: Xilinx Inc., History. Retrieved April 3, 2017.

[4] See Preface concerning anonymous stories.

[5] Ibid.

[6] Ted Smith, interviews by Carl Wilmsen, 2000. Copyright 2003 by the Regents of the University of California. Title: Pioneer Activist for Environmental Justice in Silicon Valley, 1967-2000: oral history transcript/ 2003. Used by permission.

Chapter 17

[1] Jenny Du, from her Quora post, June 22, 2014. Permission to quote per e-mail to author, November 8, 2015.

[2] Tony Jiang, from his Quora post, 2014. Permission to quote per e-mail to author, November 22, 2015.

[3] Matt Williams, from his Quora post, November 20, 2013. Permission to quote per e-mail to author, July 23, 2015.

[4] D.M., from her Quora post, January 20, 2016. Permission granted by e-mail August 18, 2016.

[5] See Preface concerning anonymous stories.

[6] Ain Phan, interview by author, March, 2017.

[7] Angelina M., from her Yelp post, December 12, 2013. Permission to quote per e-mail to author, December 21, 2015.

Chapter 18

[1] See Preface concerning anonymous stories.

[2] María García Herrero, *Archie and Me: Memories of Love*, Seattle: CreateSpace, Copyright © 2013 by María García Herrero. archieandme.weebly.com. All rights reserved.

[3] Doug McNeil, telephone interview by author, February 28, 2016.

[4] Stan Hanks, from his post on Quora, updated July 29, 2015. Used by permission granted in October 21, 2016 e-mail to author.

[5] From *Bloomberg Businessweek*, June 15-28, 2015, pg. 40.

[6] Dennis Hayes, *Behind the Silicon Curtain: The Seductions of Work in a Lonely Era*, pgs. 31-32.

[7] Greg Kemnitz, from his Quora post, 2015. Permission to quote per e-mail to author, November 4, 2015.

[8] See Preface concerning Unknown stories.

[9] Cousette Copeland, *Silicon Valley: Fact and Fiction*, pgs. 358, 360, 365. At the author's request I included the name in the last paragraph. She is right; by doing so I tell an important part of the story.

[10] Statistics are from the June 15-28, 2015 issue, page 21.

Chapter 19

[1] See Preface concerning Unknown stories.

2 Conversation, 1990s.

3 See Preface concerning anonymous stories.

4 IPO data is from Jay R. Ritter, University of Florida, "Number of Technology IPOs: 1990 to 2013."

5 Lawrence Coburn, from his Quora post, 2015. Permission granted in May 17, 2015 e- mail to author.

6 Michael Stricklen, from his Quora post, 2015. Permission granted in April 20, 2015 e-mail to author.

7 Sean Corfield, from his Quora post, 2015. Permission granted in EarthLink e-mail to author, April 16, 2015.

8 Webvan story is from a few sources: Arun Rao, *A History of Silicon Valley*, pages 345-346; CNN Money, March 10, 2010, "10 Big Dot-com Flops"; and C/Net, January 2, 2002, Greg Sandoval, "Webvan bags HomeGrocer for $1.2 billion."

9 Information about the IBM-Hitachi deal is from *Bizjournals*, April 21, 2002.

Chapter 20

1 From the Bible, I Cor. 6:12

2 Steve Jobs, interview by Gary Wolf. *Wired Magazine*, February 1996.

3 Nick Bilton, "Steve Jobs Was a Low-Tech Parent," *Disruption* (blog), *New York Times*, September 10, 2014.

Bibliography

Books

Battelle, John. *The Search: How Google and Its Rivals Rewrote the Rules of Business and Transformed Our Culture*. New York: Portfolio, 2005.

Beers, David. *Blue Sky Dream: A Memoir of America's Fall From Grace*. New York: Doubleday, 1996.

Campbell, Al, and Mimi Real. *Growing Orbit: The Story of FMC Corporation*. Philadelphia: FMC, 1992.

Chapman, Robin. *California Apricots: The Lost Orchards of Silicon Valley*. Charleston, S.C.: History Press, 2013.

Christensen, Terry, Charlene Duval, Ellen Garboske, Phil Grasser, Mary Jo Ignoffo. *Reflections of the Past: An Anthology of San Jose*.

Coleman, Charles. *PG&E of California: The Centennial Story of Pacific Gas and Electric Company, 1852-1952*.

Copeland, Cousette. *Silicon Valley: Fact and Fiction*. Charleston, S.C.: BookSurge, 2007.

Couchman, Robert, *The Sunsweet Story*. San Jose, CA; Sunsweet Growers.

Hayes, Dennis. *Behind the Silicon Curtain: The Seductions of Work in a Lonely Era*. Boston: South End Press, 1989.

Herrero, María García. *Archie and Me: Memories of Love*. Seattle: CreateSpace, 2013. Copyright © 2013 by María García Herrero.

Ignoffo, Mary Jo. *Milestones: A History of Mountain View, California*. Cupertino: California History Center & Foundation, 2002.

Lausten, Gloria Beasley. *The Shirtsleeve Invention: The Story of a Man and an Idea*. Bloomington, Ind.: Xlibris, 2010.

Lecuyer, Christophe. *Making Silicon Valley: Innovation and the Growth of High Tech, 1930-1970*. Cambridge, Mass: MIT Press, 2006.

Maher, Tom. *Silicon Valley Road*. College Station, TX:
Virtualbookworm.com, 2005.

Rao, Arun, and Piero Scaruffi. *A History of Silicon Valley: The Greatest
Creation of Wealth in the History of the Planet. 2nd Edition.* Silicon
Valley, CA: Omniware, 2013.

Saxenian, AnnaLee. *Regional Advantage: Culture and Competition in
Silicon Valley and Route 128*. Cambridge, MA: Harvard University
Press, 1994.

Smith, Randall. *The Prince of Silicon Valley: Frank Quattrone and the
Dot-Com Bubble*. New York: St. Martins, 2009.

Stanley, Tim. *The Last of the Prune Pickers: A Pre-Silicon Valley Story*.
Irvine, CA: 2 Timothy, 2010.

Steinberg, Goodwin, and Susan Wolfe. *From the Ground Up: Building
Silicon Valley.* Stanford, CA: Stanford University Press, 2002.

Tower, Clarence Robert. *Seventy Years in the Silicon Valley: An
Anecdotal History*. James Stevenson, 2002.

Twain, Mark. *Life on the Mississippi*, 1883.

Voshage, Harold. *A Grateful Mennonite: A Memoir.* Neche, N.D.:
Friesenpress, 2014.

Wolff, Michael. *Burn Rate: How I Survived the Gold Rush Years on the
Internet*. New York: Simon and Schuster, 1998.

Company Booklets and Other Limited Publications
Lockheed Missiles and Space Company. *40 Years of Leadership,
Lockheed Missiles and Space Comp*any, 1994.

Lockheed Star. *A Chronology of LMSC History*, 1992.

Moffett Field 60th Anniversary, 1933-1993.

Joshua Hendy Iron Works. *This Is Hendy*, 1945(?)

California Department of Transportation. *Tract Housing in California, 1945-1973: A Context for National Register Evaluation*, 2011.

Periodicals
Bloomberg Businessweek
New York Times
San Jose Mercury News
Wired

Some websites consulted
Bancroft Library, University of California, Berkeley
Bizjournals
Computer History Museum
Institute of Electrical and Electronics Engineers
Quora
Santa Clara Water District
Silicon Genesis
Silicon Valley History Online
Stanford Historical Society
US Census
US Department of the Interior
US Department of Labor
US Department of Veterans Affairs
US Geological Survey
US National Park Service
Wikipedia
World War II Magazine

Photo Credits

Preface
Downtown San Jose   Tim Stanley

Chapter 1
Valley view	Courtesy of San Jose Public Library, CA Rm.
Prune pickers	Courtesy of San Jose State University
Workers at canning tables	Courtesy of San Jose State University
Aerial of SJ, 1940	Courtesy of Santa Clara University Library Arch.

Chapter 2
Student soldiers at SCU	Courtesy of Santa Clara University Library
Ration card	US government office
WWII posters	US government office
Hendy, large gears	Hendy Iron Works
Hendy, 500th Liberty engine	Courtesy of Sunnyvale Historical Society
FMC LTV	US Navy
Blimp deflating	US Navy
Blimps in hangar	US Navy
Joe Stanley and Ed Parker	From collection of Tim Stanley
GIs with young lady	Courtesy of Sunnyvale Historical Society
Victory Garden Certif.	Courtesy of Linda Lester

Chapter 3
Welcome Home blimp	From collection of Tim Stanley
Bus ticket	From collection of Tim Stanley
Airport Village	Courtesy of History San Jose
Valley Homes (2)	Courtesy of Sourisseau Academy for State and Local History, SJSU
Cupertino train station	Courtesy of California History Center

Chapter 4
Aerial of Owens Corning, 1949	Courtesy of Santa Clara City Library
Aerial of Tully Road, 1953	Courtesy of History San Jose
Aerial of Fremont HS, 1955	Courtesy of Sunnyvale Historical Society

Chapter 5
Vacuum tubes	Courtesy of IBM Archives
IBM's San Jose card plant	Courtesy of IBM Archives
IBM Ramac 305	Courtesy of Sourisseau Academy for State and Local History, SJSU

IBM Cottle Road facility   Courtesy of History San Jose
HP and Lockheed, SIP   Courtesy of Sunnyvale Historical Society

Chapter 6
Lockheed, Sunnyvale, 1959   Courtesy of Sunnyvale Historical
                               Society
Polaris launch   US Navy
UTC rocket motor test   Courtesy of Pratt and Whitney

Chapter 7
Sign at new tract   Courtesy of Mountain View Historical
                           Association and Library
New housing tract   Los Angeles Times Photographic Archive,
                           Library Special Collections, Chas E. Young
                           Library, UCLA
Tropicana Village brochure   Courtesy of History San Jose
Ford Plant, Milpitas   Courtesy of San Jose Public Library, CA Rm.
Saratoga, Campbell Aves, 1959   Courtesy of History San Jose
Aerial of Lockheed, 1969   Courtesy of Sunnyvale Historical
                               Society

Chapter 8
Cutting 'cots   Courtesy of Peter Wolfe
Bookmobile   © San Jose Public Library
High school typing class   Courtesy of San Jose State University

Chapter 9
Silicon wafer   Tim Stanley
Fairchild chart   Tim Stanley
Wafer scribing machine   Deborah Stanley

Chapter 10
Navy P3 Orion   US Navy
Early computer lab   Courtesy of Santa Clara University

Chapter 11
Alum Rock Park bridge   Tim Stanley
Vasona Reservoir   Tim Stanley
Snow play at Sara. Summit   From collection of Tim Stanley
SC County Fairgrounds   Courtesy of History San Jose
Montalvo   Deborah Stanley
Paul Masson Cellars   Courtesy of Saratoga Historical Foundation

No Cruising sign   Tim Stanley

Chapter 13
Quito Rd. widened   Tim Stanley
Mt. View high rise   Courtesy of Mountain View Historical
                                 Association and Library
Gas Crisis, 10 gallon limit   © Owen Franken

Chapter 14
Xerox Alto   Deborah Stanley
Apple II   Deborah Stanley

Chapter 16
Abandoned plant   Tim Stanley

Chapter 18
Yahoo building   Tim Stanley
Apple building   Tim Stanley
Google building   Tim Stanley

Chapter 19
NASDAQ chart   Tim Stanley

Epilog
Saratoga Creek   Tim Stanley
Fog over hills   Tim Stanley

Acknowledgements

Writing a book is always a humbling experience for me. I need the help of many people if the result is to be of any quality.

A special thanks to all who shared their stories with me. There would be no book without your kind contributions. I regret that I could not use all the stories that were sent to me.

Collecting all the stories and photographs for this book was a huge endeavor. Many people who did not contribute a story gave me a lead or sent something helpful to me. In several cases, I contacted a few people before getting a story I was looking for. Many, many people were helpful, and I am sorry I cannot name you all.

I owe a big debt of gratitude to my dear wife, Deborah, who has been a huge support to my writing endeavors. She has been my IT person for more than a decade, and the keenness of her ear was proved countless times as I read and reread the manuscript to her. ("Wait a minute! Wait a minute!") There would be no book without her.

But that is only half the story. Deborah has put up with this "yo-yo man," who too frequently gets up during the night to write down what has sifted up in his mind before it evaporates. She has also been a "book widow" at times when I have been holding an entire book in my head for organizational purposes. At such times—and they can last several days—I have little capacity for her, or anything else, for that matter. Thank you, Deb, for putting up with that!

That is an unpleasant part of writing. Andrew Murray said he felt like a hen that needed to lay an egg until he finished a book he was working on. I hear you, brother!

A big thank you to the many local libraries and historical associations, and the people who staff them: to Catherine Mills and Nadine Nelson from History San Jose; Annette Stransky and Katie Alexander from the Saratoga Historical Foundation; Jeanine Stanek and Johan Koning from the Sunnyvale Historical Society; Candice Bowers, Nick Perry, and Bob Weaver from the Mountain View Historical Association; Sydney Gulbronson from the Computer History Museum in Mountain View, CA; Lisa Christensen from the California History Center at De Anza College; Nancy Reynolds and Beth Wyman from the Morgan Hill Historical Society; Bill Stubkjaer from Moffett Field Historical Society and Museum; Charlene Duval and Leilani Marshall from Sourisseau

Academy for State and Local History, San Jose State University; Diane Malmstrom and Rebecca Kohn from San Jose State University; Sheila Conway from Santa Clara University; Mary Boyle from the City of Santa Clara Library; Michele Huie from Santa Clara County Public Library; Erin Herzog from the California Room, San Jose Public Library; Julia Butler from Heritage Park Library in Irvine, CA; Chrystal Miles from the Bancroft Library of the University of California at Berkeley; Daniel Hartwig from Stanford University; Ariane de Pree from Stanford University Press; Pam Gorelow from *Stanford Magazine*; Dawn Stanford from IBM Corporate Archives; Robert Colburn from the Institute of Electrical and Electronics Engineers History Center; Bill Abbott from the Lockheed Old Timers Association; Bernard Bruand and John Minck from the Hewlett Packard Retired Employees Club; and Javier Garibay from the UCLA Library.

A big thanks to Quora for its website which was helpful in filling in some gaps, to the Stanford Historical Society for their Oral History Project, and to the Stanford University Libraries for their Silicon Genesis project. This book would be lacking without all of you.

Thanks to our son, James, who sent helpful articles, loaned pertinent books, and offered thoughtful comments. He's an engineer and thinks like one. I'm not, and don't; and he helped bridge the gap.

Thanks to my brothers and sisters who all offered something that helped the book along and were encouraging to me as well.

To my copy editor I am greatly indebted. She did a wonderful job whipping what was a much rougher manuscript than I thought it was into shape. Although she preferred to remain anonymous because I did not want to follow some of her advice, it is to her credit that the book is in as good a shape as it is. I cannot say how much I appreciate not only her skill in the craft but also her tenaciousness, although in the end the book must be mine.

Thanks also to my proofreader, Tammy Ditmore, who did a great job. Any remaining errors or awkwardness in the text are mine.

One final word of thanks is to all who have purchased one of my books and written to thank me for writing the book, to share their stories, or to give additional insight. I've learned a lot in this way and am indebted to all of you.